THE ETIM

China's Islamic Militants and the Global Terrorist Threat

J. Todd Reed and Diana Raschke

PSI Guides to Terrorists, Insurgents, and Armed Groups
James J. F. Forest, Series Editor

PRAEGER

AN IMPRINT OF ABC-CLIO, LLC
Santa Barbara, California • Denver, Colorado • Oxford, England

Library of Congress Cataloging-in-Publication Data

Reed, J. Todd.
   The ETIM : China's Islamic militants and the global terrorist threat / J. Todd Reed and Diana Raschke.
     p. cm. — (PSI guides to terrorists, insurgents, and armed groups)
   Includes bibliographical references and index.
   ISBN 978–0–313–36540–9 (hard copy : alk. paper) — ISBN 978–0–313–36541–6 (ebook)
   1. Terrorists—China. 2. Uighur (Turkic people)—China. 3. Muslims—China. I. Raschke, Diana. II. Title.
HV6433.C552U357   2010
363.325089′94323—dc22   2010000161

ISBN: 978–0–313–36540–9
EISBN: 978–0–313–36541–6

14 13 12 11 10   1 2 3 4 5

This book is also available on the World Wide Web as an eBook.
Visit www.abc-clio.com for details.

Praeger
An Imprint of ABC-CLIO, LLC

ABC-CLIO, LLC
130 Cremona Drive, P.O. Box 1911
Santa Barbara, California 93116-1911

This book is printed on acid-free paper ∞

Manufactured in the United States of America

Contents

Preface

This is the first book to focus specifically on the East Turkistan Islamic Movement (ETIM). Our intended audience is broad and includes anyone interested in China or counterterrorism, particularly members of the U.S. defense and intelligence communities.

Our backgrounds are in journalism, China studies, and counterterrorism analysis. We examine the phenomenon of the ETIM from a counterterrorism perspective, relying primarily on media accounts and government documentation. Our book includes what we believe to be the most comprehensive published open-source list of ETIM attacks and members compiled to date.

This is not a book about the Uyghur ethnic group. Nor is this a book about the territory known as Xinjiang and its long history, present-day social conditions, or related Chinese policy. We address those broad topics and draw on the work of the scholars who analyze them only to provide context for our study of the ETIM.

We direct the interested reader to "The Xinjiang Project" for more on the history, religion, demography, education, economics, ecology, and ethnic identity issues related to northwest China. The Xinjiang Project's authors and their 2004 compilation volume *Xinjiang: China's Muslim Borderland* figure prominently in our bibliography.

—*J. Todd Reed and Diana Raschke*
September 2009

Acknowledgments

The authors would like to thank Dr. James Forest for his encouragement and excellent advice on the manuscript; Dr. Elizabeth Raschke for her editing help; Camilo Geronimo, Brahim Elkamel, and Neil Westman for their work in translating Arabic to English; and Bascom "Dit" Talley III, Michael Houck, and Liesl McNeal at Johns Hopkins University for facilitating our access to research materials.

1

———— ∞∞∞ ————

Introduction

The first explosion rocked the oasis city of Kuqa in northwest China's Xinjiang region before dawn on Sunday, August 10, 2008. The blasts kept coming, at least a dozen of them in all, erupting near a police station, a bank, a hotel, a shopping center, and several government buildings. Eyewitnesses said the attackers threw homemade bombs and police fired on suspects racing through Kuqa's back alleys. Two people were killed and several others injured.

When the explosions stopped the manhunt started. Police launched a full-fledged dragnet, wearing black body armor and toting machine guns. They cordoned off the city, evacuating some residents and warning others not to leave their homes. By the end of the day Chinese police had killed eight suspected terrorists. Two more blew themselves up to avoid capture.[1]

This incident made headlines around the world, in part because of the international attention fixed on Beijing, 2,500 miles to the east, where the Summer Olympics had begun just two days before. The East Turkistan Islamic Movement (ETIM) claimed responsibility for the deadly bombings in Kuqa.[2]

WHAT IS THE ETIM?

The ETIM is a terrorist organization that demands an independent fundamentalist Muslim state for the Uyghur ethnic minority in northwest China. The ETIM is China's most infamous militant group, known in the West for its links to Al-Qaida, its suspected members' detention at Guantanamo Bay

Naval Base (GTMO), and its threats to attack the 2008 Beijing Olympics. Western, Russian, and Chinese media sources have documented the ETIM's existence for nearly 20 years. While its present size and capabilities are largely unknown, the ETIM has developed an online propaganda presence aligned with Al-Qaida's.

The ETIM is only one of the most recent—and certainly the most sensationalized—combatants in a centuries-old ethnic conflict over China's northwest territory, specifically the Xinjiang Uyghur Autonomous Region (XUAR). Figure 1.1 shows the XUAR, also known as Xinjiang, East Turkistan, and Uyghuristan.

After 9/11, the Chinese government publicized the previously obscure ETIM as a significant domestic terrorist threat with international reach. Like Al-Qaida, the ETIM subscribes to a violent form of fundamentalist Islam; its then-leader, Hasan Mahsum, knew Osama bin Laden and trained Uyghur fighters in Afghanistan's Tora Bora mountains. (Some of those fighters were later detained at GTMO.) In the all-consuming post-9/11 effort to secure the U.S. homeland, a united front against the ETIM became the cornerstone of a counterterrorism partnership between the United States and its old Cold War rival, the People's Republic of China (PRC).

This partnership is complicated. The Chinese government clearly manipulates information about its domestic terrorism problem, and about the ETIM in particular, to suit its own policy objectives. The PRC blurs distinctions

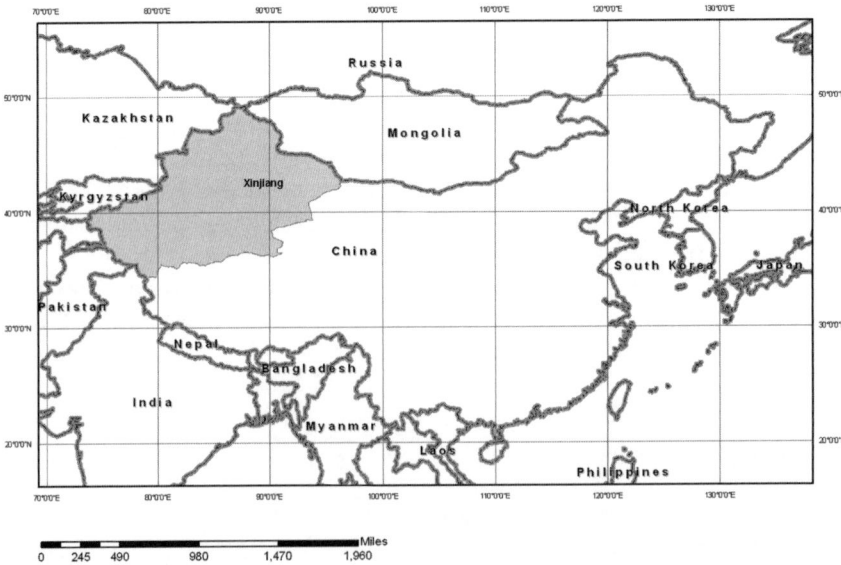

FIGURE 1.1.   The shaded area in northwest China is Xinjiang Uyghur Autonomous Region (also called East Turkistan or Uyghuristan). Map created by the author in ArcGIS.

between the ETIM, other Uyghur militants, and nonviolent Uyghur human rights advocates. Furthermore, Chinese officials' rhetoric suggests an artificial unity between different forms of dissidence and separatism. The PRC refers to pro-democracy and Falun Gong advocates in the same breath as Uyghurs, and links East Turkistani independence to Tibetan and Taiwanese separatism, implying that these different causes constitute a consolidated threat to China's security and territorial integrity. Such rhetoric forces U.S. policy makers to look for ways to condemn the ETIM without going too far and appearing to endorse harsh security crackdowns in China. Since 2002, the United States has placed the ETIM on two terrorism blacklists—one for finance and one for immigration—and lobbied for its inclusion on a UN blacklist, but refrained from adding the group to the State Department's high-profile list of Foreign Terrorist Organizations (FTOs). This seeming inconsistency reflects the complex nature of the U.S. counterterrorism partnership with the PRC.

The United States must understand the ETIM's capabilities and intentions in order to engage Beijing effectively on counterterrorism issues. This book is an attempt to describe the group's objectives, origins, leadership, ideology, and tactics while placing the ETIM in the appropriate historical and contemporary contexts.

We posit that while the ETIM itself represents no serious challenge to Beijing's power, the group may be able to provoke the PRC into harsh security crackdowns that abrogate human rights, exacerbate ethnic tensions, and precipitate further violence in Xinjiang.

Militant Uyghur separatism is a long-standing phenomenon unlikely to subside without substantial Chinese government reform. The ETIM has so far survived despite a relatively small core membership, and even if it were virtually extinguished, we project that militant Uyghur separatists would likely reassemble essentially the same organization.

Some Xinjiang observers have questioned whether the ETIM remains active, or even whether it ever existed at all. They point out that most of what we know about the ETIM comes either from the group itself or from the PRC, and each has its own incentives to fabricate information. We assess that the ETIM *is* a viable organization, although its strength is unclear. Its name has appeared in media reporting for nearly 20 years. The U.S. government identified the ETIM as a terrorist organization in 2002 and affirmed that decision in 2009 by blacklisting current ETIM leader Abdul Haq al-Turkistani. Both the Chinese government and Al-Qaida apparently believe the ETIM is real. Accused ETIM members detained at GTMO provided information that supported claims of the organization's existence, in part by volunteering the names of known ETIM figures as the leaders of their training camp in Afghanistan. Finally, some entity mounted a terrorist campaign in Xinjiang in August 2008. The ETIM claimed responsibility for it. While some of the ETIM's claims are dubious, the group likely perpetrated at least some of the attacks.

The ETIM has its own media organization called "Islam Awazi" in Uyghur, which is "Voice of Islam" in English and "Sawt al-Islam" in Arabic. The ETIM has published online statements not only in Uyghur but also in English and Arabic, probably in an effort to reach a broader audience.

We assess that the terms "East Turkistan Islamic Movement" (ETIM), "Islamic Movement of East Turkistan," "East Turkistan Islamic Party" (ETIP), "Islamic Party of East Turkistan," "Turkistan Islamic Party" (TIP), and "Islamic Party of Turkistan" (IPT) all refer to the same group once led by Hasan Mahsum. We further assess that the similarly named "East Turkistan Islamic Party of Allah" (ETIPA) is actually a separate organization.[3]

The U.S. and UN blacklists recognize "ETIM" and "ETIP" as equivalent references to the group formerly led by Mahsum, and Western media outlets generally use ETIM and ETIP interchangeably. According to the group's now-defunct website, the ETIP and the TIP are the same organization; the group dropped "east" from its name in 2000 in order to encompass both east and west[4] and include all Turkic peoples, not just Uyghurs. A TIP propaganda video released in January 2009 relays the same message.[5] Some Western scholars give a slightly different but expanded explanation for the name change, saying Mahsum dropped "east" from the group's name in 1999 after agreeing to coordinate actions with leaders of Al-Qaida (including Osama bin Laden), the Taliban, and the Islamic Movement of Uzbekistan (IMU).[6]

"IPT" is just a slightly different way of rendering the group's current name in English ("Islamic Party of Turkistan" instead of "Turkistan Islamic Party"). The group seems to use "TIP" and "IPT" interchangeably. Its website's URL (http://tipislamyultuzi.com) contained the initials "TIP," but its logo (see Figure 1.2) includes the full name "Islamic Party of Turkistan" in English. Both the initials "TIP" and the full name "Islamic Party of Turkistan" appear in videos posted on the site.[7]

Name change notwithstanding, Western media outlets continued calling the group the ETIM or ETIP, and the United States and United Nations added these names to their blacklists. Only in 2008, when the group released a series of videos threatening the Beijing Olympics and calling itself the Turkistan Islamic Party (TIP), did analysts connect the ETIM/ETIP with the TIP/IPT.

The names ETIM, ETIP, TIP, and IPT can be rendered several ways in translation and transliteration between various languages. Versions of the ETIM/ETIP's name include *Hizbul Islami Li-Turkistan Ash-Sharqiyah* in Arabic and *Doğu Türkistan İslâm Hareketi* in Turkish. *Sharqiyah* and *Doğu* mean "East" or "Eastern," so removing them from the group name changes it from "East Turkistan" to just "Turkistan."

Even though the group's current name would be the Turkistan Islamic Party (TIP) or the Islamic Party of Turkistan (IPT) in English, we use the term "ETIM" for the rest of this book because it is more familiar and less confusing to a Western audience.

FIGURE 1.2. The Islamic Party of Turkistan is another name for the ETIM. The Arabic writing on its emblem includes the *shahada*, or Muslim profession of faith ("There is no god but Allah; Muhammad is the prophet of Allah") and two verses from the Quran. The first reads, "O ye who believe! / Obey Allah, and obey the Messenger, / And those charged / With authority among you." The second reads, "And fight them on / Until there is no more / Tumult or oppression, / And there prevail / Justice and faith in Allah." Logo captured from the ETIM's website, http://tipislamyultuzi.com.

We use the term "East Turkistan Islamic Movement" and its acronym, "ETIM," only to refer to the militant Uyghur separatist group Mahsum once led. In some contexts, "East Turkistan Islamic Movement" can instead refer to all those who advocate for an independent Uyghur state based on shared Muslim identity. In still other contexts, "ETIM" can stand for "East Turkistan *Independence* Movement," a reference to all Uyghur separatists regardless of whether they want to establish a theocratic or secular state.[8]

WHO ARE THE UYGHURS?

Today, the term "Uyghur" refers to the Turkic, predominantly Muslim people who speak their own language and are concentrated in the oases of Xinjiang. The Uyghurs are one of the PRC's 55 officially recognized ethnic minorities.

Beyond that practical, contemporary definition, the notion of the "Uyghur" is much more complex. Although the term "Uyghur" has existed for millennia, the Chinese state essentially created Uyghur identity as we know it today by adapting the Soviet Union's minority policy, which aimed both to appease and to subjugate minority ethnic groups by assigning them special status.

The term "Uyghur" dates from at least 300 BCE,[9] but the ethnonym vanished from the fifteenth century until the Chinese government resurrected it in the mid-1930s. This resurrection was something of a reinvention as well.

From 744 to 840 CE, the term "Uyghur" referred to a collection of Turkic nomads living on the steppes of Mongolia. These nomads established an empire that eventually extended into northwest China, Junggaria, and at times as far west as the Ferghana Valley. Their empire fell to the Kyrgyz in 840 CE, and many of them resettled near the Tian Shan mountains. These Uyghurs' religious beliefs included Manichaeism and shamanism, but not Islam. From 844 to 932 CE, "Uyghur" referred to a sedentary people based in the Turpan oasis. They included Manichaeists, Buddhists, and Christians, but they did not tolerate Islam. From 932 to 1450 CE, "Uyghur" referred to an elite Turkic society in Turpan. These people were mostly Buddhists, and the term "Uyghur" actually distinguished them from the Muslim Turks to their west. When the Buddhist Uyghurs converted to Islam in the fifteenth century, the ethnonym "Uyghur" disappeared for nearly 500 years.[10]

The Chinese government revived the term as part of a broader initiative to control ethnic tension as the Soviets had in Central Asia. The PRC eventually identified 56 Chinese nationalities,[11] including the "Uyghurs," defined as the Turkic Muslims living in Xinjiang's oases. Under the PRC's policy, minority nationalities receive special recognition and limited discretion in governing specifically designated autonomous areas. This policy was probably intended to reward the minorities for their support in China's Civil War, make them more likely to support the PRC in the future, confine their political activities to specific locales, and separate them from other ethnic minorities who might otherwise serve as allies against the state. However, the PRC did *not* intend to preserve a distinct Uyghur identity in perpetuity. As the Xinjiang scholars Graham E. Fuller and S. Frederick Starr write,

> Mao's decision to create an autonomous Uyghur region was rooted in the strange dialectics of Communism, specifically in Stalin's nationality policies. Stalin, and later Mao, viewed the creation of autonomous regions as the Communist Party's transitory recognition of local identities that would

eventually become obsolete under socialism, and of independent cultural identities that would soon be assimilated in all but a folkloric sense. The creation of autonomous regions was therefore merely a tactic, as the idea of national autonomy would itself ultimately become a meaningless political concept under Communism.[12]

In other words, the PRC intended its autonomous region to appease the Uyghurs until the very notion of nationality itself dissolves in the perfectly cooperative social order of Communism.

In the Uyghurs' case, the PRC's minority policy actually fostered a sense of shared nationality in a historically divided people. The territory now known as Xinjiang has rarely constituted a unified political entity;[13] in times of relative independence, it resembled a collection of city-states more than a country. Most Uyghurs live near the oases in Xinjiang's vast territory, separated from other oases by high mountains and forbidding deserts. Uyghurs traditionally identify themselves as residents of one oasis or another rather than as members of a larger ethnic group. Internal fault lines include not only rivalries between oases, but also clan conflicts, culture clashes between sedentary farmers and nomadic herders, competing religious orders, and varying degrees of devotion to Islam.[14] In addition to the internal barriers to unity, the foreign powers that struggled for land, wealth, and influence in Central Asia over the centuries often manipulated and divided Xinjiang's population to suit their own ends. "Until challenged by their incorporation into the Chinese nation-state, the people of the oases lacked any coherent sense of identity," writes the Xinjiang scholar Dru C. Gladney.[15]

Although coherent, the sense of identity that emerged from the PRC's nationality policy is in some ways distorted. All the Turkic history of the Xinjiang region has been rebranded as "Uyghur,"[16] however anachronistic or otherwise inappropriate that designation may be. For example, the PRC's official version of Xinjiang's history identifies key figures of the seventeenth and eighteenth centuries as "Uyghur" even though the term would have been entirely foreign to them.[17] Many Uyghur nationalists take their ethnonym to mean they are directly descended from the empire builders of the eighth century, but this is unlikely; their ancestors would also include Iranian and Indo-European peoples.[18] (This mixed ancestry explains the dramatic variation in Uyghurs' appearance. Some have dark eyes and black hair, while others have hazel or even blue eyes and brown or even blond hair.) Furthermore, the Muslim identity so integral to the modern concept of the Uyghur ethnicity comes not from the Uyghurs of antiquity but from the later Karakhanid rule over Xinjiang.[19]

Most Uyghurs are Sunni Muslims. Islam entered Xinjiang in the tenth century and took root by absorbing elements of other religions, including Buddhism. Today, northern Xinjiang is more secular and southern Xinjiang is more orthodox. Southern Xinjiang includes a number of Sufis, adherents of a mystical form of Islam the PRC regards with particular suspicion. Sufism's hierarchical leadership structure operates independently of the state-monitored mainstream mosques, and it has a long history of political activism and resistance to Chinese rule in Xinjiang.[20] Southern Xinjiang also includes a small but potentially growing community of Wahhabis, who practice a fundamentalist form of Islam.[21]

Uyghurs speak their own language, also called Uyghur. It is a Turkic tongue written in a modified Arabic script, although in the 1950s, 1960s, and 1970s the PRC mandated Uyghur use the Cyrillic or Latin alphabets instead. The Uyghur language is similar to Uzbek. (Uyghurs pronounce their ethnic group's name "ooey-GHUR," but Americans generally say "WEE-gur" instead.)

Nearly 10 million Uyghurs live in Xinjiang.[22] They were once a majority there, but today they make up only a plurality of Xinjiang's population and may even be a minority as a result of Beijing's long-running campaign to encourage Han Chinese, the national majority, to settle in Xinjiang. Between 500,000 and 600,000 Uyghurs[23] live abroad in the "Uyghur diaspora," which includes Central Asia (especially Kazakhstan), Europe (especially Turkey), and the United States (especially Washington, DC). Munich, Germany, is home to a vocal expatriate community of about 500 to 600 Uyghurs[24] and includes the headquarters of the World Uyghur Congress (WUC) advocacy umbrella group.

Elements within the Uyghur population have fought Chinese rule in one form or another ever since the Qing dynasty claimed the territory in the eighteenth century. Unrest in Xinjiang generally runs in cycles, with periods of heightened ethnic tension leading to violence, followed by harsh security crackdowns. Uyghur activists today regard Beijing's governance as a sustained program of assimilation and exploitation enforced by human rights abuses. They argue the PRC's policies systematically erode the Uyghurs' identity as a distinct cultural group; inhibit the practice of Islam, which is a central component of Uyghur ethnic identity; concentrate Xinjiang's wealth in the hands of the Han Chinese; and exploit Xinjiang's abundant natural resources without regard for the local environment.

WHY DOES XINJIANG MATTER?

The ETIM's namesake "East Turkistan" is a vast, varied landscape of geopolitical, economic, and symbolic significance. It is roughly synonymous with China's northwestern Xinjiang Uyghur Autonomous Region (XUAR), sometimes called Xinjiang Province.

By an accident of geography, Xinjiang—historically home to nomads, farmers, and traders—borders several restive regions whose stability is critical for international security. Noted China scholar Owen Lattimore famously termed Xinjiang the "Pivot of Asia" in 1950. He wrote, "It is a whirlpool in which meet political currents flowing from China, Russia, India and the Moslem Middle East. . . . Once more, as in the days of the rise of the Han Empire, more than two thousand years ago, Sinkiang has become in fact a pivot around which revolve politics, and power, and the fates of men."[25] Lattimore's Cold War assertion still rings true in the age of information, globalization, and counterterrorism. Today Xinjiang borders the eight countries shown in Figure 1.3: Mongolia, Russia, Kazakhstan, Kyrgyzstan, Tajikistan, Afghanistan, Pakistan, and India. Three of the eight (India, Pakistan, and Russia) are nuclear powers, and two (Afghanistan and Pakistan) have provided safe haven to terrorists. All except Mongolia face threats from fundamentalist Muslim militant groups like the ETIM.

The border with India includes the disputed territory of Aksai Chin, which the PRC has administered since the 1962 Sino-Indian war. India claims Aksai Chin belongs to its state of Jammu and Kashmir but respects a "line of actual control" that favors the PRC. (Pakistan does not contest Chinese administration of Aksai Chin, although Pakistan claims other parts of Jammu and Kashmir in a long-standing conflict that has pushed Pakistan and India to the brink of nuclear war.) Xinjiang's administration obviously plays a key role in the PRC's diplomatic relations with India and the other seven border countries.

Within China, Xinjiang borders Qinghai and Gansu provinces and the Tibet Autonomous Region. Chinese officials allege an alliance between

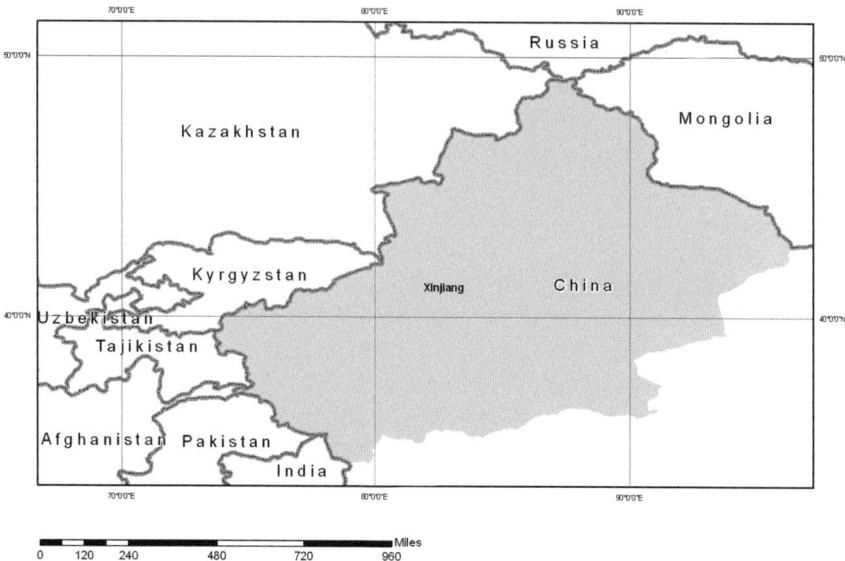

FIGURE 1.3. Xinjiang (East Turkistan) borders eight countries. Map created by the author in ArcGIS.

Tibetan activists and East Turkistan militants but have not produced evidence of it; such an alliance would make little sense, since Tibetan advocates for independence claim part of East Turkistan as "Greater Tibet."

Xinjiang's strategic location is important not only for China's power projection but also for China's economic development. Xinjiang is China's gateway to trade with Central Asia. Xinjiang had the highest export growth in all of the PRC in 2007 at more than 60 percent.[26] In addition, Xinjiang's role as the country's largest cotton production base helps curb the PRC's reliance on cotton imports. (The PRC is the world's biggest cotton importer.[27])

Xinjiang's abundant natural resources—including oil, natural gas, coal, copper, and gold—have been a keystone of China's economic growth strategy since then-President Jiang Zemin announced the "Great Western Development" economic initiative in 1999. The energy-rich Tarim, Junggar, and Turpan-Hami basins made Xinjiang China's largest oil and gas production base in both 2007 and 2008.[28] Xinjiang has 20.8 billion tons of oil and 10.8 trillion cubic meters[29] of natural gas, according to the Chinese government; based on those figures, Xinjiang accounts for 30 percent or more of the country's total oil and gas land deposits.[30] Xinjiang also has significant coal deposits projected at more than 2 trillion tons, accounting for 40 percent of China's total coal reserves.[31] Xinjiang's nonfuel mineral resources include gold, copper, nickel, lead, and zinc.[32]

Xinjiang's symbolic significance is more difficult to measure than its natural wealth. Mummies discovered in the Taklamakan Desert show Xinjiang was home to civilization more than 3,000 years ago. Xinjiang later occupied an important section of the ancient Silk Road and became an economic and cultural crossroads for civilizations from China, India, Persia, Arabia, and the West. The region developed a rich, diverse culture by fusing the musical, artistic, and literary traditions that accompanied the fabrics, spices, precious metals, and other luxury items carried along the historical trade routes.

Trade centers and other settlements in Xinjiang have traditionally clustered around its oases. Northwest China is a land of deserts, mountains, steppes, rivers, and basins. The Taklamakan is the world's second-largest shifting-sand desert. Xinjiang contains both the second-highest point on earth (the K2 mountain, more than 28,000 feet high on the China-Pakistan border) and the second-lowest land point on earth (the Turpan Depression, more than 500 feet below sea level about 100 miles southeast of Urumqi). Most of Xinjiang's population is concentrated in the oases of the Tarim Basin in the south, the Junggarian Basin in the north, and the Turpan Basin in the east. Xinjiang is more a collection of localities than a single, unified territory.

Xinjiang measures about 637,000 square miles, which is more than twice as big as Texas. It is China's largest administrative region and makes up about a sixth of China's land, but most of Xinjiang is sparsely populated and the entire region is relatively remote. More than 2,000 miles separate Kashgar in western Xinjiang from China's bustling capital. (As the Xinjiang scholars Fuller and Jonathan N. Lipman note somewhat wryly, Kashgar is closer to Baghdad than Beijing.[33]) High mountains and vast swaths of desert have historically kept China's northwest isolated from the rest of the country. Not until 1999 did China open a rail line connecting Kashgar with Xinjiang's capital, Urumqi. Additional projects building highways and otherwise improving the region's transportation infrastructure followed with the Great Western Development initiative, more thoroughly integrating Xinjiang with China proper.

WHAT DOES "EAST TURKISTAN" MEAN?

The name "Xinjiang" and the abbreviation "XUAR" refer to roughly the same territory as "East Turkistan," but the terms have vastly different connotations. "Xinjiang" and "XUAR" are the official names, used by the Chinese government and recognized by the international community. Using these names can imply either support for or mere acknowledgment of Beijing's control over the region. In contemporary usage, "East Turkistan" and its sister term, "Uyghuristan," are separatists' defiant references to the same land as if it were *not* a part of China.

The name "Xinjiang"—like much else about the region—is controversial. "Xinjiang" in Chinese translates roughly to "New Frontier" or "New Dominion" in English. This name dates from the late 1700s and it alludes to the region's identity as an outer limit, a borderland perhaps not fully subdued. Critics of China's Xinjiang policy note that the term "new" belies Beijing's claims that Xinjiang has belonged to China since ancient times. For example, the Chinese government's 2003 white paper on Xinjiang, an attempt to project institutional respect for human rights, states in its fore-word, "Since the Western Han Dynasty (206 B.C.–24 A.D.), [Xinjiang] has been an inseparable part of the unitary multi-ethnic Chinese nation."[34] If that were the case, China's critics argue, then this area would not have been called a *new* frontier in the late eighteenth century.

The Qing dynasty made Xinjiang a province of China in 1884. In 1955, Mao Zedong designated Xinjiang one of five special "autonomous regions" created to recognize the predominance of a minority ethnicity in a specific geographic area, in this case the Uyghurs in Xinjiang. Xinjiang Province then became the Xinjiang Uyghur Autonomous Region, or XUAR. The Communists had courted China's minorities during the Chinese Civil War; the Communists' autonomy policy, adapted from Joseph Stalin's, was partly a reward for the minorities' cooperation and partly an attempt to pre-empt any thoughts of secession. As China's 2005 white paper on ethnic regional autonomy puts it, "The practice of regional autonomy not only ensures the rights of the ethnic minorities to exercise autonomy as masters of their homelands, but also upholds the unification of the state."[35]

The other ethnic groups with their own autonomous regions are the Mongols in Inner Mongolia (established in 1947), the Zhuang in Guangxi (established in 1958), the Hui in Ningxia (also established in 1958), and the Tibetans in Tibet (established in 1965). China has also designated autonomous prefectures, counties, and townships within its provinces.

China's policy offers limited freedom at best. As a nominally autonomous region, Xinjiang can petition to modify or disregard Chinese government policies that do not suit its needs, but Xinjiang is not allowed to secede from the Chinese state.[36] Although the head of Xinjiang's government must be a Uyghur, the powerful head of the Chinese Communist Party in the area need not be. The Uyghurs are officially guaranteed the right to speak their own language, follow their own religion, and practice their own folkways, but in daily life displays of ethnic identity are often discouraged. As China's 2005 white paper on ethnic regional autonomy states, "The ethnic minorities are encouraged to adopt new, scientific, civilized and healthy customs in daily life."[37] Xinjiang is autonomous in name only.

Perhaps not surprisingly, many Uyghur activists refuse to call the territory the XUAR or even just "Xinjiang" because they consider the term a relic of Chinese imperialism. " 'Xinjiang' or 'XUAR' are Chinese names forcibly imposed by the Han Chinese. Therefore, we have considered these names illegal and have never admitted and will never admit to them," wrote Hashir Wahidi in an article posted on the Uyghur American Association's website. (Wahidi founded the Uyghur Liberation Organization, a group accused of murder, kidnapping, and arson[38]; he died in 1998, allegedly from injuries inflicted by unidentified intruders who beat him in his home in Kazakhstan.[39])

Those who refuse to use "Xinjiang" and "XUAR" typically refer to roughly the same territory as either "East Turkistan" or "Uyghuristan." Some people use "East Turkistan" and "Uyghuristan" interchangeably, but the two terms connote subtly different claims to ethnic sovereignty.

"East Turkistan" means "Land of the Eastern Turks," a reference to the inhabitants' identity as a Turkic—but not specifically Uyghur—people. It not only emphasizes local ethnic identity but also suggests association with other peoples (Turks in general) who share a common ancestry.

"Turkistan" was originally a nonpolitical, purely geographic term for the part of Central Asia east of the Caspian Sea, west of the Gobi desert, south of Siberia, and north of Tibet, India, Afghanistan, and Iran.[40] Mountain ranges divide this region into two parts: "West Turkistan," also called "Russian Turkistan," and "East Turkistan," also called "Chinese Turkistan." "West Turkistan" includes present-day Turkmenistan, Uzbekistan, Tajikistan,

Kyrgyzstan, and southern Kazakhstan. (The term "West Turkistan" has not been politicized as "East Turkistan" has.) "East Turkistan" usually encompasses all of present-day Xinjiang in contemporary usage. The Uyghurs who briefly attained independence during the Chinese Civil War called their country "East Turkistan." "East Turkistan" is *Sherqiy Türkistan* in the Uyghur language and *Dongtu* in Chinese.

"Uyghuristan" means "Land of the Uyghurs." It clearly identifies the territory as the Uyghur ethnic homeland, just as Kazakhstan is the land of the Kazakhs, Tajikistan is the land of the Tajiks, etc. An independent Uyghuristan would be based on shared Uyghur ethnic identity. The term suggests autochthony. It does not reach out to make common cause with other Turkic peoples.

Both violent and nonviolent Uyghur activists struggle with the choice between "Uyghuristan" and "East Turkistan." This debate was one of many dividing the members of Hashir Wahidi's Uyghur Liberation Organization.[41] Wahidi himself preferred "Uyghuristan." He found the name "East Turkistan" problematic because it refers to geography instead of a people or a nation, historically excludes the Uyghur territory of Junggaria from its geographic purview, and begs the somewhat confusing question, "What about 'West Turkistan'?"[42] Other groups try to evade the name issue altogether. For example, the banner of a 2001 worldwide gathering of Uyghur leaders read, "East Turkestan (Uighuristan) National Congress"—a somewhat clumsy attempt at compromise.[43] In general, Uyghur activists from northern Xinjiang favor the term "Uyghuristan."[44] Uyghur activists from southern Xinjiang, who are more influenced by Turkey, the Middle East, and Afghanistan, generally prefer the term "East Turkistan."[45]

By incorporating "East Turkistan" in its name, the ETIM signals the separatist element of its ideology. Choosing "East Turkistan" over "Uyghuristan" to communicate this message avoids circumscribing the ETIM's separatism as a strictly Uyghur cause, thus expanding the array of the ETIM's potential allies and benefactors. Indeed, the group's constitution says its members "carry out jihad cooperatively with the mujahideen Muslims from all over the world."[46] The ETIM has allegedly cooperated with non-Uyghur terrorist groups including Al-Qaida, the Taliban, and the IMU.[47] The suspected ETIM members detained at GTMO often used the term "East Turkistani" instead of "Uyghur," characterizing themselves as nationals of the state they sought rather than as members of one of China's 55 official minority groups.

Before 9/11, the PRC refused to use either "East Turkistan" or "Uyghuristan" or to acknowledge the separatist movement in Xinjiang.[48] After 9/11, Chinese officials began discussing their domestic terrorism problem, using the term "East Turkistan" to refer to Uyghur separatists. This term distinguishes the separatists from the general population of Xinjiang and avoids identifying separatism with Uyghur ethnicity.[49] By using the term "East Turkistan," the PRC can refer pejoratively to Uyghur separatists without condemning all Uyghurs.

Where appropriate, the authors of this book use "East Turkistan" instead of "Uyghuristan" because both the ETIM and the PRC do so. However, we usually refer to the territory in question as "Xinjiang." While it is not entirely neutral, "Xinjiang" is certainly a more neutral term than the alternatives, and its meaning is more widely understood than that of "East Turkistan" or "Uyghuristan." For the same reasons, we refer to the ethnic group as "Uyghur" instead of "East Turkistani." We also use a number of names transliterated from Chinese, Uyghur, and other languages, including Arabic. In each case, we adopt the version we believe is most familiar to the modern reader.

A NOTE ON THE AVAILABLE INFORMATION

Information in this book comes from the ETIM's now-defunct website and public statements; media reports from all over the world; PRC news releases, white papers, and statistical data; reports by human rights groups; academic accounts of Xinjiang's history; published U.S. Defense Department documentation on the Uyghurs detained at GTMO; and contemporary analyses by China scholars, counterterrorism experts, strategic think tanks, and congressional researchers. However, any credible analysis of this general topic—including ours—must acknowledge significant information gaps.

The PRC maintains strict control over the information coming from Xinjiang. Apart from the ETIM's statements, we have essentially only two sources for what we know about the region today: Uyghur expatriates and the PRC itself.

Uyghur expatriates typically leave Xinjiang because they object to the PRC's policies. Expatriates who seek a public voice generally advocate independence for Xinjiang, and so they have a powerful incentive to exaggerate the scope and intensity of Uyghur dissidence in an effort to muster support for their cause and pressure the PRC to change its policies. Furthermore, as expatriates these sources cannot provide firsthand accounts of current events in Xinjiang.

The PRC both restricts and manipulates information coming from Xinjiang. For example, the PRC's "Golden Shield Project," better known in the West as the "Great Firewall of China," blocks access to websites Beijing deems objectionable, including blogging and networking sites that could serve as an immediate conduit for information.[50]

The state news agency, Xinhua, makes no attempt at objectivity. The official media report on ethnic and religious violence only to state that the offenders have been detained and punished.[51] Foreign journalists must apply for permission to visit Xinjiang;[52] once there, they operate in an atmosphere of pervasive surveillance and censorship fueled by ethnic tension.

Xinjiang has no permanent media presence,[53] so journalists reporting on it seldom have the historical knowledge required to place events in the appropriate context.

Social scientists studying the area face strict controls on field research and can conduct only limited surveys and interviews inside the PRC. For example, after a period of relative freedom, the social ethnographer Justin Jon Rudelson found his work in Xinjiang sharply curtailed in 1990. PRC officials interrogated him for six hours, searched his bags, and harassed his friends. The officials also seized his photocopies of 250-year-old records on irrigation practices, claiming they were "secret," and told him he could no longer stay more than 10 days in one place, must have an official guide, and would need to submit any photos and videos he took for official vetting.[54]

Religious or ethnic minority issues are generally considered "state secrets,"[55] as are statistics on arrests, detentions, and executions.[56] Fuller and Lipman go so far as to say, "The logistics of armed struggle and the specifics of contact with radical Islamic groups abroad have proved impenetrable to outside investigation."[57] Because of constraints like these, reports on present-day conditions in Xinjiang rely heavily on anecdotal evidence in lieu of systematically gathered, statistically valid information.

Westerners receive few raw data from Xinjiang because only the Chinese government is in a position to collect such data. Much of what we know of Xinjiang, we know either because the PRC told us or the PRC allowed us to learn. Whatever the PRC releases is almost guaranteed to support Beijing's current official position, even if that means suppressing or exaggerating key information. Officials minimize the unrest in Xinjiang when they want to attract foreign business and inflate it when they want to legitimate a security crackdown or make common cause with the United States on counterterrorism issues. At times, officially released information seems inconsistent or plainly false, but the reason for the distortion is unclear. For example, Chinese officials provided several versions of an official statistic on terrorist attacks in Xinjiang. In all three versions, 162 people were killed and more than 440 wounded in at least 200 terrorist attacks. However, officials have provided these same numbers for three different intervals: 1992–2001, 1990–2001, and 1995–2005.[58]

The PRC has been refining its counterterrorism message and building the ETIM's international "brand" for years. Beijing's first news release on "East Turkistan" militancy, in November 2001, alleged that the ETIM was one of more than 40 Uyghur separatist groups involved in terrorism. By contrast, a similar news release from 2008 focused exclusively on the ETIM. This focus could lead Chinese officials to attribute incidents to the ETIM even when other groups are actually responsible. Naming the same adversary time after time reinforces the message that China faces a genuine terrorist threat. The ETIM has already achieved name recognition in the West because of its alleged ties to Al-Qaida and the Taliban, so it is the PRC's most logical choice for the face of Uyghur separatism.

In this book, we note where the PRC is the sole or a disputed source for our information. We also make every effort to identify information gaps and clarify what we do not know.

While the PRC has probably overattributed terrorist acts to the ETIM, the U.S. government may have originated and certainly exacerbated the attribution problem by misreading a key Chinese statement. In 2002, the PRC released a lengthy document titled " 'East Turkistan' Terrorist Forces Cannot Get Away with Impunity." This document contains one of the references to at least 200 East Turkistan terrorist attacks that killed 162 people and wounded more than 440 (in this version, from 1990 to 2001). The document goes on to detail dozens of these attacks, attributing some to the ETIM, attributing others to different East Turkistani organizations, and describing some attacks without blaming them on any specific group. Many of the descriptions of attacks not blamed on any specific group use a phrase translated to English as "the 'East Turkistan' terrorist organization," which some analysts interpreted as a reference to the ETIM. However, in Chinese, this phrase has no definite article (no "the") and could be either singular or plural.[59] Thus, the specific-sounding "the 'East Turkistan' terrorist organization" could also have been translated as the more generic " 'East Turkistan' terrorist organizations" or "an 'East Turkistan' terrorist organization." Perhaps due to this confusing translation problem, U.S. officials mistakenly blamed all 200-plus attacks, all 162 deaths, and all 440-plus injuries on elements of the ETIM.[60] The PRC had actually attributed these events to "the 'East Turkistan' terrorist forces inside and outside Chinese territory,"[61] a broad term not limited to the ETIM. The U.S. attribution artificially raised the ETIM's profile, perhaps permanently. Without access to alternative credible, accessible sources to cross-check the information, journalists and academics unwittingly reproduced the error.

The restricted, distorted available data on Xinjiang make such misinformation practically inevitable. Those able to disseminate information on current events usually have an agenda and seldom have firsthand access. The PRC's grip on information flowing out of Xinjiang only tightens when—as now—the world is watching.

The ETIM has never had a higher profile than it does today. However, it is only one of several militant groups on the radical fringe of the centuries-old Uyghur separatist movement. In order to understand the ETIM, we must look beyond the headlines and examine the contemporary and historical contexts of Uyghur separatism.

2

---⊶⊷⊷⊷---

The Contemporary and Historical Contexts of Uyghur Separatism

This chapter places the ETIM in the contemporary and historical contexts of Uyghur separatism. The first section summarizes the Uyghurs' current grievances. The second section sketches Uyghur nationalism in general and describes specific organizations, both nonviolent and militant, that claim to act on behalf of the Uyghur people. The third and final section outlines key events in the long history of militant Uyghur separatism and discusses the factors shaping Uyghur separatism today.

UYGHUR GRIEVANCES

Uyghur separatists claim the right to independence from China based on their shared ethno-religious identity and a history of unfair treatment by the Chinese state. The Uyghurs' long-standing grievances against Beijing are cultural, religious, economic, and environmental. The Han Chinese dominate Xinjiang's local government, education system, and commercial sector. Uyghur activists regard Beijing's governance as a sustained program of assimilation and exploitation. They argue that the PRC's policies systematically erode the Uyghurs' identity as a distinct cultural group; inhibit the practice of Islam, which is a central component of Uyghur ethnic identity; concentrate Xinjiang's wealth in the hands of the Han Chinese; and exploit Xinjiang's resources without regard for the local environment. Uyghur activists also claim human rights abuses are routine in Xinjiang, as the government suppresses dissent (including peaceful protest) in the guise of anticrime and counterterrorism operations.

Cultural Grievances

Uyghurs deeply resent the PRC's sustained efforts to settle Han Chinese in Xinjiang. They fear Uyghur culture is dying, as their majority dwindles to a plurality or even a minority of the local population, Uyghur children take classes in Mandarin Chinese instead of their ancestral language, and the PRC promulgates a sanitized and self-serving version of Uyghur history.

The Chinese Communist Party (CCP) took over Xinjiang in 1949. In 1950, the newly established PRC launched a major resettlement project that transformed Xinjiang's demographics from 80–90 percent Uyghur and 5–10 percent Han[1] to approximately half Han today. The proportion of Han steadily increased over several decades, going from about 11 percent of Xinjiang's total population in 1955 to 28 percent in 1962 to 40 percent in 1971.[2]

The PRC's official statistics show that Xinjiang was still about 40 percent Han in 2007 (see Figure 2.1). Another 46 percent of the population was Uyghur, and the remaining 14 percent included various other ethnic minorities.[3] However, these numbers do not include members of the army and paramilitary units stationed in Xinjiang or any of the "self-drifters," unregistered laborers who come to Xinjiang looking for work and stay for varying lengths of time. Those individuals are nearly all Han. When their ethnicity is factored into the assessment, the Han probably outnumber or at least equal the Uyghur population.[4]

Regardless of the actual demographics, many Uyghurs perceive that their share of Xinjiang's population is dwindling by the day and fear they will soon be a minority in their homeland. Media reports on this issue are filled with bleak statements by ordinary Uyghurs afraid to give their real names. In a representative 2008 article from the *Christian Science Monitor*, an Urumqi teacher nicknamed "Batur" said, "We feel like foreigners in our own land. We are like the Indians in America."[5]

The PRC initially directed the Han settlers to unoccupied parts of Xinjiang rather than encouraging them to live side by side with the Uyghurs. (The central government's true motive in this approach may have been to minimize disruption to the local population and mitigate charges of encroachment, but some Uyghurs perceive this settlement pattern as deliberate and sinister encirclement.[6]) Early Han migrants settled in northern Xinjiang, including Urumqi, Ili, and the northern ring of the Tarim Basin,[7] leaving southern Xinjiang to the Uyghurs. But in the late 1990s Han migrants moved southwest, following construction of the South Xinjiang railway connecting Urumqi to Kashgar. Han settlers now live in all the larger cities of Xinjiang and even the oases south of the Taklamakan desert, considered the Uyghur heartland.[8]

Ethnicity	Population
Uyghur	9,650,629
Han	8,239,245
Kazakh	1,483,883
Hui	942,956
Kyrgyz	181,862
Mongol	177,120
Tajik	44,824
Xibo	42,444
Manchu	25,626
Uzbek	16,138
Russian	11,609
Daur	6,678
Tatar	4,728
Others	124,158
Total	20,951,900

FIGURE 2.1.   The PRC's official statistics show that Xinjiang was 46 percent Uyghur in 2007. However, these statistics do not include "self-drifters" or members of military and paramilitary units stationed in Xinjiang, who are almost all Han. Statistics Bureau of Xinjiang Uygur Autonomous Region, *Xinjiang Statistical Yearbook 2008*, table 3–7.

The stated goal of the PRC's Han migration campaign was to facilitate economic development, not to force demographic change. As corollary benefits, the migration campaign would distribute China's population (and labor pool) more evenly and stabilize the political climate in the restive border region. Many of the Han settlers have been affiliated with the Xinjiang Production and Construction Corps (XPCC), or *Xinjiang shengchan jianshe bingtuan* (*bingtuan* for short). The *bingtuan* was created from demobilized Nationalist and Communist army units after China's civil war to, in the PRC's words, "cultivate and guard the frontier areas."[9] The *bingtuan* still serves as a paramilitary force, keeping order and managing prisons, and as an industrial group, running farming, land reclamation, and construction projects. The overwhelming majority of its members are Han. For example, in 2006 the PRC reserved 808 of 840 open *bingtuan* jobs for Han Chinese.[10]

PRC propaganda of the late 1950s and early 1960s depicted "heroic migrants opening up vast wastelands and transforming parched deserts into fertile fields,"[11] in the characterization of cultural geographer Stanley Toops. Young people from eastern cities settled in Xinjiang's countryside under Mao's "Great Leap Forward" collectivization and industrialization campaign.[12] The last major movement of Han settlers completely organized and supervised by the PRC took place in 1964,[13] but the migration did not end then. The state continued to encourage Han professionals to move west with tax breaks and other incentives. The PRC's 2003 white paper on Xinjiang alludes to the Han migration campaign as follows: "Since the founding of New China, considering Xinjiang's remoteness, backwardness and shortage of high-caliber personnel, the state has assigned, transferred or encouraged over 800,000 intellectuals and professional and technical personnel from inland regions to work in Xinjiang."[14] The PRC's open and aggressive campaign to settle Han in Xinjiang has ended, but Han self-drifters continue to flood Xinjiang in search of work.

Many Uyghurs believe the Han population will soon dominate Xinjiang, and that a dominant Han majority will destroy Uyghur cultural identity and replace it with a self-serving version of Uyghur history. Uyghur intellectuals have long endured the prospect of persecution for their cultural achievements. For example, in 1992 the PRC banned works by the popular Uyghur author Abdurehim Otkur, whose historical novels contain passages that seem to advocate separatism when taken out of context. In the mid-1990s the PRC held historian Turghun Almas under house arrest for publishing an account of the Uyghur past that contrasted with the CCP's official version. Fuller and Lipman lament the " 'Disneylandization' of Islam and Uyghur culture in China," which they say "has been emasculated, folklorized, prettified, Hanified, and cast into the nationwide museum of safely packaged ethnicity that serves up exoticism and charm to tourists in China but precludes any hint of opposition in the past or present."[15]

Today, Uyghur educational and professional advancement often necessitates a compromise of cultural identity. The PRC maintains parallel school systems in Chinese and in minority languages. Uyghur parents in Xinjiang choose whether to send their children to Uyghur schools, where they will use the Uyghur language, or to mainstream Chinese schools, where they will learn Mandarin Chinese. Graduates of the Chinese system are much more likely to succeed in the professional world, because proficiency in Chinese is a prerequisite for any professional success outside exclusively Uyghur enclaves. (Many Uyghur families solve this dilemma by sending their sons to Chinese schools and their daughters to Uyghur schools.[16] This practice anoints the females as the conservators of the Uyghur language but curtails their potential for academic and economic achievement.) Chinese proficiency also becomes more important as the student progresses in school.

Xinjiang University stopped teaching in Uyghur in 2002.[17] The PRC has established affirmative-action-style policies to help minorities gain acceptance at China's increasingly expensive universities, but statistics indicate Xinjiang's minorities (including Uyghurs) are less likely to continue their education beyond elementary school than Han living in the same district.[18]

Even in Uyghur schools, the study of language favors Mandarin speakers and the curriculum emphasizes Han culture.[19] Minority students are required to study Chinese as a second language, while Han students who were raised speaking Chinese typically study English or another language that might help them succeed outside China.[20] In addition, the PRC's dramatic shifts in foreign policy have played havoc with the written form of the Uyghur language. When the Communists came to power in China, Uyghurs used a modified Arabic script. The PRC—which, at the time, had a close relationship with the Soviet Union—changed the Uyghur script to Cyrillic, then changed it to the Latin alphabet after Sino-Soviet relations began to sour in 1958. The Latin alphabet was never popular among Uyghurs, so the PRC reinstated the modified Arabic script in 1980 (after Mao's death). These three major changes in the language provoked confusion, suspicion, and resentment among the Uyghur population. Uyghurs educated in the 1950s and 1960s knew a script no longer being taught to their own children, and some believed these switches were part of a deliberate effort to divide generations from each other.[21]

In the aftermath of China's civil war, the chief aims of the PRC's education program were to foster national unity and instill loyalty in minority populations.[22] Both aims endure today, often at the expense of historical accuracy. For example, nearly all accounts of Islam in China end with the victory of the CCP in 1949.[23] The curriculum, which is standard throughout the country, emphasizes Han Chinese culture,[24] and in postsecondary school students are required to pass an exam on the PRC's official history of Xinjiang.[25]

Chinese education also includes a strong element of political indoctrination.[26] It certainly demands assimilation. For example, female students even in Uyghur schools are not allowed to wear traditional Muslim clothing, such as head scarves and floor-length skirts.[27] Public school students can be expelled for celebrating religious holidays or studying religious texts,[28] like a young woman caught praying in her dormitory room at the Kashgar Teachers' Training College in 2001.[29] Men who work in schools can even be forced to shave their facial hair, although beards and mustaches are symbols of manhood in Uyghur culture.[30] Forced accommodations like these are deeply troubling to the Uyghur population. In the words of Fuller and Starr, "In a cultural, religious, and linguistic sense, [the Uyghurs] fear that to assimilate is to die."[31]

Uyghur advocates fear their future will look like Inner Mongolia's present. In the parts of Mongolia under PRC rule, the ethnic Mongol population is less than 20 percent. Mongols have almost no control over the region's affairs, and their folkways scarcely exist outside of tourist attractions.[32]

Religious Grievances

The CCP is, of course, officially atheist, and it prohibits its members from believing or participating in religion. However, China's 1982 constitution promises religious freedom. In practice, the PRC permits religious expression that does not threaten state power. China's prohibitions on "illegal religious activities" are broad enough to allow provincial and local authorities tremendous latitude in their posture toward religious communities.

Beijing frequently conflates Uyghur Islam with separatism and regulates the practice of Islam more strictly in Uyghur Xinjiang than elsewhere in the country.[33] The Muslim Hui, who speak Chinese and are generally more culturally assimilated, are allowed more freedom to worship. (Hui and Uyghurs maintain separate mosques.) A 2005 report from Human Rights Watch and Human Rights in China notes that "Islam is perceived as feeding Uighur ethnic identity, and so the subordination of Islam to the state is used as a means to ensure the subordination of Uighurs as well."[34]

The CCP initially tolerated Islam in Xinjiang but soon co-opted its sources of power and revenue, eliminating tithes, putting religious authorities on the state payroll, and transferring land endowments from the church to the state.[35] Mao's regime repressed Muslims and many other sectors of society during the Cultural Revolution (1966–1976). The PRC shut down and repurposed religious buildings all over China, including Xinjiang (for example, by converting a mosque courtyard to a slaughterhouse for pigs, which Muslims consider unclean animals[36]). Deng Xiaoping's "Reform and Opening" campaign ushered in an era of renewed tolerance in the late 1970s, but in the mid-1990s, China "reverted to the strictest controls and outright repression," according to Fuller and Starr.[37] In 1998, China's central government directed Xinjiang authorities to develop more stringent policies on religious matters. The "October 1998 Instructions" tightened rules related to religious professionals, places, and teachings.[38] Official punishments range from mandatory indoctrination courses to fines to prolonged detention, sometimes without charge. Harassment is commonplace. Today, the PRC's program of surveillance, regulation, and intimidation extends beyond the clergy to the laity, severely curtailing the practice of Islam in Xinjiang.

The Chinese state is deeply suspicious of Muslim people and perceives a potentially serious political threat in Muslim gatherings, especially in Xinjiang. Chinese law requires all religious associations to apply for state authorization, but Xinjiang authorities frequently deny these applications and then place the applicants under surveillance.[39] (This pattern of denial and surveillance creates a catch-22 situation for the would-be association members. If they fail to apply for state authorization, their group is illegal; however, if they do apply they are likely to be denied, in which case their group is still illegal and they have attracted unwelcome attention from the local authorities.)

All mosques and religious schools must register with local officials or risk forced closure.[40] Government informers attend prayer services. During Ramadan, police drop in on gatherings for the postsunset meal known as *iftar*, monitoring who is observing the Muslim fast.[41] In 1995, Xinjiang outlawed *mashrap*—a Uyghur Muslim version of the Knights of Columbus—after the social clubs crossed the line into political activism by successfully boycotting liquor in Yining.[42] In 1996, the PRC limited the number of its citizens who could travel to Mecca, Saudi Arabia, for the obligatory Muslim pilgrimage known as the *hajj*.[43] (The respect and prestige conferred on a *hajji* after his return to Xinjiang may be one reason for this restriction. Uyghurs who have completed the *hajj* can become influential religious figures capable of mobilizing their communities and, therefore, capable of challenging the PRC at the local level.)

Xinjiang law prohibits children younger than 18 from practicing religion and bans adults from preaching to them. These laws are rigidly enforced, and most mosques have a sign above the door barring minors.[44] Xinjiang's authorities treat religion like the United States treats legal vices such as smoking, drinking, and gambling. These laws seem targeted specifically at the Uyghur Muslim population, as children elsewhere in China (even in Tibet) are allowed to worship more freely.

The state must preapprove any publications that discuss religion. A 2000 manual for implementing religious guidance in Urumqi reads as follows: "Any item to be published (including news and articles) related to research and appraisal of Islamic religion must uphold the Marxist point of view of religion, and use the yardstick of the Party's and the government's religious policies and regulation."[45] (Marx famously termed religion "the opiate of the masses." Marxists believe religion will gradually disappear as society evolves toward the ideal of Communism.) How a document that upholds the Marxist view of religion could contain genuine research and appraisal is not addressed.

Religious professionals live under regular surveillance. PRC officials monitor their behavior for signs that they are preaching Islam to minors, spreading "fundamentalism" (which is defined at the whim of the state), or connecting China's Muslim community to other Muslim communities abroad. Those acts are "illegal religious activities" punishable by a prison term.[46] The October 1998 Instructions directed local authorities to create "a political verification dossier to make sure imams meet political requirements" and to keep "a handle on the imam's ideological state at all times."[47]

The PRC also exercises control over Muslim leadership by requiring official imams to hold a degree from the Institute for the Study of Islamic Texts in Urumqi. The institute's faculty all work directly for the Chinese state, and a government-funded organization called the Islamic Association of China establishes the institute's curriculum from Beijing.[48]

The imams of major mosques are all government employees subject to removal if their preaching somehow offends the state. For example, in 1995 the PRC replaced two imams in Hotan, Xinjiang, for applying Quranic teaching to current events; their replacement began advocating for improved women's rights, and he was arrested as well.[49] (These events led to a major public demonstration that morphed into a riot, which police suppressed with tear gas and beatings.[50]) To retain their accreditation, imams must attend annual training that amounts to political indoctrination. Under Xinjiang's sustained "re-education" campaign, clerics spend about three weeks listening to CCP speeches and taking exams on religious law and CCP doctrine. They meet in small groups to confess their knowledge of illicit religious or separatist activity, admit any personal thoughts about opposing party doctrine, and point out each other's errors. Confessing too big a violation brings harsh sanction, but an imam who confesses nothing is suspected of hiding the truth. The officials running the re-education session record the clerics' actions and send the records to the local religious affairs bureaus.[51]

Those who work for the state in a nonreligious capacity know their professional advancement depends on avoiding mosques and eschewing any close association with religious authorities.[52] Much like public school students, public sector employees are not allowed to wear traditional Muslim clothing, including headscarves for women or the embroidered *doppa* skullcap for men.[53] (The *doppa* is a Central Asian version of the Muslim prayer cap known as the taqiyah, kufi, topi, and many other names elsewhere in the world.)

In its 60 years of rule in China, the CCP has moved quickly to neutralize the potential political power of organized Islam and maintained steady surveillance of Muslim religious leaders. Faith is not only marginalized but stigmatized. Many Muslims, particularly Uyghurs, are forced to choose between publicly observing the tenets of their faith and rising in China's socioeconomic strata.

Economic Grievances

In the 1990s, the PRC began a concerted effort to develop Xinjiang, believing development would not only enrich the country but also curb ethnic nationalism and engender a greater sense of national unity. In 1999, then-President Jiang Zemin announced the "Great Western Development" ("Xibu Da Kaifa") economic initiative, also called "Develop the West," "Open Up the West," or the "Great Leap West." It focused on exploiting Xinjiang's abundant natural resources. Today, Xinjiang is one of China's more prosperous regions overall, but the distribution of Xinjiang's wealth clearly favors the Han population. Uyghurs believe the Han Chinese discriminate against them in the working world (despite the PRC's attempt at affirmative-action-style policies to promote Uyghur economic achievement) and that the PRC exploits Xinjiang's natural resources without reinvesting in the region.

The limited economic data available from the PRC clearly indicate economic disparity in Xinjiang. The gross domestic product (GDP) of a given region in Xinjiang correlates with the concentration of Han in that area's population.[54] In general, Han occupy Xinjiang's most prosperous areas, while the predominantly Uyghur areas in southern Xinjiang have the region's lowest GDP per capita.[55] The Xinjiang scholar Michael Dillon writes, "Poor rural Uyghurs are at the bottom of the social hierarchy whilst the government, party and military bureaucracies, which are mostly but not exclusively Han, have a monopoly of political authority and access to the lion's share of better quality housing, well-paid employment and consumer goods."[56]

In this stratified society, many economically disadvantaged Uyghurs view their more successful brethren as collaborators in the Han-dominated socio-economic system. Some Han also resent upwardly mobile Uyghurs as the beneficiaries of ethnic advancement policies, even as the Uyghurs resent the Han for flooding the labor market. (Rudelson's 1990s fieldwork indicates the presence of self-drifters—who are typically impoverished Han willing to accept the most menial of jobs—actually mitigates Turpan residents' hostility toward the Han in general,[57] by demonstrating that some Han also live in difficult circumstances.)

The sustained influx of Han Chinese to the Xinjiang region means Uyghurs must compete with Han for jobs in Xinjiang. This competition takes place on increasingly Han terms, despite a 1995 antidiscrimination law and recent affirmative-action-style policies designed to help ethnic minorities advance in the workplace. Han supervisors discriminate in favor of workers who speak their language and share their culture. Prospective Uyghur employees must overcome a prevailing stereotype of Uyghurs as dim, lazy, and backward.

Many specialized jobs are reserved for the *bingtuan* and other Han-dominated work units.[58] Uyghurs who find work and perform well often hit a glass ceiling.[59] Currently, Han occupy about 80 percent of Xinjiang's jobs in the manufacturing, transport, communications, oil and gas, and science and technology sectors, as well as 90 percent of the jobs in the booming field of construction.[60] Xinjiang's unemployed are disproportionately ethnic Uyghurs, Kazakhs, and Kyrgyz[61]; its entrepreneurs are mostly Han and Hui.[62]

The PRC controls development more tightly in Xinjiang than elsewhere in China, directing intellectual and financial capital toward building infrastructure and extracting minerals.[63] Han direct the exploitation of Xinjiang's natural resources, and Han are the primary beneficiaries of energy wealth. Han are also monopolizing the economic opportunities created by a more open western border, and Han merchants have established permanent agents in all the principal markets in Almaty, Bishkek, Osh, and Tashkent.[64] Most of the profits from the oil and gas industry go to Beijing, and the portion that remains in Xinjiang funds projects that many Uyghurs believe further threaten the region's environment and the Uyghur way of life.

Environmental Grievances

Rudelson recounts a Uyghur joke about the train from Beijing to Urumqi. On the trip west, the train's chuffing sounds like "ach, ach, ach" ("I'm hungry"); headed back east, the chuffing sounds more like "toq, toq, toq" ("I'm full").[65] Many Uyghurs believe Beijing cares only about extracting Xinjiang's natural resources and pays little attention to the potentially disastrous effects on local ecology. They point to China's only nuclear test facility at Lop Nor as proof of Beijing's disregard for Xinjiang's environment.

Xinjiang has China's largest oil and natural gas reserves, as well as a large cotton industry. Unfettered development in the energy and agricultural sectors raises serious questions about environmental sustainability and preservation. The most pressing concern is whether Xinjiang's limited water resources can accommodate the growing local population under the increased strain of development.

Xinjiang's climate is arid, its oasis aquifers are a nonrenewable resource, and its most important river is threatened. The Tarim River provides more than half of Xinjiang's irrigation water, and in 2007 22 percent of the river's course ran dry. In recent decades, six of the Tarim's nine historical tributaries have dried up. Furthermore, glaciers that feed the Tarim from the Tian Shan and Kunlun mountain ranges are retreating.[66]

Fossil fuel exploitation is a thirsty business. For example, the hydraulic processes involved in getting oil out of the ground can require a significant amount of water (although just how much is open to debate). Drilling for oil and gas can also contaminate the existing groundwater supply, and groundwater is a precious commodity for the agrarians of Xinjiang.

Agriculture in Xinjiang has always been a matter of irrigation, but the PRC has permanently changed how local farmers bring water to their fields and what they grow. For centuries, Uyghur farmers used an efficient irrigation system called *karez*. *Karez* are underground aqueducts engineered to collect groundwater and direct it to surface canals that water the fields of an oasis.[67] However, the *karez* system is in jeopardy today. Over the past 50 years, the PRC has largely replaced the *karez* with motor-pumped tube wells, which overexploit the aquifers, causing the water table to fall and the remaining *karez* to dry up.[68]

Under PRC leadership, Xinjiang has moved away from subsistence farming and toward commercial agriculture, particularly cotton production. Cotton is such a lucrative crop in the belt between Turpan and Hotan that its production more than doubled between 1995 and 2000.[69] However, cotton requires intensive irrigation, and Xinjiang cannot sustain a cotton monoculture for long. Without crop rotation, the land will be ruined by desertification and salinization. (About a quarter of Xinjiang's cultivated land is already too salinated to farm.[70]) Today's cotton farmers also use fertilizers, herbicides, and pesticides that contribute to water pollution and erosion.[71] In general, a more developed style of agriculture has put traditional Uyghur agrarian life at risk.

Uyghurs harbor another, unrelated environmental grievance: China's sole nuclear test site is located in Xinjiang, and Uyghurs have suffered from the associated radioactive fallout. The PRC conducted more than 40 nuclear explosions both above and below ground at Lop Nor between 1964 and 1996.[72] Some of them were 300 times more powerful than the bomb the United States dropped on Hiroshima, Japan, during World War II.[73]

Foreigners may venture no closer than Turpan[74], about 150 miles north of Lop Nor, so objective reporting on the area is difficult, but mainstream news accounts claim that as many as 210,000 people have died from the radiation.[75] Some Uyghur activists claim half a million deaths.[76] Untold numbers of people have been affected by cleft palates and other birth defects, as well as increased rates of cancer. By 1990, cancer rates near Lop Nor were more than 35 percent higher than the national average.[77]

While Chinese officials have acknowledged an increase in liver, lung, and skin cancer around Lop Nor, they have not attributed these health problems to nuclear radiation.[78] The PRC has made no special provisions for health care in this area, and Uyghur advocates believe Beijing has dismissed Lop Nor as a Uyghur problem. In this sense, the Lop Nor issue is both an environmental grievance and a human rights complaint.

Human Rights Abuses (Strike Hard)

Uyghur advocates accuse the PRC of widespread and long-term human rights abuses in Xinjiang, particularly in connection with the "Strike Hard, Maximum Pressure" campaign launched there in 1996.

"Strike Hard" (*Yan Da* in Chinese) is a nationwide anticrime campaign that specifically targets separatism in Xinjiang. Uyghurs argue that the PRC's definition of "separatism" includes legitimate religious activity as well as almost any form of political dissent, even the veiled or oblique. For example, a man who translated the United Nations' Universal Declaration of Human Rights into Uyghur reportedly received a 20-year jail term.[79] A better-known example of China's hard-line stance on dissent is the case of Rebiya Kadeer, a wealthy Uyghur businesswoman sentenced to eight years in prison in Urumqi for "providing secret information to foreigners." She was arrested in 1999 for sending copies of publicly available newspapers, including the *Kashgar Daily, Xinjiang Legal News, Yili Daily*, and *Yili Evening News*, to her husband in the United States, who openly advocated independence for Xinjiang. Many believed her real offense was organizing a grassroots movement called the Thousand Mothers Association, which was modeled on the American Mothers Against Drunk Driving (MADD) and operated independently from the PRC government.[80] The PRC released Rebiya Kadeer in 2005, after her case garnered worldwide attention from human rights groups.[81]

Under the banner of Strike Hard, the PRC has conducted mass arrests, torture, summary trials, and hundreds of executions.[82] Police conduct house-to-house sweeps, demanding papers and scanning for any kind of objectionable material. These raids often have a strong antireligious tone, with police confiscating unauthorized religious materials such as pamphlets and cassettes.[83] Some claim the police are given arrest quotas. Detainees may be maltreated or subject to torture. For example, a Uyghur the United Nations recognized as a political refugee claimed that police in Xinjiang beat him with shackles, shocked him in an electric chair, and pushed metal nails under his toenails.[84]

People detained in Strike Hard sweeps can be held without charge indefinitely at undisclosed locations[85] and sentenced without trial to years in the PRC's "re-education through labor" camps.[86] A charge is tantamount to a conviction; about 98 percent of China's criminal cases end in a "guilty" verdict.[87] Under the aegis of Strike Hard, the PRC often accelerates its judicial procedures. For example, in 1996, PRC senior military and law enforcement officers allotted 10 days to determine which detainees would be executed after the first iteration of the Strike Hard campaign.[88] Chinese authorities try Uyghurs charged with political offenses at the same time as others accused of violent nonpolitical crimes, such as murder, rape, and armed robbery,[89] blurring the distinction between political dissent and violent crime.

In addition to inspecting private homes, Strike Hard forces in Xinjiang close or repurpose any unregistered religious sites. For example, 105 "illegal" madrasahs and 133 "illegal" mosques were closed in the Strike Hard campaign of 1997.[90]

Uyghur advocates argue that at the national level, the PRC uses counterterrorism as a cover for suppressing dissent and forcing cultural assimilation; at the local level, officials use Strike Hard as a pretext to intimidate the Muslim population, elicit bribes, levy arbitrary fines, and blackmail ordinary people terrified of the PRC's criminal justice system.[91] Observers of Xinjiang believe human rights abuses disguised as counterterrorism operations have escalated since September 11, 2001, and the start of the U.S.-led war on terror. Xinjiang's security crackdowns intensified still further around the 2008 summer Olympics, when China most needed to project a national image of stability and harmony. The PRC arrested almost 1,300 people on state security charges in Xinjiang in the first 11 months of 2008. That is nearly twice the number of similar arrests for all of China in 2007.[92]

Xinjiang's government periodically proclaims new crusades in the Strike Hard campaign, sometimes with a time limit (100 days, two years, etc.), but does not announce when an existing iteration is drawing to a close. In 2004, Xinjiang announced it would extend Strike Hard indefinitely.[93]

Other Objections to PRC Governance

Uyghurs have the lowest life expectancy of any ethnic group in Xinjiang,[94] and as the anthropologist Jay Dautcher writes, "Among Xinjiang's Uyghurs, health issues take on social meaning as they are refracted through the lens of ethnicity."[95] Most medical professionals are Han who speak only Chinese, and their standard practice is to treat a patient only after receiving a large cash payment,[96] which is beyond the means of many impoverished Uyghurs. Uyghur advocates perceive deliberate neglect in Beijing's failure to combat Uyghur alcoholism, rising drug use, and disproportionately high rates of HIV and AIDS.[97]

In addition to concerns specifically related to their ethnicity and religion, the Uyghurs' grievances include general objections that could be levied by other factions of Chinese society. These include the PRC's repressive political climate, rampant censorship, stringent family-planning policy (although Uyghurs and other ethnic minorities are permitted at least one more child than Han families in similar circumstances[98]), and the legacy of famine, fear, and purges associated with Mao-era campaigns such as the Cultural Revolution and the Great Leap Forward.

When the CCP came to power it treated Uyghurs no differently than members of other ethnic groups, dispossessing powerful landholders and redistributing lands once held as private endowments.[99] However, today the PRC controls religion and development more tightly in Xinjiang than elsewhere in the country, and that control has increased dramatically since the late 1990s.[100] The PRC genuinely fears Uyghur separatism—or "splittism," as PRC bureaucrats call it—as a threat to China's national unity and territorial integrity.

UYGHUR SEPARATISM TODAY

Not all Uyghurs are separatists, obviously. In general, we can characterize present-day Uyghur ethno-political thought in four ways: apathist, assimilationist, autonomist, and separatist.[101]

Apathist. Many modern Uyghurs simply do not care about politics; instead, they focus on the personal concerns of their daily existence. The apathists barely figure in our current discussion of separatism, but any successful separatist movement would need the support of this population, however tacit it may be.

Assimilationist. A minority of Uyghurs simply want equality with the Han and would not object to being wholly absorbed into the Chinese state. They prize modernity over the preservation of their native culture. They believe in the promise of a multiethnic China, and they do not object to the degree of autonomy the PRC currently affords the XUAR. Assimiliationists are generally secular Uyghurs fluent in the Chinese language.[102]

Autonomist. Autonomists want Uyghur ethnic identity to remain intact, with its own culture and language. They believe in pursuing these goals within the construct of the Chinese state. Autonomists value the role of Islam in Uyghur life, but they do not object to secular government. Most politically active Uyghurs fall into this category.

Separatist. Separatists have the same basic goal as the autonomists—to preserve Uyghur ethnic identity—but they believe this is impossible within the construct of the Chinese state. They want political as well as cultural independence, and they advocate full political separation from the PRC. Many of them consider the PRC's cultural, religious, economic, environmental, and law enforcement policies in Xinjiang tantamount to "ethnic cleansing" or genocide. "The opposition to Chinese rule in Xinjiang has not reached the level of a Chechnya or an Intifada, but similar to the Basque separatists of the ETA in Spain or former IRA in Ireland and England, it is one that may erupt in limited, violent moments of terror and resistance," Gladney told a U.S. congressional subcommittee in 2009.[103] The true breadth and depth of separatist sentiment are almost impossible to assess because of the PRC's repressive political climate, but Xinjiang experts believe only a small percentage of Uyghurs wants independence.

East Turkistan's flag is a white crescent and five-pointed star on a Turkish blue background. (See Figure 2.2; Turkey's flag bears the same symbols, but its background is red.) This flag is also known as the *gök bayrak*, which is a Turkish phrase that means both "blue banner" and "heavenly flag" in English. Chinese officials consider East Turkistan's flag a manifestation of separatist sentiment, and so it is forbidden in the PRC.

Nonviolent and militant groups alike have appropriated this emblem. The ETIM created its own version in about 2000 by adding the *shahada*, or Muslim profession of faith, to the top of the flag[104] (see Figure 2.3). The *shahada* translates roughly to, "There is no god but Allah; Muhammad is the prophet of Allah." These beliefs are the first pillar of Islam, and Muslims recite the *shahada* daily. The flag of Saudi Arabia and the flag of the former Taliban regime in Afghanistan both also incorporate the *shahada*.

FIGURE 2.2.   East Turkistan's flag is a white crescent and five-pointed star on a Turkish blue background. (Turkey's flag bears the same symbols, but its background is red.) Wikipedia [permission granted at http://commons.wikimedia.org/wiki/File:Flag_of_Eastern _Turkistan.svg.png]).

The ETIM's now-defunct website notes that the mainstream Uyghur separatist movement disapproved of the changed flag: "This caused uproar amongst the ranks of the secular and democratic parties working for reform in Eastern Turkestan. These groups viewed such a move as a 'defacement' of the national flag and they objected to the fact that there had been no consultation over this."[105]

Until the 1990s, most Uyghur separatists were secular. Secular separatists may be Muslims, but they want an independent *ethnic* state, whereas religious separatists want an independent *Muslim* state. For some, this desired Muslim state is entirely Uyghur; for others, it involves union with the larger Muslim community known as the *ummah*.

Many Uyghur separatists, and Uyghur advocates in general, seek U.S. support. Much like those in the Free Tibet Movement, they appeal to the United States' avowed commitment to freedom, equality, and human rights. (Uyghur advocates sometimes lament the publicity gap between their cause and the Tibetans', suggesting that Westerners would champion Uyghurs

FIGURE 2.3.   The ETIM created its own version of the East Turkistani flag in about 2000 by adding the *shahada*. Captured from the ETIM's website, http://tipislamyultuzi.com.

alongside Tibetans if Uyghurs were Buddhist instead of Muslim.[106]) Uyghur activists regard the United States as the only country capable of pressuring China into real change in Xinjiang. However, at least one analyst speculates that U.S. foreign policy since 9/11, particularly the U.S.-China counterterrorism partnership, has prompted more anti-American sentiment among the Uyghur population.[107]

Most Uyghur separatists are peaceful activists who want to achieve independence through political means. Thus, violent separatists are a minority (those advocating violence) of a minority (those who want full independence from China). The ETIM is but one faction within this minority of a minority.

The PRC does not recognize such distinctions; its rhetoric and policy routinely conflate terrorism with separatism and separatism with dissent. They also fail to distinguish extremism from religious belief. Chinese government officials refer to "the three evils" of terrorism, separatism, and extremism in Xinjiang, thus linking the three concepts rhetorically and working to elide the distinction between terrorism and nonviolent dissent. In the words of the political scientist and Xinjiang scholar Yitzhak Shichor: "China's efforts to combine all Uyghur groups under one 'Eastern Turkestan' umbrella that promotes terrorism do not reflect the reality. To be sure, a small minority of these organizations do endorse terrorism but they are small, marginal and—to judge by the outcome—not terribly effective. Moreover, they have been disregarded and excluded by the mainstream Uyghur organizations that have never promoted terrorism."[108]

Uyghur Attempts at Political Unity

Uyghur advocates have long struggled to develop a united front for effective action. Violence and threats like the ETIM's generally undermine Uyghur political efforts, which already struggle to bridge geographical and ideological divides.

The only Uyghurs able to agitate for change publicly live outside China, removed from daily life in Xinjiang and often far removed from one another. The key issue dividing them is whether to push for outright independence or just greater autonomy. They have called conference after conference and formed a number of umbrella organizations to try to unify the dozens of diaspora advocacy groups. The WUC, currently led by Rebiya Kadeer, represents Uyghur nationalists' most united front in more than a decade.

In order to be effective, Uyghur advocates must operate outside the PRC, in a country relatively insulated from China's stifling influence. Over time, the Uyghur political base has shifted farther west. Rising Chinese influence in Kazakhstan, Kyrgyzstan, and Uzbekistan curtailed Uyghur advocacy there and pushed the center of East Turkistan nationalism to Turkey.[109] In the mid-1990s, Beijing began pressuring Turkey to suppress its East

Turkistan nationalists, and so the movement shifted westward once again, this time to Munich, Germany.[110] Munich was a relatively central location within Europe, under a democratic government,[111] and already home to a number of Uyghur expatriates. (Several Uyghurs, including prominent activist Erkin Alptekin, had been hired by Radio Free Europe/Radio Liberty's Munich headquarters in the 1970s. Other Uyghurs had gradually joined them.[112]) Some Uyghur leaders also moved to the United States to court American support. Today, Munich and Washington, DC, are the epicenters of Uyghur political action.

The key issue dividing Uyghur leaders is whether to demand total independence from China or to urge increased autonomy, democracy, and the right of "self-determination." They assume that, given a vote, Xinjiang's Uyghurs will choose to secede from China. Those who demand total independence are the idealists. For them, compromise is betrayal. Those who urge increased autonomy, democracy, and self-determination are still nationalists. Their ultimate goals are not very different from the separatists' goals, but they have crafted their agenda to avoid the "separatist" label (at least outside China) and to avoid alienating potential supporters. They are pragmatists open to compromise if it will advance the cause.

This polarization—idealism versus pragmatism, intransigence versus compromise—is a relatively new phenomenon. The Uyghur political community has long been a pluralistic one. Expatriate Uyghur organizations proliferated in the 1980s and especially the 1990s, partly due to the rise of the Internet. Some of these organizations offered information about the cause, some urged action, and some combined information with advocacy. They numbered in the dozens and were scattered around the globe. Most were small and poor; some existed only on their own letterhead or website. In their sheer numbers, they offered Uyghur advocates a variety of ways to join the cause, but they struggled to achieve results. Some (but not all) of these organizations regarded Isa Yusuf Alptekin, a Uyghur who fled Xinjiang when the Communists took over in 1949, as their leader. When he died in 1995, the movement was practically faceless.

Uyghur leaders held conferences and formed umbrella organizations to try to unite the movement, even before Alptekin's death. In 1992, they gathered in Istanbul for the Eastern Turkistan World National Congress, later called the First National Assembly, and called for independence.[113] (The PRC alleges this assembly formed a three-phase plan for revolt, in which the Uyghurs would accumulate forces for the first two years, activate their forces in the following three years, and mount a full-scale offensive in 1997 with the goal of achieving independence in 2000.[114] We have no evidence such a plan existed.) The assembly resolved to set up an umbrella organization to represent Eastern Turkistanis' interests,[115] but this organization did not materialize until six years later.

In 1998, more than 40 Uyghur leaders established the Eastern Turkistan National Centre (ETNC), an umbrella organization of groups that advocate independence but not violence. Extremist groups that believe force is the only way to achieve independence excluded themselves from the ETNC. One year later, the East Turkistani political community held its Second National Assembly in Munich and renamed the Eastern Turkistan National *Centre* the Eastern Turkistan National *Congress*, electing Uyghur leader Enver Can as its president.[116]

The number, membership, and activity of Uyghur advocacy groups seemed to drop after 9/11.[117] The Uyghur political movement essentially split in 2004, when competing groups of moderates and hard-liners each launched their own umbrella organizations. Both umbrella organizations are secular and disavow violence, but they differ in strategy.

In April 2004, the moderates established the WUC in Munich by merging the ETNC with a group called the World Uyghur Youth Congress (WUYC). The WUC advocates not for outright independence but for democracy and the right of self-determination. According to the group's website, "The main objective of the World Uyghur Congress is to promote democracy, human rights and freedom for the Uyghur people and use peaceful, nonviolent, and democratic means to determine their political future."[118] The WUC selected Erkin Alptekin, son of the late Uyghur exile leader Isa Yusuf Alptekin, as its first president.

Five months later, in September 2004, a group of separatists announced they were forming the East Turkistan Government-in-Exile, based in Washington, DC. The separatists named Anwar Yusuf Turani as their first president and a full cabinet to complement him. Turani launched the organization with an extended appeal to the United States. "We turn to the United States of America, as the leader of liberty, justice, and wisdom, hoping that the United States of America will recognize the just cause of freedom and independence of millions of East Turkistanis," Turani said.[119] The government-in-exile—unlike the WUC—stresses that its goal is independence, not just democracy or self-determination. Shichor writes:

> The emergence of *two* competitive umbrella organizations underlines what has become the nature of the Uyghur national liberation movement all along, namely, ongoing splits and disunity. To a great extent, it is China's repeated attempts to "unite" these diverse groups under one "Eastern Turkestan" organization and to accuse them of terrorism, separatism and radicalism that contributed more than anything else to the improvement of their international and public image.[120]

The WUC is the more influential and respected of the two rival umbrella organizations. Its current president is Rebiya Kadeer, the wealthy Uyghur businesswoman and activist formerly detained by the PRC. She also leads the Uyghur American Association (UAA) and International Uyghur Human Rights and Democracy Foundation (IUHRDF), both based in Washington, DC. The WUC, UAA, and IUHRDF all receive funding from the U.S. National Endowment for Democracy (NED).[121]

Kadeer, sometimes called "the mother of all Uyghurs," is probably the most widely recognized Uyghur leader today. The PRC has clearly targeted her as the face of Uyghur separatism, publicly accusing her of orchestrating the July 2009 ethnic riots in Xinjiang from her home in the United States. Immediately after the riots, a CCP newspaper condemned her "ferocious terrorist nature" and called her "an ironclad separatist colluding with terrorists and Islamic extremists and an instigator unceasingly fanning unrest among her followers within and outside of China." The same newspaper also compared her to the Dalai Lama, the spiritual leader of Tibet,[122] which would be a high compliment in many other contexts. While these and similar accusations were surely attempts to sully Kadeer's reputation, they also raised her international profile. By singling her out with extreme criticism, the PRC has supported Kadeer's status as an influential and unifying force among Uyghurs worldwide.

Uyghur Militant Groups

Uyghur militant groups are much more difficult to characterize than the political organizations that pursue publicity to further their cause. Militants often seek the shadows, and if the groups are based in Xinjiang the only information Westerners receive about them is what Beijing chooses to release. In general, PRC officials and media outlets have focused closely on the ETIM since about 2002 and report little new information about other militant groups. Such groups merge, splinter, or fade away over time, and so older information may no longer be reliable.

The following are brief descriptions of the major Uyghur militant groups noted by the PRC and the mass media over the past 15 years (excluding the ETIM, which is covered in depth in the rest of this book). Several of these groups were mentioned once or twice in 2001 and never addressed again; they may have been confused with other groups or simply invented in the post-9/11 push to identify and target terrorist organizations.

East Turkistan Liberation Organization (ETLO), aka *Shärqiy Türkistan Azatliq Täshkilati* (SHAT). This was probably the most prominent of the Uyghur militant groups until the U.S. blacklisting raised the ETIM from obscurity. The PRC blames the ETLO for a long list of incidents dating back more than a decade. These incidents include masterminding a rash of deadly poisonings in Kashgar in January and February 1998[123]; committing 15 cases of arson in

Urumqi on May 23, 1998[124]; committing bomb attacks in Kyrgyzstan between May and June 1998[125]; murdering four Uyghurs to keep them from leaking information about the ETLO in Almaty in June 1998[126]; shooting and killing a Uyghur leader who refused to cooperate with the ETLO in March 2000[127]; robbing the Almaty World Bank on May 18, 2000[128]; shooting at two officials investigating a fire at the "Tur Bazaar" in Bishkek on May 25, 2000, killing one and injuring the other[129]; murdering two local police on duty in Almaty in September 2000[130]; murdering Chinese diplomat Wang Jianping in Bishkek on June 29, 2002[131]; and hijacking a bus, killing all 22 people on board, and burning the vehicle with the bodies inside on March 27, 2003.[132]

The ETLO's funding allegedly comes from armed robbery, drug trafficking, arms smuggling, and Al-Qaida donations.[133] The PRC claims the ETLO trained and fought in Chechnya[134] and ran special training camps at Mazar-e-Sharif and Khost, Afghanistan, with Taliban support.[135] The ETLO also allegedly provided funds and personnel to the IMU in 1999.[136]

The ETLO and ETIM are occasionally confused with each other. The PRC claims the two groups established an alliance at a four-day meeting in Bishkek in March 1998.[137] The ETLO's leader, Mehmet Emin Hazret, has denied any association with the ETIM, Al-Qaida, or Osama bin Laden.[138] In a January 2003 interview with Radio Free Asia, Hazret said, "We have not been and will not be involved in any kind of terrorist action inside or outside China." His other remarks clarified that while the ETLO might disavow terrorism, it remained militant: "Our principal goal is to achieve independence for East Turkestan by peaceful means," Hazret said. "But to show our enemies and friends our determination on the East Turkestan issue, we view a military wing as inevitable."[139]

The ETLO released a threatening video on the Internet in October 2005, just before the fiftieth anniversary of the founding of Xinjiang Uyghur Autonomous Region. In the video, three masked men holding automatic weapons and standing in front of the East Turkistani flag read a statement saying that the group will launch an all-out war against China's government.[140]

Observers in the West have heard little from the ETLO since the 2005 video. Some analysts question whether the group still exists.[141]

Uyghuristan People's Party. The Uyghuristan People's Party is a self-described political organization in Kazakhstan created by the merger of two militant groups.[142] The party publicly rejects terrorism. According to its platform, the party's purpose "is to contribute to the political struggle of our nation for the restoration of the sovereign, civic, and democratic state in its historic homeland (the Xinjiang Uighur Autonomous Province of the People's Republic of China) . . . in its activities [the party] will use only political methods" and "decisively will refuse and expose appearances of terrorism, extremism, and religious fanaticism in any kind."[143] However, the party's leader, Kakharman Khozhamberdi, says the group differentiates between civilians and legitimate targets in the pursuit of national liberation.[144]

Although the Uyghuristan People's Party and the ETIM share a common goal, Khozhamberdi and the ETIM's late founder, Hasan Mahsum, despised each other. Khozhamberdi suspected Mahsum was a Chinese agent, and Mahsum called Khozhamberdi an infidel.[145]

The Uyghuristan People's Party formed in September 2001, when the United Revolutionary Front of East Turkistan (URFET) merged with the Uyghur Liberation Organization (ULO).[146] The URFET was established in the 1970s, probably with Soviet assistance.[147] Its leader, Yusupbek Mukhlisi, sought publicity and even met with U.S. State Department officials in 1996.[148] Then, in 1997, he announced the URFET was beginning an armed campaign against China.[149] He made a number of probably exaggerated claims to the media about the size, capability, and ferocity of the Uyghur militant movement.[150]

The ULO was founded by Hashir Wahidi, who claimed in 1996 to have more than 1 million supporters in Xinjiang and 12,000 more abroad in Central Asian countries.[151] The PRC accused the ULO of kidnapping a Xinjiang businessman for ransom, murdering the businessman's nephew, setting fire to the Bishkek Market of Chinese Commodities in May 2000, and then murdering the Xinjiang investigator sent to Kyrgyzstan to work on the case.[152] The ULO also allegedly killed two Kazakh police officers in September 2000.[153]

The Uyghuristan People's Party cannot register itself in Kazakhstan because Kazakh law bans parties based on ethnicity.

East Turkistan People's Party. As of 1999, the East Turkistan People's Party reportedly had more than 60,000 members and 178 underground branches in Xinjiang.[154] In 2004, the PRC executed two members of the group after convicting them of separatism and weapons charges; 16 other party members received sentences ranging from five years to life in prison.[155]

A 1994 book by a PRC-sponsored research group contains a lengthy passage on an East Turkistan People's Party established in the 1960s with Soviet aid.[156] This passage concludes with a warning that some of the party's old members have become active again. It is unclear whether the East Turkistan People's Party reported in 1999 and 2004 is a revival of the 1960s group by the same name.

Islamic Reformist Party, aka Party of Islamic Reformers. The PRC claims the "Shock Brigade" of the Islamic Reformist Party established a training base in Basheriq Township, Yecheng County, in 1990 and trained more than 60 people in terrorism and religious extremism.[157] This group allegedly also masterminded a bus explosion in Urumqi on February 5, 1991, that resulted in more than 20 casualties, according to a PRC statement from 2001.[158] PRC media reported that the Islamic Reformist Party conducted another bombing in Urumqi in 1992, killing three people and wounding 23.[159] In the early to mid-1990s, the PRC imprisoned and executed several Uyghurs accused of forming this group in October 1990 or later joining it.[160]

The Islamic Reformist Party is one of four groups mentioned in a 2002 Chinese television program on East Turkistan terrorism. The Xinjiang expert who watched the Chinese television program wrote that the Islamic Reformist Party is "hardly known outside China. At best, they are—or were—a small and loosely organized [group] of little operative value. At worst, they may have been a figment of Chinese imagination or even invented by Beijing."[161]

Tigers of Lop Nor, aka Lop Nor Tigers. The late URFET leader Yusupbek Mukhlisi claimed the Tigers of Lop Nor blew up two airplanes and several tanks inside the PRC's nuclear zone on May 15, 1993, and destroyed an official vehicle in Urumqi, killing nine Chinese officials, in late February 1996.[162] However, Mukhlisi was prone to exaggeration,[163] and this group was not mentioned in the PRC's later statements on East Turkistan terrorism. A Kazakh newspaper alleged in 2002 that the Tigers of Lop Nor had close links with Uzbek fighters and attributed this information to "various countries' special services."[164]

The group takes its name from the PRC's nuclear test site in Xinjiang, where the local population suffers from increased rates of cancer and birth defects.

Wolves of Lop Nor. This group is perhaps even more obscure than the similarly named Tigers of Lop Nor. The Wolves of Lop Nor allegedly bombed a Beijing bus in March 1997, but Xinjiang authorities have denied Uyghurs were involved in that attack.[165] A 2002 U.S. Congressional Research Service report says the Wolves of Lop Nor claimed a number of train bombings and several assassinations in Xinjiang. According to this report, the Wolves released a statement to Taiwanese radio saying all their attacks are a response to the PRC's "suppression of proindependence activism" in Xinjiang.[166]

East Turkistan National Solidarity Union, aka East Turkistan National Unity Alliance. Multiple sources claim this group bombed buses in Urumqi on the day of former Chinese leader Deng Xiaoping's funeral (February 25, 1997), killing 9 people and injuring 74.[167] The group was also accused of 25 cases of poisoning in southern Xinjiang that killed 4 people and sickened 40 in early 1998.[168]

Islamic Holy Warriors. This group provided training in shooting, demolition, and assassination in Afghanistan in 1998, according to a 2002 PRC statement. The Islamic Holy Warriors then sent members back to Xinjiang to recruit, raise funds, collect arms, and plan violence.[169] In 2003, the PRC executed an accused leader of this group named Ujimamadi Abbas after convicting him on subversion, terrorism, and weapons charges.[170]

East Turkistan Opposition Party. This group's propaganda declares its intent to "take the road of armed struggle" and "conduct various terrorist activities in densely populated regions," according to a 2002 PRC statement.[171] A 2002 article in *Foreign Affairs* mentions the East Turkistan Opposition Party as one of several groups with links to small guerilla cells based in the oasis towns of Xinjiang's Taklamakan Desert. These guerilla cells have allegedly raided government laboratories and warehouses for explosives and manufactured various types of bombs.[172]

Free Turkistan Movement. At least two news reports blame this group for the 1990 Baren Rebellion, which killed 22 people, although other sources blame the ETIM for the same incident. One of these news reports notes that the Free Turkistan Movement, led by Abdul Kasim, acquired weapons from the Afghan mujahideen.[173] The Free Turkistan Movement is not mentioned in any other context.

Spark, aka Spark of the Motherland, aka Homeland Spark. Several news reports from the late 1990s and early 2000s mention that a group called Spark coordinates between different Uyghur militant organizations. Spark allegedly formed at an illegal congress in Moscow in September 1994.[174] In 1997, the group was reportedly raising funds to buy weapons for Uyghur militants.[175] Spark allegedly claimed responsibility for bombings in Xinjiang in 1998.[176] The late URFET leader Yusupbek Mukhlisi identified Spark's leader as of 1997: Colonel Abdul Gapar Shakhyar, who allegedly attacked the Lop Nor nuclear test site in 1993.[177]

The Xinjiang expert James Millward mentions Spark or Spark Alliance as a separatist network organized by teenagers who stockpiled weapons in Akto and Yining in the 1980s.[178] It is unclear whether this network had morphed into a coordinating center by the late 1990s or whether it was a separate group altogether.

Spark is also the name of an online newspaper affiliated with the nonviolent East Turkistan Information Center (ETIC).[179]

East Turkistan Democratic Islamic Party. This group reportedly formed in 1991 and carried out a series of bombings in southern Xinjiang between June and September 1993, killing 2 people and injuring 36.[180] In the mid-1990s, the PRC arrested several people for belonging to this group.[181]

Uyghur Youth Association of Kazakhstan. The PRC claims the Uyghur Youth Association of Kazakhstan robbed a bank vehicle in Almaty, Kazakhstan, in May 2001.[182] The group apparently preaches nonviolence; it sent a delegate (Yasin Samedi) to the Unrepresented Nations and Peoples Organization international conference on nonviolence and conflict in Tallinn, Estonia, in July 1997.[183]

East Turkistan Islamic Party of Allah, aka East Turkistan Islamic Party of God, aka East Turkistan Islamic Hizballah, aka *Doğu Türkistan İslamcı Allah Partisi.* This group was reportedly founded by Alerken Abula in 1993 and crushed by the PRC in 2001.[184] The PRC blamed the East Turkistan Islamic Party of Allah for the deadly riots in Yining in February 1997.[185] The PRC also accused the group of targeting 32 Chinese officials, Communist Party members, and officially sanctioned clerics.[186] The PRC executed Abula in 2001 and claimed to have destroyed his 113-member group,[187] which is sometimes confused with the ETIM.

East Turkistan International Committee. The PRC claims the East Turkistan International Committee ordered the smuggling of arms and ammunition into China 17 times in 1998.[188] Based on their similar names, the East Turkistan International Committee might be the same as the Committee for East Turkistan.

Committee for East Turkistan. All the information on this group comes from a 1993 news report, which identifies the Committee for East Turkistan as "the most radical national movement in Central Asia." At that time, the group claimed several thousand volunteers who were ready to fight the Chinese in Xinjiang. The group's leaders said the Committee for East Turkistan had supported a raid on a military warehouse in Kashgar in June 1993. The group was operating illegally in Kazakhstan because the Kazakh Justice Ministry refused it permission to register. It distributed its own newspaper in Central Asia, Xinjiang, Germany, and Turkey. Its original members were Uyghurs who fought the Chinese Communist takeover in Xinjiang from 1944 to 1949, and its leaders as of 1993 were Yusupbek Mukhlisi and Taynutdin Basakov.[189] Mukhlisi, who died in 2004,[190] also led the United Revolutionary Front of East Turkistan (URFET), which later became part of the Uyghuristan People's Party. Either the URFET or the Uyghuristan People's Party may have absorbed the Committee for East Turkistan. Based on their similar names, the Committee for East Turkistan might be the same as the East Turkistan International Committee. Either or both may be affiliated with URFET.

Uyghur Liberation Party. This group made headlines in 1997 when a spokesman named "Akhmed" talked to reporters in Almaty. Akhmed claimed the Uyghur Liberation Party was an umbrella group responsible for the Urumqi bus bombings that coincided with Deng Xiaoping's funeral,[191] although other sources blamed the East Turkistan National Solidarity Union for this attack.[192] Akhmed said the Uyghur Liberation Party operates all over western Xinjiang, from Yining in the north to Hotan near the Pakistani border.[193] Akhmed told reporters his group's creed was to kill the Chinese even if that means dying or killing fellow Uyghurs in the attempt.[194]

East Turkistan Gray Wolf Party, aka *Sharki Turkistan Bozkurt Partiyesi.* A Uyghur news report mentions that this group and four other militant organizations "unified their efforts" after a secret meeting in Yining in September 1994. According to the news report, the East Turkistan Gray Wolf Party is based in Urumqi and supported by young intellectuals, teachers, and students.[195] The group was established in the 1970s[196] and is probably pan-Turkic, based on its name. (The gray wolf is a symbol of Turkic identity.)

Home of the Youth. This group's name appears in a 1999 news report. According to the report, the Home of the Youth is known as "Xinijang's Hamas." The group claims more than 2,000 members, mostly young people, many of whom have served in the Turkish military. Some know how to launch missiles, fly jets, and operate tanks.[197]

Allah Party of East Turkistan, aka Hizballah of East Turkistan, aka *Dongtu Yisilan Zhenzhudang.* According to a 2002 Chinese television program, the Allah Party of East Turkistan participated in a 1996 conference of Muslim East Turkistan terrorists in Hotan.[198] The Xinjiang expert who watched the Chinese television program wrote that the Allah Party of East Turkistan is "hardly known outside China. At best, they are—or were—a small and loosely organized [group] of little operative value. At worst, they may have been a figment of Chinese imagination or even invented by Beijing."[199]

Based on its name, this group may be the same as the East Turkistan Islamic Party of Allah.

Central Asian Uyghur Hizballah, aka Central Asian Uyghur Party of God. The PRC claims this group is partially financed by Osama bin Laden, has about 1,000 armed members, and is based in Kazakhstan with training camps in Afghanistan.[200]

East Turkistan Islamic Justice Party. The PRC claims the East Turkistan Islamic Justice Party engineered a prison rebellion in Xayar County on July 15, 1996, as well as a riot in Yining on February 5, 1997. The prison rebellion killed 15 and the riot resulted in more than 300 casualties.[201]

Uyghur National Army. A 2001 PRC statement claims this group received terrorist training in July and August 1999 at Taliban bases in Afghanistan.[202] The Uyghur National Army allegedly practiced using conventional weapons with live ammunition and learned tactics such as assassination, bombing, and poisoning.[203] The group does not appear in the 2002, 2003, or 2008 PRC statements naming specific terrorist organizations and individuals.

Central Asian Uyghur Jihad Party. This is one of several East Turkistan groups reportedly mentioned by Chinese foreign ministry spokesman Zhu Bangzao at a briefing on terrorism on or about November 18, 2001. Zhu alleged that Osama bin Laden had trained all East Turkistan groups (including the Central Asian Uyghur Jihad Party) and influenced them with his thought.[204] However, this group was not included in the PRC's list of terrorist organizations released later that month, nor did it figure in the PRC's 2002, 2003, or 2008 statements naming specific terrorist organizations and individuals.

Turkistan Party, United Committee of Uyghurs' Organizations, and East Turkistan Islamic Resistance Movement. A 2001 PRC statement identifies these three distinct groups as organizations that openly advocate violence in their political platforms, but the statement does not provide further details.[205] The Turkistan Party is reportedly based in Pakistan; the United Committee of Uyghurs' Organizations, in Central Asia; and the East Turkistan Islamic Resistance Movement, in Turkey. These groups do not appear in the 2002, 2003, or 2008 PRC statements naming specific terrorist organizations and individuals.

A Brief History of Uyghur Separatism

The ETIM and other Uyghur groups active in the 1990s and 2000s are only the most recent players in a centuries-old conflict over China's northwest territory. Xinjiang's political past is a story of repression and revolt, marked by two brief periods of Uyghur independence (1933–34 and 1944–49). Over the past hundred years, pan-Turkic, Marxist, and Islamist ideologies have shaped Uyghur separatist thought.

The territory now known as Xinjiang became part of China in 1759, when the Qing dynasty invaded it. The Qing installed military governors at Yining and garrisons at key locations but otherwise left local government in the hands of the region's native leaders.[206]

About century later, a local warlord named Yakub Beg was the first of many Uyghur leaders to demand independence based on appeals to shared religion and ethnicity.[207] He briefly established a kingdom centered on Kashgar before being defeated in 1877.

The Qing dynasty fell in 1911. The years from about 1916 to 1949 are often called China's "warlord period," marked by an unstable central government.

A series of dictatorial provincial governors ruled Xinjiang. During this time Xinjiang's society split along religious, ethnic, economic, and political lines to form a number of quarrelling factions—Muslim, Chinese, Uyghur, Hui, Kazakh, warlord, commoner, Nationalist, Communist, etc.[208]

Pan-Turkic ideals took root in Kashgar and other parts of Xinjiang in the 1910s and 1920s, carried by visiting intellectuals from Russian Turkistan and the Ottoman Empire.

When Xinjiang's government tried to interfere in the affairs of Hami's traditional ruling family in 1931, local Muslims rebelled, beginning a series of insurrections that culminated in the proclamation of the Eastern Turkistan Republic (ETR) in Kashgar on November 12, 1933. The ETR is sometimes also called the Turkish-Islamic Republic of Eastern Turkistan, or TIRET. The ETR's constitution both proclaimed sharia law and professed modern, democratic principles.[209] The ETR lasted less than a year before it fell to the Chinese-speaking Muslims known as Hui.[210]

Then, from 1944 to 1949, a Uyghur government called the second Eastern Turkistan Republic governed the three westernmost prefectures of Xinjiang.[211] Some consider this small state a successful Turkic nationalist or Islamic movement; others believe it was only a puppet of the Soviet Union.[212]

With the Communists winning China's Civil War, representatives of the second ETR planned to visit Beijing in August 1949 to try to negotiate with the Communist leadership.[213] Their plane from Almaty crashed mysteriously, killing the second ETR's top leadership.[214] Later that same year, the Communists "peacefully liberated" Xinjiang, reaching a settlement to liquidate the second ETR and incorporate all of Xinjiang into the newly formed PRC.[215]

Xinjiang's Uyghurs have periodically protested specific government policies and resisted Bejing's control more generally. In recent years, Uyghurs demonstrated in Urumqi in 1989 over the publication of an anti-Muslim book; in Baren in 1990 over a variety of government policies; in Hotan in 1995 over the arrest of a respected local cleric; in Yining in 1997 over a government ban on a traditional social gathering of Muslim men known as the *mashrap*; and in Urumqi in 2009 after two Uyghurs died in a factory brawl, touching off riots that killed hundreds and injured more than 1,000 people. The Hotan demonstrations, coupled with Uyghur political action and unrest in Yining beginning around the same time, turned Beijing's policy in Xinjiang from accommodation to repression in the 1990s.[216]

Key Factors Shaping Present-Day Uyghur Separatism

Three key factors combined to galvanize and transform Uyghur separatism in recent decades: increased ties between China and the rest of the world, the collapse of the Soviet Union, and the rise of the Internet.

After Mao Zedong's death in 1976, Deng Xiaoping consolidated power and embarked on a course of "reform and opening." Deng's policies forged new ties between the PRC and the international community. The phenomenon of globalization that began in the 1980s brought further economic, cultural, and political integration. Now Uyghur separatists could more easily move people, information, and money across national borders. Nongovernmental organizations (NGOs) proliferated in the 1990s, promoting Western-style democracy, demanding transparency in government, and criticizing the PRC for its treatment of ethnic minorities and religious dissidents. The NGOs' advocacy helped publicize the Uyghurs' grievances to an increasingly interconnected world.

Until 1991, the Uyghurs were just one of several Central Asian ethnic groups subjugated to a Communist world power and governed from a distant capital. But when the Soviet Union dissolved into 15 independent states, the Kazakhs got their Kazakhstan, the Uzbeks got their Uzbekistan, the Kyrgyz got their Kyrgyzstan, and so on. Only the Uyghurs are left without a homeland in Central Asia. The predominantly Muslim countries of the former Soviet Union became beacons of hope in the drive to establish an independent Uyghuristan.

The rise of the Internet in the 1990s gave Uyghur separatists a medium ideally suited to their cause. Online, Uyghur advocates can share information, exchange opinions, and coordinate activities efficiently. They can also work to preserve their cultural legacies, especially the Uyghur language.[217] Violent groups, particularly the ETIM, have also used the Internet to issue threats, claim attacks, and disseminate other propaganda.

Now Uyghur separatists can communicate instantaneously regardless of the physical distance between them. Those who want to remain anonymous can use proxy servers and other countermeasures to obfuscate their identities. Shichor calls the proliferation of online networks and websites since the mid-1990s "by far the most significant change and important development for Uygur-interest articulation . . . the message of Eastern Turkestan no longer depends on conventional means such as conferences, meetings, or printed matter. The proliferation of Uygur websites expands its transmitting horizons almost endlessly, with a capacity to effortlessly penetrate the Great Wall of China, and apparently with little risk."[218] Gladney notes the increased role of the Internet in forging virtual communities dedicated to Xinjiang's independence, a phenomenon he terms "cyber-separatism." Gladney argues that while cyber-separatists could never unseat a local government on their own, similar virtual communities have facilitated the flow of information and funds in other restive regions, including East Timor, Aceh, Chechnya, and Bosnia.[219]

The efficacy of cyber-separatism remains unknown. Uyghur separatists may communicate more because of the Internet, but that does not assure an increase or improvement in their political action. Online communities can be unstable, with members joining and dropping out whenever they want. Online communities are more vulnerable to PRC infiltration than are in-person gatherings. An increased emphasis on Internet communication could add an element of elitism to Uyghur separatism by excluding Uyghurs without the funds or opportunity to establish a presence online. For example, cyber-separatism is far more prominent among Uyghur émigrés than among Uyghurs in Xinjiang, where the PRC tries to block access to websites critical of China's government. (The so-called "Great Firewall of China" is hardly impenetrable, but access to separatist sites is at least spotty, if not barred altogether.) Even without the PRC's censorship, Internet access in Central Asia is often unreliable, and it can be prohibitively expensive. Finally, Shichor suggests the medium of the Internet could actually undermine independence efforts by placating separatists with a virtual "site" to congregate and air their grievances, which may mute their drive to establish real territory.[220]

CONCLUSION

Uyghur activists regard the PRC's governance as a sustained program of cultural and religious assimilation coupled with economic and environmental exploitation. Despite their common grievances, Uyghur advocates have long struggled to make common cause with one another.

The moderate majority advocates for increased autonomy in Xinjiang. Today the WUC, led by Rebiya Kadeer, represents Uyghur nationalists' most united front in more than a decade. This organization eschews the "separatist" label, instead advocating for democracy and the right of self-determination. However, more radical thinkers believe the only way to preserve Uyghur identity, rights, and even dignity is to secede from the Chinese state. They cite the historical precedent of the Eastern Turkistan Republic that existed from 1933 to 1934 and again from 1944 to 1949. Even among the outright separatists, many believe in pursuing their goal through political means. Others commit or endorse violence (often undermining political activists' efforts in the process).

The ETIM is by far the most internationally notorious Uyghur militant group. A distant second is the secular ETLO, which some analysts consider defunct. Dozens of other militant groups were identified after 9/11, but most faded back into obscurity.

These groups of the 1990s and 2000s are only the most recent players in a centuries-old conflict over China's northwest territory. Xinjiang's political past is a story of repression and revolt, influenced over the past hundred years by pan-Turkic, Marxist, and Islamist ideologies. Three key factors have combined to galvanize and transform Uyghur separatism in recent decades: increased ties between China and the rest of the world, the collapse of the Soviet Union, and the rise of the Internet.

As the next chapter illustrates, the ETIM took advantage of two of these factors—increased ties between China and the rest of the world and the rise of the Internet—to seek support abroad and broadcast its message around the globe.

3

The ETIM's Origins, Evolution, Ideology, Rhetoric, and Activities

The ETIM is a terrorist organization that demands an independent fundamentalist Muslim state for the Uyghur ethnic minority in northwest China. The ETIM has been blamed or claimed responsibility for a variety of terrorist attacks dating back to 1989, including bombings and assassinations. Most of these attacks occurred inside China, with a few in other Central Asian countries. The ETIM has yet to engineer a large-scale terrorist event, but its threats indicate that it intends to do so. While its present size and capabilities are largely unknown, the ETIM has developed a significant online propaganda presence aligned with Al-Qaida's.

The ETIM considers itself the modern-day descendant of a militant group founded in 1940, but the group has changed its name, ideology, and tactics over time, as its leaders have been killed or detained. In 1997, Hasan Mahsum re-established the ETIM in its current form. Abdul Haq al-Turkistani took over the group's leadership after Mahsum was killed in an Al-Qaida stronghold in 2003.[1]

The ETIM attained international notoriety after 9/11, when the PRC began issuing news releases on terrorists operating inside China[2] and successfully urged other governments to blacklist the group. The ETIM has sought more international attention by increasing its use of electronic communications. In recent years, the group released a website (now defunct),[3] recruiting videos, threat videos, and an electronic magazine.

Before 9/11, the ETIM was obscure but not unknown. Western, Russian, and Chinese media sources have documented the ETIM's existence for nearly 20 years. At least four 1990 accounts of a rebellion in Baren Township, southwest of Kashgar, referred to the Islamic Party of East Turkistan.[4] A 1990 BBC translation of a Xinjiang newspaper article also mentioned the East Turkistan Islamic Party.[5] In 1994, a Western news report referred to "a militant group known as the East Turkistan Movement."[6] In 2000, a Russian newspaper published at least three articles referring to the East Turkistan Islamic Movement.[7] Boaz Ganor of Israel's International Institute for Counter-Terrorism also mentioned the ETIM in 2000.[8]

THE ORIGIN AND EVOLUTION OF THE ETIM

The ETIM's website traces the group's lineage to the Turkistan Islamic Party (*Hizb ul Islami Li-Turkistan*) formed in 1940 by Abdul Azeez Makhdoom, Abdul Hameed, Abdul Hakeem, and other scholars. Throughout the 1940s and 1950s, this group engaged in battles and other uprisings against the Chinese government's military forces. Around 1956, the group changed its name to the East Turkistan Islamic Movement (*Hizb ul Islami Li-Turkistan Ash-Sharqiyah*). Leaders named Mullah Baqee and Mullah Muhammad led the group into a large battle in 1956 but were defeated. The ETIM's leaders were killed or imprisoned, and the group remained inactive until the 1980s.[9]

One of the group's founders, Abdul Hakeem, was released from prison in 1979. Deng Xiaoping had recently initiated sweeping reforms in China, and the PRC's policies toward Uyghurs and Muslims were relatively permissive at the time. Abdul Hakeem went on to establish Islamic schools in Kargharlak that carried forward the ETIM's ideas. Hasan Mahsum, who would become the ETIM's most notorious leader, studied at one of these schools from 1984 to 1989.[10]

In the late 1980s, the ETIM was revived under the leadership of Dia Uddin bin Yousef.[11] The group increased its recruiting, training, and procurement efforts in early 1990. On April 5–6, 1990, the ETIM led a rebellion in Baren Township, Akto County, Xinjiang. Hasan Mahsum participated in the rebellion and was arrested for it.[12] (Adel Noori, one of the Uyghurs detained at GTMO, also mentioned that one of his friends, Abdulhanlid, was killed in the Baren Rebellion.[13]) The Baren Rebellion was small, but it had long-lasting effects.[14]

The Baren Rebellion led the PRC to deal more harshly with the Uyghur population and launch an aggressive campaign of arrests and imprisonment. Not surprisingly, this approach failed to have the intended effect. Xinjiang's prisons became a fertile recruiting and training ground, with Islamic militants, students, criminals, and bystanders sharing close quarters for long periods.[15]

Instead of intimidating the Uyghurs into submission, the Chinese government created an atmosphere of animosity and heightened ethnic tension. At least one analyst has surmised that the government's treatment of local Uyghurs after the Baren Rebellion actually bolstered the ETIM's support base in Xinjiang.[16]

Abdul Hakeem, the last of the scholars who founded the ETIM in 1940, died in 1993. After his death, Abudu Rehmen and Muhanmmed Tuhit led the group briefly, but it collapsed again later that year.[17] Hasan Mahsum revived the group in the late 1990s.

Mahsum had studied in one of Abdul Hakeem's schools and was involved in the 1990 Baren Rebellion. He was imprisoned from May 1990 to November 1991[18] and again from late 1993 to early 1996, sentenced to three years of labor "re-education" on terrorism charges. His philosophy grew more militant during this period.[19] Mahsum was detained yet again in one of the Chinese government's Strike Hard campaigns in August 1996. He was released and left Urumqi in January 1997.[20]

Mahsum had decided to form a militant group and traveled to Saudi Arabia, Pakistan, and Turkey to seek support and funding from the Uyghur diaspora.[21] All these efforts failed. According to the history provided at the ETIM website, Mahsum met with "democratically inclined groups," but they thought he was naïve.[22]

Undaunted, Mahsum and Abudukadir Yapuquan re-formed the ETIM in about September 1997.[23] They focused on correcting the "mistakes" of the previous leader, Dia Uddin bin Yousef,[24] which probably means they committed to a more militant approach.[25]

Mahsum met several times with Osama bin Laden and Al-Qaida. Al-Qaida reportedly gave the ETIM money and training.[26]

The ETIM moved its headquarters to Taliban-controlled Kabul, Afghanistan, in September 1998.[27] From 1999 to 2003, ETIM members trained in undisclosed camps in Central Asia. Videos released on the ETIM's website, YouTube, and other file-sharing Internet sites contain footage of Hasan Mahsum at various wilderness training camps with date stamps from 1999 to 2003.[28] In the video "Steadfastness and Preparations for Jihad in the Cause of Allah," the ETIM claims to have maintained a continual training camp presence. The curriculum at the ETIM training camps included "shariah, political, and military lessons—such as in explosives and tactics, heavy and light weaponry, and lessons in intelligence and other military sciences."[29]

In an interview published in the ETIM's magazine, *Turkistan al-Islamiyya*, Abdul Haq said ETIM members attended training camps in Khost, Bagram, Kabul, and Herat, Afghanistan, in the late 1990s.[30] From the testimony of Uyghurs detained at GTMO, we know the ETIM ran a training camp in Afghanistan's Tora Bora mountains from at least November 2000 until the U.S. bombing campaign began in October 2001.

Several of the GTMO Uyghurs stated that the Tora Bora training camp was for new arrivals who would need to prove themselves in order to graduate to a more advanced camp for additional training. This is consistent with the methodology published on the ETIM website, which outlines the Islamic studies new recruits must complete before they are allowed to commence military preparation. The ETIM listed eight topics a recruit must master:

1. *The meaning of shahada.* The *shahada* is the Muslim profession of faith. It translates roughly to, "There is no god but Allah; Muhammad is the prophet of Allah."
2. *The conditions of shahada.*
3. *The categories of tawheed. Tawheed* is the Muslim doctrine of monotheism.
4. *The ten things which nullify a person's faith.* This is a commonly repeated list of prohibited practices, such as believing in other gods and sacrificing to the dead.
5. *The deviant modern ideologies (including democracy, secularism, etc.).*
6. *The knowledge of some of the deviant groups (e.g., Shia, murjiah, mutazilah).* The "deviant groups" are other sects of Islam.
7. *Understanding of jihad, i.e., linguistic and legalistic (sharia) definitions, the banner of jihad, who do we fight and why do we fight, etc.*
8. *An abbreviated basic jurisprudence (fiqh) of jihad.*[31]

The Tora Bora training camp curriculum also included weapons training, martial arts, and physical fitness.[32]

Several GTMO detainees reported that Hasan Mahsum visited the Uyghur camp in Tora Bora.[33] He also reportedly ran an ETIM safe house in Kabul.[34]

Mahsum was killed in Pakistan in 2003 by a joint U.S.-Pakistani operation against multinational militants in Angoor Adda, South Waziristan.[35] After Mahsum's death, little new information about the ETIM reached the public until the PRC reported several raids on ETIM locations in 2007. We do not know if the ETIM was mostly dormant during this period or if the Chinese government changed its public information strategy in preparation for the 2008 Summer Olympics in Beijing. Only in fall 2008 did the PRC resume making public statements about the group, and the ETIM—following in the footsteps of other Islamic militant organizations, including Al-Qaida— began releasing propaganda videos and publishing an Arabic-language magazine called *Turkistan al-Islamiyya.* The group used these forums to introduce its new leader, Abdul Haq al-Turkistani, and to demonstrate its ties to the past with references to its previous leader, Hasan Mahsum.

Abdul Haq al-Turkistani is likely the same "Abdul Haq" several of the GTMO Uyghurs named as the person running the day-to-day operations of their training camp in 2001.[36] Abdul Haq al-Turkistani heads the ETIM's

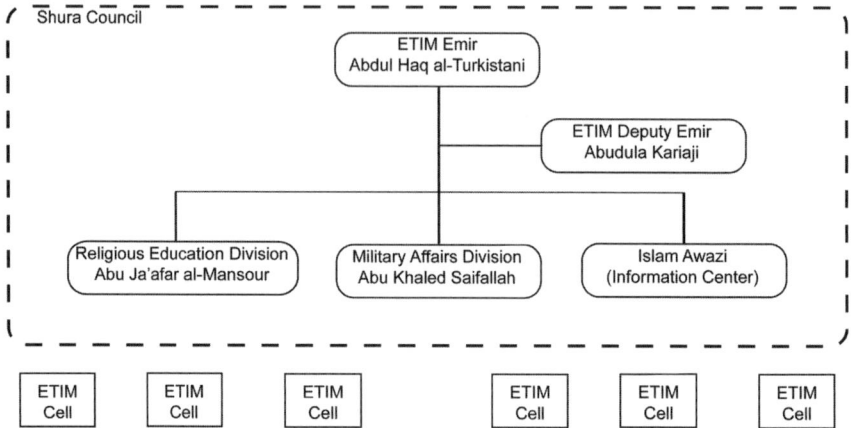

FIGURE 3.1. Based on the limited data available, the ETIM appears to be governed by a Shura Council under Abdul Haq al-Turkistani. Alexeyev, "A Tough International"; Intel-Center, "Turkistan Islamic Party (TIP): Threat Awareness Wall Chart"; Turkistan Islamic Party, "Regarding the Death of Hesen Mexsum."

Shura Council, which is the leadership group consisting of the emir, the deputy emir, and the heads of at least three divisions: the Religious Educa-tion Division, the Military Affairs Division, and the Information Center. One report indicated the ETIM also has an Intelligence/Counterintelligence Division and a Logistics Division.[37] See Figure 3.1 for an organization chart.

THE ETIM'S IDEOLOGY AND RHETORIC

The ETIM espouses a militant form of fundamentalist Islam. The group's political goal is to establish a state of East Turkistan, but its ultimate spiritual goal is to re-establish the Caliphate and install its particular brand of Islam as the supreme law of the land. Like Al-Qaida, the ETIM claims jihad is a divinely ordained obligation for every Muslim. Unlike Al-Qaida, the ETIM primarily targets China instead of the West. The ETIM claims the right to use any means necessary to drive the Chinese out of East Turkistan. The group has threatened and attacked unarmed civilians as well as Chinese military and police targets, but ETIM spokesmen deny accusations of terrorism. The ETIM's rhetoric implicitly justifies the group's violence against unarmed civil-ians by defining the enemy as *all* Chinese people in East Turkistan, calling them "invaders" and "infidels." In the case of the 2008 Beijing Olympics, the ETIM also issued broad, cryptic warnings admonishing the truly innocent to avoid the entire event.

The ETIM believes in applying Islamic rule to all of society, either by con-verting nonbelievers or by levying the tax known as *jizya* on non-Muslims as a sign of their subjugation.[38] (The ETIM considers democracy "cursed by Islam"[39] because it is secular.) According to the group's constitution, the ETIM's "criteria for action are to follow all the teachings of the Holy Koran and all the teachings of the Prophet Muhammad. This requires the implementation of comprehensive Islamic education, including faith, worship, morality, integrity, knowledge, [and] understanding, as well as implementing relevant principles explained in the Islamic tradition and Shari'a law."[40]

The present-day incarnation of the ETIM believes militant action is the only viable approach to establishing an East Turkistani state governed by fundamentalist Islam. The emphasis on militancy was a philosophical change Mahsum introduced in 1997. According to the ETIM's website, "The understanding of Hasan Makhdoom underwent a radical transformation in that he decided alongside other group members, that peaceful, non-resistant . . . efforts were only producing limited success."[41] (Many of these group members reached this conclusion after being imprisoned,[42] presumably in China; their radicalization in prison parallels countless similar stories in other countries around the world.)

The ETIM has evolved from critiquing the efficacy of peaceful resistance to declaiming that violent struggle is the Uyghurs' only path to self-preservation. For example, the narrator of a 2009 ETIM video declares that "speeches and writings won't have any impact" and "[a]nyone who is familiar with the battles that the mujahideen are engaged in today will know that the path of Jihad is the only path to prevent attacks and injustice."[43]

The ETIM claims violent jihad is not only a means to achieve a political objective but also a divinely ordained duty for all Muslims. The obligation to wage violent jihad has been a consistent theme in ETIM statements dating at least to 2003,[44] and it remains prominent in current rhetoric. For example, in a 2009 video an ETIM spokesman identified as Abdullah Mansur says, "Making preparations to fight these Atheist Communists is an obligation on every Muslim, and that includes scaring them, frightening them, and [also] causing horror in their hearts . . . every Muslim in East Turkestan must become involved in specifically undertaking military training."[45] The ETIM emphasizes that this mandate comes not from its own leaders but directly from Allah. In a 2008 article in *Turkistan al-Islamiyya* magazine, Abdullah Mansur (presumably the same ETIM spokesman in the video) makes this point by quoting from the Quran: "The almighty Allah said: 'Fighting is prescribed for you, and ye dislike it. But it is possible that ye dislike a thing which is good for you, and that ye love a thing which is bad for you. But Allah knoweth, and ye know not.' "[46] Al-Qaida and its affiliates commonly use a similar argument, which suggests the ETIM may have observed Al-Qaida's approach, judged it successful, and adopted the same rhetoric.[47] (The Jamestown Foundation analyst Murad Batal al-Shishani suggests the ETIM uses this argument either to associate itself with Al-Qaida or to attract Uyghurs to the Al-Qaida movement.[48])

For the ETIM, jihad is not an individual struggle, nor a local one, but instead a worldwide movement in which its members participate. According to the first paragraph of the group's constitution, ETIM members

> carry out jihad cooperatively with the mujahadin Muslims from all over the world . . . in order to re-establish the fallen Islamic Caliphate on earth. Particularly, [the ETIM] carries out jihad cooperatively with those who fight for Allah's mission of jihad in East Turkistan under the guidance of Islam.[49]

Collaboration with other Islamic militants within Xinjiang and in countries around the world is therefore among the ETIM's founding principles. The group is built for the global jihad.

While the ETIM's constitution emphasizes cooperation among holy warriors from all over the globe, remarks from one of its 2008 videos suggest other jihadis object to the ETIM's focus on East Turkistan over other, ongoing conflicts. In the video, an ETIM member named "Shaykh Bashir" says:

> To those among our brothers who disagree with us and ask: "Why are you fighting China now, while Muslims are still fighting the Americans and NATO?" We reply to this. . . . The clergy have ruled that fighting the near enemy takes precedence over fighting the far enemy—because the one who is close poses a real danger for Muslims, like in eastern Turkestan, while the far enemy does not pose an effective threat to Muslims. They have ruled that fighting an invading enemy is defensive fighting that takes precedence over offensive fighting (raiding the lands of the infidels).[50]

The ETIM apparently considers the West a legitimate but secondary target in the East Turkistani jihad. Shaykh Bashir goes on to accuse the United States, the rest of NATO, and "the other Jewish and Christian infidel factions" of hating Islam and waging "an ideological holy war" against Muslims. However, the ETIM considers the Han Chinese an invading enemy and therefore a much greater threat.

The ETIM's rhetoric reflects many of the Uyghur activists' general grievances against the Chinese state, including religious repression, economic exploitation, environmental degradation, human rights violations, and stringent population control. "China has stood against Islam and Muslims, has forced atheist Communism and communist education on them, has prevented them from holding their religious ceremonies, has outlawed religious education and closed schools, institutes and universities teaching Islam, has prevented them from immigrating to Muslim countries, and has maintained a policy of isolation, population birth control, and ethnic cleansing," Shaykh Bashir declares. An English-language document posted on the ETIM's now-defunct website describes the PRC's alleged crimes against the Uyghur population in lurid detail. Some of the more sensational charges include forcibly shaving Muslim men's beards in the streets, ripping the *hijab* off Muslim women's heads to humiliate them in public, and broadcasting pornography in order to corrupt Muslim youth. The ETIM laments PRC bans on building mosques and operating Muslim charities and schools (except for the Institute for the Study of Islamic Texts in Urumqi, which many Uyghur advocates consider hopelessly compromised; according to the ETIM's website, the institute "teach[es] a corrupt form of pro-communist Islam"[51]). The English-language document on the ETIM's website also notes, "The Turkestani people do not have control over their vast resources of raw minerals and they are not given the right to exploit and utilize them." The document further alleges that the nuclear tests at Lop Nor led to the deaths of 250,000 Turkistanis, and the PRC's birth control policy led to more than 500,000 abortions or murders in East Turkistan.[52]

The ETIM considers its actions justified by the PRC's alleged offenses. The ETIM has proclaimed its right and intention to use any means necessary to achieve its goals,[53] implicitly acknowledging its terrorist tactics while rejecting the term "terrorism." For example, in a 2009 video the ETIM's "Commander Seyfullah" says, "Dear brothers, be well aware that the path we are asking you to follow is not 'terrorism' or barbaric or hegemonic work as the infidels have claimed with their poisonous tongues. But, it is the path of preciousness and glory exactly as Allah ordained for the believers."[54] Commander Seyfullah does not elaborate on the difference between "terrorism" and "the path of preciousness and glory."

While the ETIM often targets China's military and police, the group has also targeted unarmed civilians with threats and attacks on public transportation and gathering places—acts generally considered terrorism. Justifying such acts is a challenge common to all terrorist groups. The ETIM largely skirts the issue, avoiding any explicit attempts to justify violence against innocents. Instead, the ETIM addresses the issue implicitly by defining its legitimate targets not only as agents of the Chinese state but also as any ethnic Chinese in Xinjiang and any others who support the Chinese in Xinjiang. The ETIM's constitution states that the group "believes that all Chinese immigrants' existence in East Turkistan is entirely illegal . . . they must go back to where they came from. This is the last warning for them."[55]

By issuing such a "warning," the ETIM can claim it is not responsible for any harm that might come to ethnic Chinese who remain in Xinjiang. The ETIM released many similar warnings about the Beijing Olympics, demanding a boycott and announcing its intent to attack any athletes, officials, and spectators who dared to participate. (The ETIM did commit several attacks in Xinjiang during the Olympics, but none near sites affiliated with the Games.) The ETIM sought to pre-empt accusations of terrorism by defining its prospective targets not as innocents but as collaborators in the PRC's alleged oppression. "Do you not realize that, by your silence, you are aiding the abuser in his abuse?" asks the ETIM's leader, Abdul Haq al-Turkistani, in a March 2008 video.[56] A July 2008 video claims that anyone at the Beijing Olympics "stand[s] by the Chinese infidels against your Muslim brothers in Turkestan."[57] The same July 2008 video extends the threat beyond the duration of the Games themselves: "The [ETIM] is sending another warning to China to stop these Olympics. Should they ignore our warning, we shall target places which are important to the Olympics and we shall make this our permanent target."[58] It is unclear whether the "permanent target" is the collection of Olympic-related sites in China or the Olympic Games themselves, whatever their future locations might be. In either case, the ETIM is employing the same strategy of issuing a "warning" that redefines innocent bystanders as legitimate targets.

CATALOGUE OF ETIM ACTIVITIES

We attempted to develop a complete catalogue of events attributed to the ETIM as of this writing. These events span the 1990s, with one in 2002, one in 2005, and a cluster in 2008. Based on the available data, the ETIM's tactics appear to be evolving.

The 1990s events attributed to the ETIM include a number of bombings and attempts to assassinate Muslim clerics in good standing with the local government, often by shooting or stabbing them. By 2008, the ETIM's bombings, shootings, and knife attacks focused more on police and security forces. The group had developed an online media presence and begun releasing videos to claim attacks and threaten future ones. Some of the attacks it claimed took place outside Xinjiang.

Three recent reports of ETIM activity involve female suicide bombers, which may be an emerging tactic in the ETIM's repertoire. In March 2008, a 19-year-old woman was detained trying to bomb and crash a China Southern Airlines flight.[59] In August 2008, two women were involved in a series of a dozen bombings in Kuqa, Xinjiang; one of them blew herself up to avoid capture by Chinese authorities.[60] In June 2009, authorities in Punjab, Pakistan, were looking for a female suicide bomber trained by the ETIM.[61] Female suicide bombers have proven to be devastating attackers in Iraq, and the ETIM may be appropriating this tactic. (In 2006, two academics said ETIM members in Europe were studying Al-Qaida in Iraq's tactics and technologies, presumably in order to appropriate those that proved effective.[62])

For the sake of simplicity, we recorded all events attributed to or claimed by the ETIM, ETIP, TIP, IPT, and other known translations or transliterations of the group's name as ETIM events, regardless of which variant appeared in the original reporting. One of the key sources for our catalogue of events is an ambiguously worded 2002 PRC news release titled " 'East Turkistan' Forces Cannot Get Away with Impunity." The English translation of this news release invites confusion over which group or groups are responsible for specific events in Xinjiang. The news release uses a Chinese phrase that can be translated to English as "the 'East Turkistan' terrorist organization," which some analysts have considered a reference to the ETIM. However, in Chinese, this phrase has no definite article and could be either singular or plural.[63] Thus, the specific-sounding "the 'East Turkistan' terrorist organization" could also be translated as the more generic " 'East Turkistan' terrorist organizations" or "an 'East Turkistan' terrorist organization"—clearly not a reference to the ETIM alone. We included events attributed to "East Turkistan terrorist organizations/*an* East Turkistan terrorist organization/*the* East Turkistan terrorist organization" in our catalogue but noted the ambiguity.

The following catalogue includes four categories of events:

1. Events for which the ETIM has claimed responsibility.
2. Events explicitly attributed to the ETIM or its factions.
3. Events loosely associated with the ETIM and not explicitly attributed to other groups. This category includes several events that have not been attributed to any group but that involved tactics and techniques similar to the ETIM's.
4. Events attributed to "East Turkistan terrorist organizations/*an* East Turkistan terrorist organization/*the* East Turkistan terrorist organization." We will specify when events were attributed to the ETIM as a result of this ambiguous language.

Figure 3.2 shows the locations of ETIM-related attacks and raids. Figure 3.3 shows the subset of these attacks and raids that occurred within Xinjiang.

1989–1990: Bombings

Abdul Kareem (one of the ETIM's original founders) and Shaheed Idris bin Omar led an ETIM faction called the Islamic Party of Reformation (*Hizbul Islah Al-Islami*) responsible for car and bus bombings in Urumqi from 1989 to 1990.[64]

April 5–6, 1990: Baren Rebellion

Protests over a variety of government practices in Baren Township erupted in rebellion on April 5, 1990. (Ironically, the PRC had named Baren an "Ethnic Unity Model Town" in 1984.[65]) Chinese government reports immediately after the rebellion attributed this event to the ETIM. The rebellion resulted in 22 deaths—6 police officers, 14 ETIM members, and 2 others—and 19 injuries.[66]

The rebellion began early on April 5, 1990, when Zaiyiding Yusupu led a group of approximately 200 Uyghurs in a march on the government compound in Baren. This group included one to two dozen ETIM members.[67]

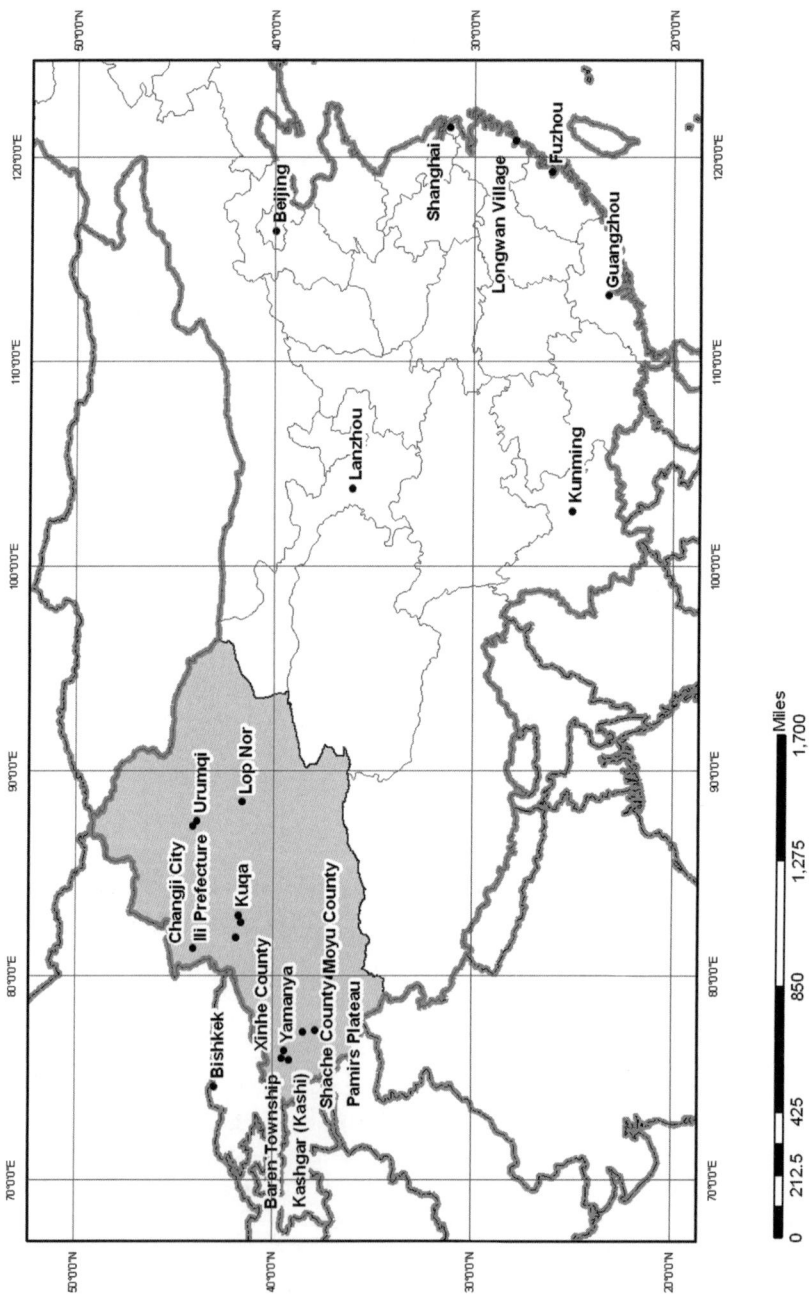

FIGURE 3.2. Dots on this map represent ETIM-related attacks and PRC raids targeting the ETIM. Most (but not all) of them occurred in Xinjiang. Map created by the author in ArcGIS.

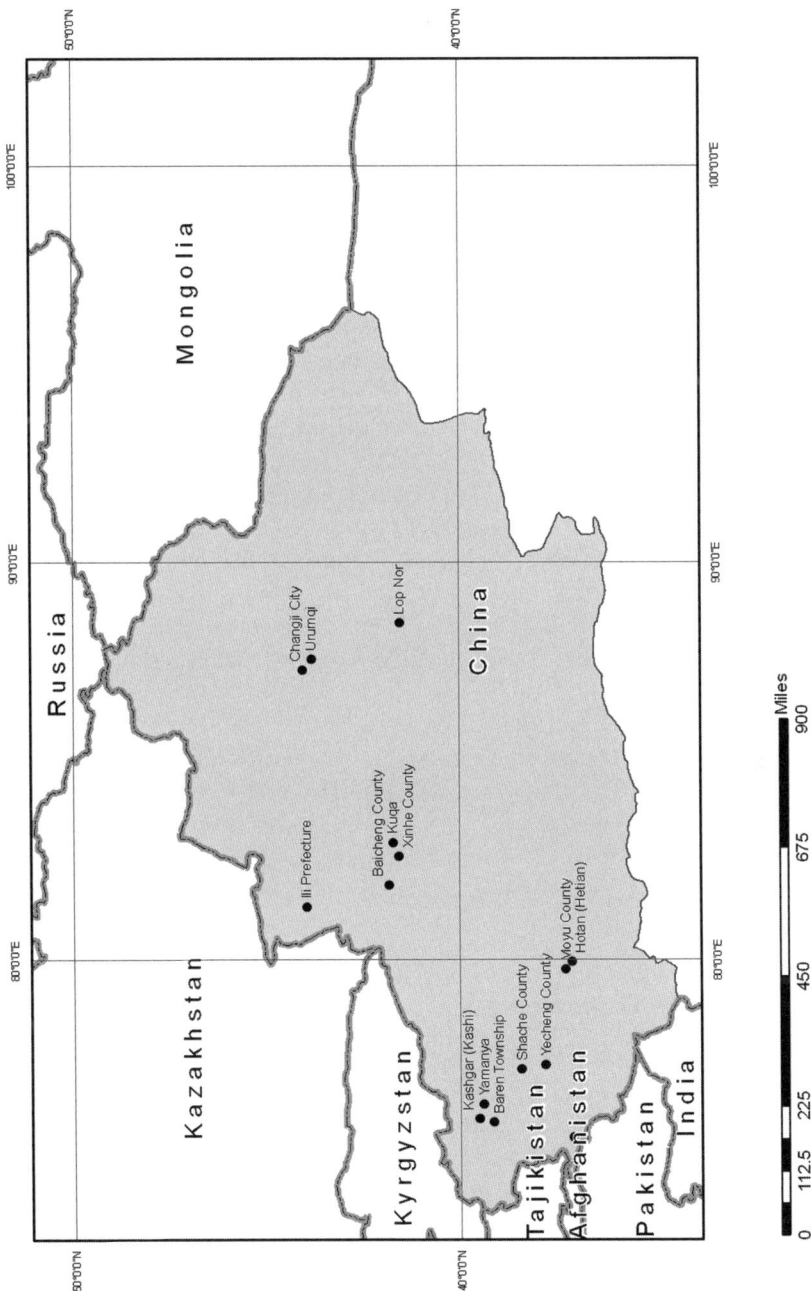

FIGURE 3.3. Dots on this map of Xinjiang represent ETIM-related attacks and PRC raids targeting the ETIM. Most (but not all) of them occurred in Xinjiang. Map created by the author in ArcGIS.

Local police intercepted the march and tried to disperse the crowd, but the police were driven into the compound along with the government employees.[68]

ETIM members controlled a bridge about a kilometer from the government compound's courtyard. They stopped four police officers responding to the rebellion, killed them, and destroyed their vehicle. The ETIM members then stopped another group of three police and killed two of them, injuring the third and again destroying the vehicle.[69]

Early on April 6, the rebels began shooting and throwing bombs into the government compound, breaching the wall in three places.[70]

Military and police reinforcements arrived on the afternoon of April 6 and quickly ended the rebellion. Three ETIM members committed suicide with hand grenades. Military and police forces killed 11 other ETIM members and arrested and imprisoned many other Uyghurs.[71] The violence spilled over to spark unrest in Urumqi, Kashgar, Hotan, Kuqa, Aksu, and Artush. According to the Xinjiang scholar June Teufel Dreyer, "The confrontations were said to have resembled real battles, and soldiers reportedly fled on occasions when they found themselves outnumbered and outgunned."[72]

The PRC claims the ETIM stockpiled weapons to use in the rebellion. The government's list indicates how limited the group's resources would have been. It includes a single submachine gun, a single rifle, 11 handguns, 117 bullets, homemade explosives, daggers, long swords, axes, and rusty tin cans.[73]

The context for the Baren Rebellion remains unclear. The PRC claims the ETIM planned it.[74] Some sources indicate Baren was only a small piece of a complex ETIM plan that involved simultaneous attacks on various government buildings; they say the plan was discovered prematurely, which led the group to attack Baren's government compound ahead of schedule.[75] Other sources argue that the Baren Rebellion was really just a spontaneous street protest that happened to include ETIM members.[76]

February 28, 1991: Bombing

The PRC reported a bombing at the video terminal of the bus station in Kuqa on February 28, 1991. The explosion killed 1 and injured 13. The PRC attributed this attack to "East Turkistan terrorist organizations/*an* East Turkistan terrorist organization/*the* East Turkistan terrorist organization."[77]

February 28, 1991: Attempted Bombing

The PRC documented another bomb in Kuqa intended to detonate simultaneously with the bus station bomb on February 28, 1991. This second bomb was planted in a private store but did not explode. The PRC attributed this attack to "East Turkistan terrorist organizations/*an* East Turkistan terrorist organization/*the* East Turkistan terrorist organization."[78]

June 17, 1993: Bombing

The PRC reported a bombing at an agricultural machinery company in Kashgar on July 17, 1993. The explosion killed two people, injured seven, and destroyed the company's offices. The PRC attributed this attack to "East Turkistan terrorist organizations/*an* East Turkistan terrorist organization/*the* East Turkistan terrorist organization."[79]

August 1, 1993: Bombing

The PRC reported a bombing at the video theater of a foreign trade company in Shache County, Kashgar Prefecture, Xinjiang, on August 1, 1993. The PRC attributed this attack to "East Turkistan terrorist organizations/*an* East Turkistan terrorist organization/*the* East Turkistan terrorist organization."[80]

August 19, 1993: Bombing

The PRC reported a bombing at a "cultural palace" in Hotan on August 19, 1993. The explosion injured six people. The PRC attributed this attack to "East Turkistan terrorist organizations/*an* East Turkistan terrorist organization/*the* East Turkistan terrorist organization."[81]

August 24, 1993: Assassination Attempt

The PRC reported an attempt to assassinate a Muslim cleric who maintained positive relations with local government officials in Yecheng County, Kashgar Prefecture, Xinjiang, on August 24, 1993. Two attackers stabbed Abliz Damolla, the imam of the Great Mosque in Yecheng County and a member of the county's Chinese People's Political Consultative Conference (CPPCC) executive committee. The PRC attributed this attack to " 'East Turkistan' terrorists."[82] This was the first of several attempts to assassinate Islamic leaders who worked with the Chinese government.

June to September 1993: Bombings

The PRC reported seven other explosions in department stores, markets, hotels, and cultural centers in southern Xinjiang from June to September 1993. (These are in addition to the bombings on June 17, August 1, and August 19.) The PRC attributed these attacks to "East Turkistan terrorist organizations/*an* East Turkistan terrorist organization/*the* East Turkistan terrorist organization."[83]

March 22, 1996: Assassination

The PRC reported the assassination of a Muslim cleric who maintained positive relations with local government officials in Xinhe County, Aksu Prefecture, Xinjiang, on March 22, 1996. Two attackers shot Hakimsidiq Haji at his home. He was the assistant imam of a mosque and the vice-chairman of the Islamic Association of Xinhe County.[84]

The PRC did not attribute this attack to a specific group, but this incident is similar to the August 24, 1993, attempt to assassinate a Muslim cleric, which the PRC attributed to "East Turkistan terrorist organizations/*an* East Turkistan terrorist organization/*the* East Turkistan terrorist organization."

May 12, 1996: Attempted Assassinations

The PRC reported an attempt to assassinate a Muslim cleric who maintained positive relations with local government officials and an attempt to assassinate the cleric's son in Kashgar on May 12, 1996. Four attackers repeatedly stabbed Arunhan Aji and his son while they were traveling to Aitga Mosque. Aji was an executive committee member of the Islamic Association of China, vice-chairman of the CPPCC Xinjiang Regional Committee, and chairman of the Kashgar Islamic Association. The PRC attributed this attack to "East Turkistan terrorist organizations/*an* East Turkistan terrorist organization/*the* East Turkistan terrorist organization."[85]

This series of attacks on Muslim clerics was followed by an increase in bombings from 1997 to 1999.[86] The PRC responded to these events by cracking down on Islamic militants and the Uyghur population in general.[87] There are numerous reports of clashes, arrests, executions, and riots during this period. Very few of these events were attributed to or claimed by specific groups at the time.

February 25, 1997: Bombings

Three bus bombs exploded and a fourth failed to detonate in Urumqi on February 25, 1997. The explosions killed 9 and injured 68. The PRC attributed these attacks to "East Turkistan terrorist organizations/*an* East Turkistan terrorist organization/*the* East Turkistan terrorist organization."[88] Press reports immediately after the attack attributed it to "freedom fighters" and "Moslem separatists coming from the cities of Kashgar and Korla."[89]

November 6, 1997: Assassination

The PRC reported the assassination of a Muslim cleric who maintained positive relations with local government officials in Baicheng County, Xinjiang, on November 6, 1997. Muhammat Tursun, a member of the

" 'East Turkistan' organization," shot Yunus Sidiq Damolla at a mosque. Damolla was the imam of the mosque in Baicheng County, a member of the Islamic Association of China, a member of the Islamic Association of Xinjiang, and chairman of the Islamic Association of Aksu. The PRC attributed this attack to "East Turkistan terrorist organizations/*an* East Turkistan terrorist organization/*the* East Turkistan terrorist organization" abroad.[90]

January 27, 1998: Assassination

The PRC reported the assassination of a Muslim cleric who maintained positive relations with local government officials in Yecheng County on January 27, 1998. Attackers shot and killed Abliz Haji, the imam of the Yecheng County Great Mosque and an executive committee member of the Yecheng County CPPCC. (He may be the same man targeted in the August 24, 1993, assassination attempt.) The PRC attributed this attack to "East Turkistan terrorist organizations/*an* East Turkistan terrorist organization/*the* East Turkistan terrorist organization" abroad.[91]

February 22 to March 30, 1998: Bombings

The PRC reported six bombings in Yecheng County from February to March 1998. The bombings injured three people. One bomb exploded a natural gas pipeline, causing a large fire and more than $120,000[92] in damage. The PRC attributed this event to "East Turkistan terrorist organizations/*an* East Turkistan terrorist organization/*the* East Turkistan terrorist organization."[93]

April 7, 1998: Bombings

The PRC reported eight separate but sequential bombings in Kashgar Prefecture in April 1998. The explosions occurred in several locations, including the homes of senior public officials, and injured eight people. The PRC attributed this event to "East Turkistan terrorist organizations/*an* East Turkistan terrorist organization/*the* East Turkistan terrorist organization."[94]

February 4, 1999: Robbery and Murder

The PRC claimed the ETIM committed robbery and murder in Urumqi on February 4, 1999. At least five people died in the attacks.[95]

March 17, 1999: Attack

The ETIM reportedly attacked a People's Liberation Army convoy in Changji City, Xinjiang, on March 17, 1999. After the attack, the PRC said those responsible had been "wiped out."[96]

June 18, 1999: Attack

The PRC blamed the ETIM for shooting and killing a police officer in Xinhe County, Xinjiang, on June 18, 1999.[97]

December 14, 1999: Murder

The PRC blamed the ETIM for a murder in Moyu County, Hotan Prefecture, Xinjiang, on December 14, 1999.[98]

May 2002: Planned Bombing of U.S. Embassy in Kyrgyzstan

The Chinese government, the Kyrgyz government, and the U.S. embassy in China all claim the ETIM planned to bomb the U.S. embassy in Bishkek on an unspecified date. However, the Kyrgyz government initially identified the plotters as members of a different group and accused them of a different crime.

On May 23, 2002, a spokesperson for the Kyrgyz government announced that Mamat Sadyk (aka Ogut Nevzay) and Mamed Yasin were detained in Kyrgyzstan on May 8 and deported to China on May 21. They were accused of playing a role in killing the chairman of the Ittipak Uyghur Association in Bishkek in March 2000 and, later, in killing a member of a Chinese trade delegation. Sadyk and Yasin were reported as suspected members of the Eastern Turkestan Liberation Front.[99]

In August 2002, the U.S. embassy in Beijing announced the ETIM planned to bomb the U.S. embassy in Bishkek. A U.S. spokesperson in Beijing identified the plotters as Mamet Sadyk (an alternative spelling of Mamat Sadyk) and Mamet Yasyn (an alternative spelling of Mamed Yasin). The spokesperson said Yasyn had surveyed several embassies and marketplaces in Bishkek. The U.S. embassy spokesperson indicated this information came from the Kyrgyz government.[100]

Kyrgyz Foreign Minister Askar Aitmatov told the *Washington Post*, "There were some suspicions that they might have been planning an attack against the U.S. Embassy." He indicated that one of the two deported men had a map showing embassies in Bishkek. The two individuals were clearly identified as ETIM members at this point.[101]

Investigations and interrogations conducted after Sadyk and Yasyn were deported to China may have uncovered additional, as-yet-unreleased evidence that they belonged to the ETIM and planned to attack the U.S. embassy. However, they were initially identified as members of a different group and accused of a different crime.

August 8, 2005: Bombing

Three years after the fact, the ETIM claimed responsibility for bombing a bus in Fuzhou, Fujian Province, on August 8, 2005. The PRC attributed this event to "a 42-year-old farmer suffering from terminal lung cancer."[102] No militant groups claimed the attack at the time. Then, in 2008, the ETIM released a video titled "Our Blessed Jihad in Yunnan." The video included images from the 2005 Fuzhou bombing.[103]

The ETIM was mostly silent from 2003 to 2007. In early 2007, the PRC began announcing raids on ETIM camps in Xinjiang. Shortly thereafter, the ETIM began issuing more public statements, including threats and attack claims.

March 7, 2008: Attempted Plane Crash

The ETIM claimed responsibility for attempting to bomb China Southern Airlines flight CZ6901 on March 7, 2008.[104] The plane left Urumqi at 10:35 a.m., bound for Beijing. Approximately 40 minutes into the flight, a 19-year-old woman named Guzalinur Turdi tried to start a fire in the bathroom. She and an accomplice had smuggled drink cans filled with gasoline through the business-class security checkpoint. Airline employees stopped Turdi from setting fire to the fuel. The plane made an emergency landing at Lanzhou, Gansu Province, at 12:40 p.m. Two other suspects were detained in the incident.[105]

March 13, 2008: Bombing

The PRC reported that an explosion at a vehicle repair plant in Guangzhou, Guangdong Province, killed 7 people and injured 30 on March 13, 2008.[106] The ETIM may have claimed responsibility for this explosion but relayed the details differently. The ETIM claimed it bombed a plastics factory in Guangzhou on July 17, 2008. The PRC refuted this claim, saying a plastics factory was not bombed on that date.[107] (There was a fire at a plastics factory on July 17, 2008, but the fire occurred in Shanghai.[108])

April 9, 2008

A video posted online April 9, 2008, reportedly shows the execution of three Han Chinese and displays the ETIM logo.[109]

May 5, 2008: Bombing

A bus exploded in Shanghai on May 5, 2008, killing 3 people and injuring 12. On July 28, 2008, the ETIM claimed it had bombed the bus. The PRC refuted this claim and insisted somewhat cryptically that although the blast was deliberate, it was not terrorism.[110]

May 17, 2008: Bombing

A tractor drove into a car and minibus, causing an explosion in Longwan Village, Wenzhou City, Zhejiang Province, that killed 19 and injured 45 on

May 17, 2008. This incident was originally reported as a traffic accident, but updated PRC reports indicate the tractor's driver was a disgruntled gambler who had loaded his vehicle with explosives and was on his way to bomb a gambling house when he crashed the tractor by mistake.[111]

On July 28, 2009, the ETIM claimed responsibility for this explosion but provided the wrong date; the ETIM said the explosion occurred on July 17, not May 17. The PRC denied the ETIM's claim.[112] (It is unlikely that the ETIM had any real connection to this bombing, although the PRC's explanation seems even more farfetched.)

July 21, 2008: Bombing

The ETIM claimed responsibility for two bombs that exploded on buses in Kunming, Yunnan Province, on July 21, 2008.[113] The attackers had taped ammonium nitrate underneath the buses' seats. The first bomb killed 1 person and injured 10; the second bomb killed 1 and injured 4.[114]

Early that morning, a mysterious text message sent to some residents of the city had warned, "The general mobilization of ants. . . . [I] hope citizens receiving this message will not take bus lines 54, 64, and 84 tomorrow morning."[115]

The PRC rejected the ETIM's attack claim, saying it had no evidence the bombings were linked to terrorism.[116]

THE ETIM AND THE 2008 SUMMER OLYMPICS

A cluster of attacks in August 2008 coincided with the Beijing Olympics, which the ETIM had threatened to disrupt in a series of videos dating back six months. The group's initial Olympics threat video, released March 1, 2008, said, "[We] have completed our preparations for striking the Olympic Games and thwarting them. We will make this year a year of grief and terror for all Chinese, turning their joy into funeral processions and tears everywhere."[117]

In July, the ETIM claimed responsibility for recent bombings in China and reiterated its intent to target the Games, including "all the participants in the Olympics as well as venues, sports facilities, and residential compounds."[118]

Another video released in August showed the Olympic flag in flames and warned Muslims not to go to China during the 2008 Olympics. The video did not make any specific threats, but it indicated that both infrastructure and modes of transportation were potential targets.[119]

The PRC's security director for the 2008 Olympics, Ma Zhenchuan, claimed the Chinese had evidence that the group had indeed plotted attacks on Olympic venues.[120] While the ETIM did not pull off a spectacular attack on the world stage in Beijing, it did execute several smaller attacks in Xinjiang.

August 4, 2008: Attack

The ETIM attacked a group of police officers in Kashgar on August 4, 2008, both by its own admission and in the assessment of PRC officials.[121] Accounts of the incident differ in the details. In one version, the attackers drove a truck into a group of about 70 police officers who were exercising at about 8 a.m. In another version, the attackers stopped the truck and then threw homemade explosives at the police officers. In both versions, the attackers then used knives to continue their attack by stabbing the injured police. The attack killed 16 and injured 16 more. One of the attackers accidentally blew off his arm.[122]

The attackers' truck reportedly contained 10 more homemade explosives, which resembled explosives the PRC had captured in a raid on an ETIM camp in 2007.[123]

August 7, 2008: Attack

The ETIM claimed responsibility for shooting at a security patrol in an unintelligible location on August 7, 2008, in a statement released three months later. The ETIM claimed it killed eight troops. No other information about this attack is available.[124]

August 8, 2008: Bombing

The ETIM claimed responsibility for bombing a police convoy in Xinjiang's Ili Prefecture on August 8, 2008, in a statement released three months later. The attack killed nine people. No other information about this attack is available.[125]

August 10, 2008: Bombings[126]

The ETIM claimed responsibility for a series of bombings in Kuqa on August 10, 2008. Two people were killed and several others injured. The explosions began before dawn in the courtyard of a police station downtown. Some sources indicate the attackers threw bombs into the courtyard, and other sources say they drove a vehicle into the courtyard and the vehicle exploded.

According to some sources, the attackers bombed 12 sites, and according to other sources they executed 17 distinct attacks. Other targets included a bank, a hotel, a shopping center with stores owned by Han Chinese, and several government buildings. According to the ETIM, the government buildings included a courthouse, a customs facility, and a building owned by the "Center for Birth Restriction." The bombs were homemade, constructed of bent pipes, gas canisters, and liquid-gas tanks. The state news agency reported that police seized dozens of unexploded bombs.

Police cordoned off the city, evacuating some residents and warning others not to leave their homes. By the end of the day Chinese police had killed eight suspected terrorists and detained either two or three, including a 15-year-old girl. Two more (including a woman) blew themselves up to avoid capture. Another two or three were believed to be at large, based on one detainee's statement that 15 people were involved in the attack.

The assailants used the same tactics as in the August 4, 2008, bombing attributed to the ETIM. No group claimed responsibility immediately, and the PRC did not blame the ETIM. The ETIM claimed responsibility for this attack in a statement released three months later.

August 12, 2008: Attack

The ETIM claimed it stabbed four security officers at a roadside checkpoint in Yamanya, Shule County, Kashgar, on August 12, 2008, killing three of them and wounding the fourth. The PRC said it had no evidence the ETIM was responsible.[127]

August 27, 2008: Attack

The ETIM also claimed responsibility for another stabbing on August 27, 2008, against police officers investigating the August 12 roadside checkpoint killings. Two investigating officers were killed and five injured in Kizilboyi, Jiashi County, Kashgar. On August 29, police returned to the scene and again encountered resistance. They found nine suspects hiding in a cornfield. The suspects attacked the police with knives, and the police killed six of them and arrested the other three. Two officers were wounded.[128]

The ETIM was able to execute these attacks despite losses suffered in PRC raids that began even before the group officially threatened the Olympics. The details of the raids are as follows.

> *January 5, 2007*: A raid on an ETIM camp in the mountains near the Pamirs plateau in Xinjiang on January 5, 2007, resulted in 18 killed and 17 captured. Xinjiang police reportedly seized 22 hand grenades and 1,500 partially constructed explosive devices.[129]
>
> *January 4–11, 2008*: The PRC claimed it arrested 10 members of an ETIM cell and seized explosives in raids conducted between January 4 and January 11, 2008. PRC officials claimed the ETIM cell trained to use poisoned meat, poisoned gas, and remote-controlled explosive devices.[130]
>
> *January 27, 2008*: The PRC claimed it raided an ETIM safe house and weapons cache in Urumqi, killing 2 ETIM members and detaining 15 others. PRC officials said the weapons were intended "to damage [the] Beijing 2008 summer Olympic Games."[131]

Chinese police say they arrested 82 people from Xinjiang in the first half of 2008 for offenses related to the 2008 Olympics.[132] It is unclear how many of those 82 belonged to the ETIM.

CONCLUSION

The ETIM was obscure before 9/11 but not unknown. The group has been blamed or claimed responsibility for a variety of terrorist attacks dating back to 1989. These include the Baren Rebellion of 1990, bus bombings, assassinations, an attempted plane crash, and a spate of attacks on police and security forces in Xinjiang during the 2008 Olympics.

The ETIM's tactics appear to be evolving. Events attributed to the ETIM in the 1990s include a number of attempts to assassinate Muslim clerics in good standing with the local government, often by shooting or stabbing them. By 2008, the ETIM's bombings, shootings, and stabbings focused more on police and security forces. The group continues to target unarmed civilians when it attacks buses, government offices, and businesses owned by Han Chinese. The ETIM's rhetoric implicitly justifies such violence by defining the enemy as *all* Chinese people in East Turkistan, calling them "invaders" and "infidels."

The present-day incarnation of the ETIM believes militant action is the only viable approach to establishing an East Turkistani state governed by fundamentalist Islam. It claims violent jihad is an obligation for every Muslim and interprets jihad not as a local struggle but as a worldwide movement aimed at reinstating the Caliphate. The ETIM's constitution commits the group to collaboration with other Islamic militants, both within Xinjiang and abroad. Indeed, the ETIM's most notorious leader, Hasan Mahsum, forged alliances with Al-Qaida and the Taliban in the late 1990s.

Perhaps influenced by Al-Qaida's investment in media operations, the ETIM began releasing propaganda videos, established a website, and started its own magazine. The ETIM's present size and capabilities are largely unknown, but its ability to execute attacks during the 2008 Olympics despite increased security measures demonstrates the group's resilience. The ETIM's enduring transnational ties—including its allegiances with terrorist groups in other countries, bases abroad, and an Internet presence—have helped insulate the ETIM from the PRC's security crackdowns.

4

———— ∞ ————

The ETIM's Transnational Presence

The ETIM has reported ties to Al-Qaida, the Taliban, and the IMU. The ETIM has allegedly been active in a number of foreign countries, including Afghanistan, Pakistan, Kazakhstan, Kyrgyzstan, Tajikistan, Uzbekistan, and Chechnya. The group has partially insulated itself from China's counterterrorism measures by establishing operational bases and sources of support outside the PRC's borders.

The ETIM has been based outside of China since Hasan Mahsum re-established the organization in 1997. From 1997 until September 2001, the ETIM maintained its base in the Tora Bora region of Afghanistan controlled by the Taliban. When the U.S.-led coalition began military operations in Afghanistan, the coalition captured 22 Uyghurs and later detained them at GTMO.

After the Taliban fell, the ETIM moved its headquarters to Pakistan. As of August 2008, the ETIM reportedly bases its operations in Nir Ali, North Waziristan, in Pakistan's lawless Federally Administered Tribal Areas (FATA; see Figure 4.1).[1] The ETIM also uses the Internet to project its message beyond the FATA, broadcasting its claims, threats, and other rhetoric around the world.

THE ETIM AND OTHER ISLAMIC MILITANT ORGANIZATIONS

A variety of sources link the ETIM with Al-Qaida, the Taliban, and the IMU. Limited reporting also links the ETIM to other militant groups, including the United Tajik Opposition, the Harkat-ul-Jihad al-Islami, the Islamic Jihad Union, and the Tehrik-i-Taliban Pakistan.

FIGURE 4.1. The shaded area shows Pakistan's Federally Administered Tribal Areas (FATA). Hasan Mahsum was killed in Angoor Adda. The ETIM ran a training camp on the Afghan side of the border, at Tora Bora. Map created by the author in ArcGIS.

Al-Qaida

The PRC, the United States, and the United Nations all assert a connection between Al-Qaida and the ETIM. Although former ETIM leader Hasan Mahsum denied this connection in 2002, the ETIM's own actions and statements indicate a sustained and even strengthening relationship.

The first published claim of a link between the ETIM and Osama bin Laden's Al-Qaida came not from the PRC but from the Russian newspaper *Nezavisimaya Gazeta* in 2000. An article by Michael Falco stated that the ETIM and the IMU twice met with bin Laden in Kandahar, Afghanistan, in 1999.[2]

After 9/11, the PRC began reporting that Al-Qaida provided funding and training to the ETIM. In a news release issued in November 2001, the PRC claimed Hasan Mahsum met with Al-Qaida in 1999, and that Al-Qaida and the Taliban gave the ETIM $300,000 between October 2000 and November 2001.[3] Later, the Chinese government further claimed the ETIM had also received training from Al-Qaida.[4]

At U.S. urging, the United Nations designated the ETIM an Al-Qaida-affiliated terrorist group on the one-year anniversary of the 9/11 attacks.[5] The U.S. press statement on this designation alleged a "close financial relationship" between the ETIM and Al-Qaida. The press statement also said many ETIM members received terrorist training financed by Al-Qaida and the Taliban.[6] However, the 2002 edition of the U.S. State Department's annual report on international terrorism was more cautious, saying the

ETIM and other, overlapping Uyghur militant groups are linked to Al-Qaida "to a limited degree." The 2002 report said the ETIM "is suspected of" receiving training and financial assistance from Al-Qaida.[7] Language on this issue grew more authoritative in later annual reports. In 2003, the State Department said the ETIM *is* linked to Al-Qaida, without qualifying that statement. The 2003 annual report also states as fact that the ETIM received training and financial assistance from Al-Qaida.[8]

Although the late ETIM leader Hasan Mahsum denied a connection to Al-Qaida in 2002, an ETIM deputy emir confirmed that connection two years later. In an interview with Radio Free Asia, Mahsum said the ETIM had "no organizational links with Al-Qaeda or the Taliban."[9] (Mahsum was killed in 2003 in an Al-Qaida stronghold in Waziristan.) However, in 2004, a man who identified himself as the ETIM's deputy emir confirmed the pre-9/11 link with Al-Qaida in a *Wall Street Journal* interview. Abudula Kariaji said he personally participated in a 1999 meeting with Osama bin Laden in Kandahar and admitted that some ETIM members fought with Al-Qaida and the Taliban against the U.S.-led coalition in Afghanistan. Kariaji also said the relationship between the ETIM and Al-Qaida was not as strong as the Chinese and U.S. governments claimed. He described a conflict between the ETIM's focus on the PRC and Al-Qaida's belief that the mujahideen's "first duty is to free Palestine and the sacred Arab lands."[10] (A 2008 ETIM statement titled "Why Are We Fighting China?" alludes to this difference of opinion between the ETIM and other jihadis.[11])

Recent ETIM propaganda indicates the link with Al-Qaida may be strengthening. In 2008, the ETIM began publishing a magazine called *Turkistan al-Islamiyya* through Al-Qaida's distributor, Al-Fajr Media Center.[12] Analysis of recent ETIM statements indicates the group is adopting Al-Qaida's rhetoric. For example, the ETIM seems to have appropriated Al-Qaida's argument that every Muslim has a moral obligation to wage violent jihad.[13] If the ETIM is moving toward a closer relationship with Al-Qaida, that relationship with a truly global and well-established terrorist group may help sustain the ETIM despite the PRC's efforts to eradicate it.

The Taliban

The ETIM has almost certainly received at least tacit support from the Taliban, if not actual funding and training. The PRC,[14] the United States,[15] and the United Nations[16] all assert a link between the Taliban and the ETIM.

Mahsum denied links to the Taliban in the same interview where he denied links to Al-Qaida.[17] However, Abudula Kariaji, the ETIM deputy emir who spoke with the *Wall Street Journal* in 2004, confirmed that some ETIM members fought alongside the Taliban against the U.S.-led coalition in Afghanistan.[18] In addition, one of the ETIM's videos essentially admits the Taliban provided the ETIM safe haven until 2001. The video, titled "Steadfastness and Preparations for Jihad in the Cause of Allah" and released in January 2009, includes the following comment:

> In 1997, the mujahideen of East Turkestan gathered under the leadership of Commander Hasan Mahsum beyond the borders of our land, and they were graced by choosing the path of training within the shadow of the Islamic Emirate of Afghanistan—as they were prohibited and forbidden from doing so in their own country because of the Chinese occupation.[19]

The "Islamic Emirate of Afghanistan" is a reference to Afghanistan under Taliban control. The ETIM could not have established its safe houses and training camps in Afghanistan—including the ETIM-run camp at Tora Bora, where 18 of the GTMO Uyghurs trained—without the Taliban's assent, since the Taliban controlled the territory at the time.

The Islamic Movement of Uzbekistan (IMU)

Under Hasan Mahsum, the ETIM maintained close ties with the IMU. Like the ETIM, the IMU wants to establish a fundamentalist Muslim state under sharia law. The IMU was reportedly severely weakened by U.S. strikes in Afghanistan,[20] but it remains operational in Uzbekistan[21] and Pakistan.[22]

The Chinese government claims the ETIM received support from the IMU.[23] Russian press reporting from 2000 indicates ETIM and IMU leaders met and jointly received funding from Osama bin Laden.[24]

The ETIM's current leader, Abdul Haq, and other Uyghur fighters fell under the IMU's military wing when they were attending training camps in Afghanistan in the late 1990s.[25] This information comes from an interview with Abdul Haq published in the ETIM's magazine.

Other Groups

Limited reporting links the ETIM to at least four other militant groups: the United Tajik Opposition (UTO), the Islamic Jihad Union (IJU), the Tehrik-i-Taliban Pakistan (TTP), and the Harkat-ul-Jihad-al-Islami (HUJI).

A Russian newspaper wrote in 2000 that the ETIM was expanding its contacts with the UTO.[26] The UTO lost Tajikistan's civil war and its leaders signed a peace agreement in 1997. However, hard-line elements within the UTO continued fighting under the group's name.[27]

The ETIM reportedly receives protection from the IJU and the TTP.[28] The IJU is an Al-Qaida-affiliated group operating in Pakistan, Uzbekistan, and Germany.[29] The TTP controls the FATA region of Pakistan, along the Afghan border, and reportedly protects the ETIM elements based there.[30] The TTP is an umbrella group formed from previously unaligned Pakistani militant organizations that support Afghanistan's Taliban. The TTP is an independent organization not subordinate to Afghanistan's Taliban.[31]

One source asserts a connection between the ETIM and the HUJI, an Al-Qaida-affiliated militant organization that operates in Pakistan, India, Afghanistan, and Bangladesh. In a 2006 article, academics Rohan Gunaratna and Kenneth George Pereire say the HUJI provided aid to the ETIM, and HUJI leader Qari Saifullah Akhtar "cemented the ETIM link with the Taliban and Al-Qaeda."[32] We are unable to corroborate this specific claim with information from other sources, but the PRC previously alleged a connection between Uyghur militants and a Pakistani group related to the HUJI. In 2001, a Kyrgyz newspaper cited the Chinese embassy in Islamabad as the source for information that Harkat-ul-Mujahideen—a HUJI splinter group—recruits and trains Uyghurs and then infiltrates them into Central Asia.[33]

THE ETIM'S FUNDING AND SUPPORT

The size and sources of the ETIM's funding stream are largely unknown. The PRC claims the ETIM receives money from "drug trafficking, arms smuggling, kidnapping, blackmailing, robbery, and other organized crimes."[34] Russian press reporting indicates that in 1997, a Saudi Uyghur named Muhammadamin Turkistan gave the ETIM and the IMU $130,000 each.[35] Osama bin Laden reportedly gave a total of $270,000 to both the ETIM and IMU in 1999[36] and an unspecified amount to the ETIM in 2001.[37] The Taliban also provided at least tacit support by allowing the ETIM to train in Afghanistan from 1997 to 2001.[38]

All these reports of funding and support date from before 9/11. We have no information on the ETIM's financial resources after the United States launched its global war on terrorism. However, the ETIM has probably sought support from elements of the Uyghur diaspora population. As many as 600,000 Uyghurs live abroad.[39] Up to 500,000 of them live in Kazakhstan, Kyrgyzstan, Tajikistan, Turkmenistan, and Uzbekistan, and about another 75,000 live in Afghanistan, Europe, Pakistan, Turkey, and the United States.[40] The ETIM has likely solicited support in all of the countries with both a diaspora population and a history of ETIM activity (Afghanistan, Pakistan, Kazakhstan, Uzbekistan, Kyrgyzstan, and Tajikistan), although we do not know how successful that solicitation has been.

Only a few interactions between the ETIM and the Uyghur diaspora have been documented. When Hasan Mahsum was re-establishing the ETIM in 1997, he approached the Uyghur diaspora in Saudi Arabia and Turkey in an attempt to gain support and was rejected. According to the ETIM's website:

[Hasan Mahsum] met numerous Turkestani migrants and key Turkestani personalities, ameers and leaders of Turkestani groups including the democratically aligned groups. He discussed his ideas and methodology of change with them, but they were not interested in his Islamic inclinations. . . . They also accused Hasan of being new to the "world scene" and naïve in his political understanding and having a warped understanding of reality. These Turkestani groups viewed any activity geared towards military action as ridiculous and unrealistic. . . . His call was not readily accepted by those he was addressing who viewed his Islamic inclinations as "backwardness."[41]

The Saudi Uyghur Muhammadamin Turkistan allegedly gave the ETIM funds three years after Mahsum made his pitch,[42] but that is the only documented instance of the ETIM's receiving money from the Uyghur diaspora.

The PRC alleges that the WUC diaspora umbrella group is a front for the ETIM. The group's leader, Rebiya Kadeer, denies these allegations, which are likely Chinese attempts to discredit all Uyghur activists by associating them with the ETIM's terrorist activities.[43]

THE ETIM AND THE GTMO UYGHURS

The United States detained 22 Uyghurs at GTMO as part of the global war on terrorism. The U.S. cases against these Uyghurs alleged they were members of a terrorist organization called the ETIM (assumed to be affiliated with Al-Qaida). At a minimum, all the GTMO Uyghurs either lived at an ETIM training camp, lived at an ETIM safe house, or admitted belonging to the ETIM.

Eighteen of the Uyghurs admitted to training at an ETIM camp in Tora Bora.[44] The other four were captured separately. Three of them had fled to Mazar-e-Sharif, Afghanistan, where Northern Alliance forces picked them up. The final GTMO Uyghur was captured in Lahore, Pakistan. He and two Arabs were caught trying to escape wearing burkas, the loose-fitting, full-length dresses worn by some Muslim women.[45]

From at least November 2000[46] through October 2001, the ETIM ran a training camp in the mountainous Tora Bora region of eastern Afghanistan, south of Jalalabad and close to the Pakistani border. (ETIM propaganda videos of Hasan Mahsum lecturing at training camps in mountainous terrain, possibly at Tora Bora, are available on the Internet.) Militants have lived and trained in this area for decades. Tora Bora's rugged mountains are difficult to penetrate, and the caves make good hiding places. Al-Qaida and the Taliban also maintained training camps in the same area.

The GTMO Uyghurs who attended the ETIM's training camp claimed they learned of its existence through word of mouth while in various places, including cities in China, Afghanistan, Kyrgyzstan, Kazakhstan, and Pakistan. Several detainees provided the name of the person who told them about the camp, but those names form no pattern.

GTMO Uyghurs followed several routes to the ETIM camp. For those coming from China, the most common route was to cross the border into Kyrgyzstan, then make their way through Pakistan to Jalalabad, Afghanistan. Finally, they would travel two or three hours from Jalalabad to the camp at Tora Bora.[47]

Some of the GTMO Uyghurs admitted they went to Afghanistan to train in military tactics and weaponry for a future conflict with the Chinese government. Some claimed they left China with the intent of doing business but ended up going to the training camp as well.[48] Several indicated they left China because they were wanted by the Chinese government; one, who stayed at an ETIM safe house in Kabul, said he was wanted by the PRC because of the 1990 Baren Rebellion.[49]

The ETIM training camp at Tora Bora consisted of four or five houses and a mosque[50] and held between 30 and 35 Uyghurs.[51] When the trainees arrived, the camp was in disarray. Most of the GTMO Uyghurs claimed they spent more time working on the camp than they spent training. Many of them discussed their work rebuilding and expanding the camp, sometimes by collecting rocks they would use to repair buildings. When they were not working on the camp infrastructure, they exercised, practiced martial arts, studied the Quran, and trained on various weapons.[52] Several indicated they did not know the Quran when they arrived, and most reported they spent more time studying the Quran than any other subject. All the GTMO Uyghurs who attended the camp claimed the amount of actual weapons training they received was limited, and several of them objected to the word "training." They said they "learned" how the weapons worked, but they did not consider this training. One of the GTMO Uyghurs said, "I wasn't really trained on the weapon, I just learned a little bit about how to use it."[53] The weapons training included the Seminov pistol, the Makarov pistol, the Kalashnikov rifle, and other rifles.[54] Most of the GTMO Uyghurs said they spent only a couple of days learning to use the weapons and focused on basic skills, like breaking down a rifle. They admitted to shooting only three to five rounds each.

Hasan Mahsum visited the camp several times. One of the GTMO Uyghurs said Mahsum led prayer, gave a speech about the condition of Uyghurs in China, and spoke about the lack of funding at the training camp.[55]

The Uyghurs abandoned the ETIM camp in October 2001, when the U.S.-led coalition began bombing Tora Bora. Most fled into the mountains and took shelter from the bombing in caves. Since they were from other regions and had only recently come to Tora Bora, they did not know how to get back to Pakistan or Jalalabad. Several noted that the camp's leaders did not return for them. After a few weeks, a group of Arabs passed by the mountains where the Uyghurs were hiding. The two groups could barely communicate because of the language barrier, but the Uyghurs discerned that the Arabs were heading to Pakistan. The Uyghurs decided to follow. In Pakistan, they stayed with a seemingly hospitable host, but one night, they were brought to a mosque where all 18 of them were picked up by Pakistani government forces.[56] One of them later reported that they were turned over to the United States in exchange for a bounty of $5,000 each.[57] They were eventually detained at GTMO.

The U.S. government initially branded the 22 Uyghurs "enemy combatants," like hundreds of others captured overseas and detained at GTMO. An enemy combatant is anyone who belonged to or supported Al-Qaida or Taliban forces fighting the U.S.-led coalition.[58] U.S. courts later determined that all 22 Uyghurs were "no longer enemy combatants" and should be released. The United States released five of the GTMO Uyghurs to Albania in May 2006.[59] Complications between the U.S. government, the Chinese government, and the Uyghur population delayed the release of the remaining 17.[60]

The United States has decided not to return any of the GTMO Uyghurs to the PRC, because the Chinese government would imprison, probably torture, and likely even execute the Uyghurs upon their return. (The Uyghurs asked to be released to any country but the PRC.) Because of this very real threat, the United States is trying to find other countries willing to accept both the Uyghurs themselves and a potentially damaged relationship with the PRC, which demands the Uyghurs back. Four of the GTMO Uyghurs were released to Bermuda in June 2009.[61] The other 13 remained at GTMO at the time of this writing.

Many of the GTMO Uyghurs admitted to training to fight the Chinese government. They did not specify a time or a location, and they did not state that they wanted to start the conflict; rather, they indicated they wanted to be prepared if such a conflict did occur. Several of the GTMO Uyghurs went into long diatribes about Chinese mistreatment of the Uyghur population. They argued that the Chinese had invaded the nation of East Turkistan and said they wanted independence from the Chinese government.

While many of the GTMO Uyghurs admitted to training for a conflict with the Chinese government, they said they had not formally joined any party, movement, or organization. They argued that since they had not undergone a formal indoctrination, the United States should not consider them members of the ETIM. Yet many of them referred to Hasan Mahsum as their leader,[62] and it is unlikely they did not know he led the ETIM. Ten of the GTMO Uyghurs named as the head of the training camp either Mahsum or Abdul Haq, likely the same Abdul Haq currently leading the ETIM. The GTMO Uyghurs who attended the ETIM-run camp must have known that some militant group was in charge of it. One of them called a witness who said the detainee would not have joined a different group (in this case the IMU), because the detainee already belonged to "the Uyghur group" (which we know as the ETIM):

Q: Do you know if Abdul Ghapper [a Uyghur detained at GTMO] was a member of the Islamic Movement of Uzbekistan?

A [Witness]:   No, I don't think he would join another organization because there were only Uighur people in that place. How can he drop that organization to join another organization?[63]

The witness's statement contains a couple of key pieces of information. First, a Uyghur organization was present at the camp. We know this Uyghur organization as the ETIM. Second, the Uyghurs at this camp belonged to this organization. This implies the Uyghurs at this camp knowingly belonged to the ETIM.[64]

One of the GTMO Uyghurs—Nag Mohammed, who was captured in Mazar-e-Sharif—actually admitted to being an ETIM member but indicated he did not know the ETIM was a terrorist group. He later chose not to participate in further tribunals after seeing U.S. evidence linking the ETIM to Al-Qaida:

> Based on a follow-up/final interview conducted on 16 Nov 04, detainee has elected not to participate in the Tribunal; instead he desires that [the personal representative] present his responses. His sudden change of mind seems to have resulted from UNCLAS exhibit R-3 that describes in detail the terrorist group ETIM and its alleged ties to [Osama bin Laden] and Al Qaeda/Taliban. Although detainee adamantly denied having knowledge of these ties, the contents of the exhibit obviously changed his mind. Detainee has previously professed to being a member of the ETIM, but not a terrorist. . . . Detainee asked when the Eastern Turkestan Islamic Movement (ETIM) was identified as a terrorist organization and that he had no knowledge of this fact.[65]

THE ETIM ABROAD

The ETIM has allegedly been active in Afghanistan, Pakistan, Kazakhstan, Kyrgyzstan, Tajikistan, Uzbekistan, and Chechnya.

Afghanistan

The ETIM moved its base to Afghanistan in 1997[66] and maintained its headquarters there until the U.S.-led bombing campaign began in 2001. Under Taliban rule, Afghanistan provided safe haven to a number of terrorist groups besides the ETIM, including Al-Qaida and the IMU. In 1999, Osama bin Laden met with the ETIM and the IMU in Kandahar;[67] this meeting, and the ETIM's connections with those two other groups, would become some of the most damning evidence against the ETIM in the Western debate over whether it should be blacklisted as a terrorist organization.

ETIM members attended training camps in Khost, Bagram, Kabul, and Herat.[68] The ETIM also ran a training camp in Tora Bora, which was destroyed by air strikes in fall 2001. Many of the GTMO Uyghurs were captured while fleeing these air strikes.

Pakistan

After losing its safe haven in Afghanistan, the ETIM moved its headquarters to Pakistan. The ETIM is currently based in Nir Ali, North Waziristan, in the FATA region of Pakistan along the Afghan border.[69] The ETIM has had connections to Pakistan since the group's re-establishment in 1997.

The ETIM's website stated that the group's leaders traveled to Pakistan in late March 1997 for a strategy session: "The brothers went to Pakistan, where they met some of the leading Islamic personalities to discuss the future direction of the movement."[70]

In 2000, a Russian paper reported that the ETIM was active in Pakistan (as well as Afghanistan, Tajikistan, and Chechnya).[71] ETIM members have been captured or killed in Pakistan from 2002 to at least 2009. For example, Pakistan deported ETIM member Ismail Kadir to China in May 2002 and ETIM member Ismail Samed to China in 2003.[72] ETIM leader Hasan Mahsum was killed in Pakistan in October 2003.[73] More recently, Pakistan deported 10 accused ETIM members to China in 2009.[74] (The ETIM issued a statement claiming these Uyghurs did not belong to the ETIM.[75])

Other Central Asian Locations

Limited reporting indicates the ETIM has also operated in several other Central Asian locations, including Kazakhstan, Kyrgyzstan, Tajikistan, Uzbekistan, and Chechnya.[76] The only specific action attributed to the ETIM in any of these other locations is the alleged plot to bomb the U.S. embassy in Bishkek, Kyrgyzstan.[77]

THE ETIM'S ONLINE PRESENCE

The ETIM uses the Internet to broadcast its claims, threats, and other rhetoric around the world. The group's members also almost certainly communicate online to coordinate strategy and tactics. The ETIM's Internet presence includes both its own media outlet and a media partnership with Al-Qaida. The ETIM has published online statements not only in Uyghur but also in English and Arabic, probably in an effort to reach a broader audience.

The ETIM's media outlet is called "Islam Awazi" in Uyghur, "Voice of Islam" in English, and "Sawt al-Islam" in Arabic. The media outlet's logo

FIGURE 4.2.   The ETIM's media outlet is called "Islam Awazi" in Uyghur, "Voice of Islam" in English, and "Sawt al-Islam" in Arabic.

is Figure 4.2. Through Islam Awazi, the ETIM has developed a website (now defunct), created a YouTube channel, and released numerous videos and other public statements. The Nine Eleven/Finding Answers Foundation considers Islam Awazi one of the primary sources of jihadi information in Central Asia.[78]

The ETIM also distributes a magazine through Al-Fajr Media Center, which is the primary publisher of Al-Qaida videos, statements, and other communications.[79]

The ETIM used its now-defunct website to post videos, statements, its own constitution, a history of the ETIM, and various other information. The website went off-line in 2008, sometime between April and August.[80] We do not know why. Perhaps the most likely explanation is a PRC cyberattack, which would be consistent with the PRC's general security crackdown in the months leading up to the August 2008 Beijing Olympics. Another government, or even another militant group, could also have been responsible. Alternatively, the ETIM could have decided to remove the site, perhaps because it revealed too much information or because it would not have a role in the ETIM's solidifying media partnership with Al-Qaida. To our knowledge, the ETIM's website had not been revived or replaced as of this writing (September 2009). Instead, the group disseminates information on other jihadi sites.

Several different URLs mapped to the ETIM's now-defunct website, including the following:[81]

- http://tipislamawazi.com
- http://tipsilamyultuzi.com
- http://islamyultuzi.com
- http://www.tipawazionline.net

We do not know whether these URLs all forwarded to the same site or whether they pointed to sites hosted on separate servers. One of these URLs used the same domain as the website of an Al-Qaida-affiliated cleric. The domain tipawazi.com hosted both an ETIM site (www.tipislamyultuzi.com, registered in Pakistan[82]) and the website of Abu Amir Abdel Hakim Hassan (http://kanzhassan.com).[83] Hassan is a cleric affiliated with Al-Qaida. Al-Qaida's second-in-command, Ayman al-Zawahiri, referred to Hassan in a recent book, and Al-Qaida's Al-Fajr Media Center published a notice about Hassan's website.[84]

The ETIM has published several e-mail addresses, including the following:[85]

- tipislamawazi@yahoo.com
- tipislamyultuzi@yahoo.com
- tipawazi@gmail.com
- info@tipislamyultuzi.com
- tipawazi2000@yahoo.com
- tipawazionline@yahoo.com

The ETIM also has its own YouTube channel, http://www.youtube.com/user/tipawazi, but this channel includes only a few of the many videos Islam Awazi has published. Some videos have been reposted by other YouTube users, and other videos are available via the standard jihadi media distribution channels. Jihadi media operatives typically place their videos and statements on several file-sharing sites and then post links to the sites on jihadi forums and blogs.

The ETIM released the first issue of its magazine, *Turkistan al-Islamiyya* ("Islamic Turkistan"), in July 2008.[86] The magazine was in Arabic, which suggests the group targeted the broader global jihadi movement rather than the Xinjiang natives who would read and write in Uyghur.

Three jihadi media outlets published the first issue of *Turkistan al-Islamiyya* almost simultaneously, which caused a cyber-disagreement between two well-known jihadi publishing forums, Al-Fajr and Madad al-Suyuf. Each accused the other of stealing the magazine. The first posting was apparently on a third forum, Faloja, and came from a user named Abdallah al-Mansur.[87] This happens to be the name of the head of the ETIM's Religious Education Division.[88]

The ETIM almost certainly uses the Internet for internal as well as public communication. We cannot prove this assertion, because private conversations, by their very nature, would be unavailable to Western researchers. However, we can infer that if the ETIM uses the Internet for public statements, the organization would also take advantage of the speed and relative anonymity offered online to coordinate internally. Such coordination could include everything from the strategic direction of the organization to the specific details of a planned attack. To the extent that the ETIM can penetrate the so-called "Great Firewall of China," the Internet may also help

ETIM members circumvent the PRC's restrictions on separatist activity inside Xinjiang.

CONCLUSION

The ETIM has partially insulated itself from China's counterterrorism measures by developing transnational ties that include alliances with other terrorist groups, operational bases abroad, and an online presence used for propaganda and probably also for internal communications. These transnational ties will likely help sustain the ETIM despite the PRC's best efforts to eradicate it.

Under Hasan Mahsum's leadership, the ETIM cultivated relationships with other groups that share its philosophy of jihad. The ETIM has documented ties to Al-Qaida, the Taliban, and the IMU, as well as more tenuous links to the UTO, the HUJI, the IJU, and the TTP. Mahsum leveraged his relationship with the Taliban to establish a Uyghur training camp in the Taliban-controlled Tora Bora mountains.

A total of 22 Uyghurs were detained and held at GTMO as part of the U.S.-led global war on terrorism. They offered uniform accounts of their time at the apparently ineffective camp, saying they focused on Quranic study and camp construction and shot only three to five rounds each. U.S. courts later determined that all 22 Uyghurs were "no longer enemy combatants," but the U.S. government has met difficulty in finding suitable locations for resettlement.

After the U.S.-led coalition unseated the Taliban in Afghanistan, the ETIM moved its headquarters to Nir Ali, North Waziristan, in the FATA region of Pakistan—where Al-Qaida's leadership is generally believed to reside. The ETIM's link with Al-Qaida appears to be strengthening. In 2008, the ETIM began publishing an Arabic-language magazine through Al-Qaida's distributor, Al-Fajr Media Center. The magazine's use of Arabic instead of the Uyghurs' native tongue suggests the ETIM is increasingly focused on appealing to the Arab-centric jihadi movement anchored by Al-Qaida. Analysis of recent ETIM statements indicates the group is adopting Al-Qaida's rhetoric.

The ETIM uses the Internet to project this rhetoric, as well as its attack claims and threats, beyond the FATA and around the world. To the extent that the ETIM can penetrate the so-called "Great Firewall of China," the Internet may also help ETIM members circumvent the PRC's restrictions on separatist activity inside Xinjiang.

The PRC perceives separatism of all kinds as a threat to China's territorial integrity. For Chinese officials, the Uyghur separatist movement is only one in a constellation of movements that demand reform or even independence on political, religious, or ethnic grounds. The next chapter will attempt to illuminate Beijing's perspective on Uyghur separatism in general, and the ETIM in particular.

5

⊶⊷

The ETIM and the PRC's Political Agenda

The Chinese government's primary political objective is to maintain control of its vast territory. This chapter is an attempt to place the Chinese government's approach to the ETIM in the context of the PRC's larger political agenda. The first section discusses the PRC's treatment of dissenters, including pro-democracy advocates and dissenting religious groups (including Falun Gong practitioners, Christians, and Muslims). The second section addresses the PRC's problems with separatism, specifically movements in Taiwan and Tibet. The third section outlines some of the PRC's countermeasures, including media censorship, Internet censorship, surveillance, and protest law. The fourth and final section addresses the PRC's rhetoric on Uyghur separatism, terrorism, and the ETIM.

The PRC has relaxed some of its restrictions on political and especially economic activity over the past 30 years. Under Mao Zedong, the PRC was a truly socialist system; everything was state-owned and state-run. Now, the public sector is still large, but the private sector has more businesses and more workers. Chinese citizens are allowed a number of personal freedoms; for example, they can start their own businesses, educate themselves, and marry and divorce as they please. However, the Chinese government still faces internal dissent and separatism, and it cracks down harshly on any activity that may threaten its control.

The Chinese government is strong enough to repress any small movement that challenges its control. However, it would be difficult for the government to combat either a large and well-organized movement or many simultaneous small movements scattered across its vast territory. Therefore, the PRC tries to prevent dissenting groups from growing large or organized enough to form a real alternative to the Communist Party.

The PRC does not tolerate public dissent or separatism. It strictly controls the release of and access to information at both the national and local levels, including publications, broadcasts, and online media. The PRC also uses its economic resources to help prevent dissatisfaction among its citizens. Many central government strategies are designed to facilitate economic growth and create jobs. The government allows state-run enterprises to hemorrhage money, functioning as a kind of welfare system. The Chinese citizens who owe the state their jobs also owe the state their allegiance. (If the state released these enterprises, many would go bankrupt. This could transform the workers from supporters of the state into its unemployed and dissatisfied critics.) In addition, food and housing are heavily subsidized.

The Chinese government's attention to Xinjiang has resulted in remarkable economic growth for the past 30 years, and Chinese officials may use the improving economy as a carrot to maintain control of Xinjiang. However, many of the best jobs and the top salaries go to Han Chinese instead of to Uyghurs or other minorities. Some Uyghurs have benefited from the PRC's economic policies, but others resent the onslaught of modernity that threatens their traditional way of life.[1] Many believe the PRC ignores environmental and legal issues to propel economic growth at all costs.

PROBLEMS WITH DISSENT

The PRC's authoritarian form of government allows it to silence opposition quickly. However, this authoritarianism leaves ordinary citizens who want to voice their objection to some policy or practice no choice but to work against the PRC's system.

Pro-Democracy Movements

The PRC is a one-party state. Like other authoritarian regimes, the Chinese government opposes democracy. It was a democratic movement that led to the largest single instance of political dissent in recent Chinese history: the Tiananmen Square protest of June 1989. After using tanks to remove more than 100,000 protesters demanding economic and political reform, the government changed its stance on democracy. Prior to this event, the PRC acted as if it could manage a slow transition toward a democratic system. It tolerated high-level officials who advocated some measure of democratic reform. After the Tiananmen Square protest, national-level discussions about democracy were off the table.

Democracy would surely mean challenges to the CCP's supremacy and likely the end of its solitary hold on power. In a democratic system, other political powers could investigate and pass judgment on the CCP, which is notorious for rampant corruption, including soliciting bribes, accepting kickbacks, and stealing from state coffers. In 2005, the CCP reprimanded more than 115,000 of its members for corruption and prosecuted more than 15,000 of them.[2] In January 2008, PRC president Hu Jintao warned that corruption might bring down the CCP.[3]

The PRC recognizes this corruption as a threat to its power. In an effort to pacify democracy advocates, the PRC has experimented with methods of enfranchising citizens locally without giving them a voice in national politics. In some sections of the country, the Chinese government has allowed citizens to help elect local leaders. In other locations, citizens have been able to nominate the leaders. However, the pool of eligible leaders is usually limited to CCP members.[4]

The semblance of democracy in selected localities does not translate into tolerance of national-level democracy advocates. Many Chinese democracy activists are eventually arrested or must flee the country. Even the democratic freedoms the people of Hong Kong enjoyed before the transfer back to Chinese control on July 1, 1997, have been severely limited. Hong Kong activists are pressing the Chinese government to reinstate full democracy by 2020, but the Chinese government has not agreed to do so.[5]

Religious Dissent

In discussions about China, the issue of religious freedom is often combined with the issue of political freedom. Because of this, many in the West have the misconception that the PRC prevents people from practicing religion in China. This is not exactly the case.

In 1982, the PRC issued its official policy on religion, known as "Document 19." While Communism is an atheist philosophy, Document 19 explicitly protects five religions: Buddhism, Daoism, Islam, Catholicism, and Protestantism. (Document 19 does not protect so-called "cults" like Falun Gong, which is banned.) Chinese citizens are free to attend Buddhist temples, mosques, Christian churches, and other religious sites. Members of religious groups are free to live and congregate near each other.[6] However, religious organizations are restricted in the areas of proselytizing and fund-raising,[7] and the government does not guarantee that believers will not face discrimination.

The Chinese government often discriminates on the basis of religion or other characteristics. For example, members of religious groups are ineligible for most government jobs, because those jobs go only to CCP members and the CCP requires its members to be atheists. This means overt believers are effectively barred from political office. In the 1990s, the CCP discovered that some of its members were actively practicing religion and quickly issued directives calling for members to comply with party rules or risk becoming ineligible for government positions.[8]

The PRC tends to treat all the adherents of a religion, no matter how large, as a unified political force. When some members of a religious group use the group to further a political end, the PRC often cracks down on *all* the group members in response. In 2005, Gretchen Birkle, acting principal deputy assistant secretary of the U.S. Department of State's Bureau of Democracy, Human Rights and Labor, testified to Congress, "Chinese authorities remained quick to suppress religious, political and social groups that they perceived as threatening to government authority or national stability."[9]

Falun Gong

Falun Gong (also called Falun Dafa) started as a subset of the larger *qigong* movement in China. *Qigong* is an exercise that includes meditation, breathing, and controlled movements. The Falun Dafa Information Center defines Falun Gong as "a combination of exercises, meditation, and moral living."[10] The addition of "moral living" and its specific moral beliefs—such as the belief that negative experience comes from bad karma—are what make Falun Gong a religious movement. Officially, *qigong* is a sport,[11] but the PRC considers Falun Gong a cult because of the moral beliefs it entails.

Li Hongzhi founded Falun Gong in 1992.[12] He traveled freely around China for years and lectured to groups of thousands about Falun Gong,[13] growing the movement to an estimated 70 million members.[14] Falun Gong practitioners remained free to act as they wanted until 1999, when the PRC banned the movement. Falun Gong had become powerful and demonstrated the potential for effective political action; if someone made a negative public statement about Falun Gong, the group would organize protests to force the source to retract.[15] The turning point that led the PRC to ban Falun Gong came on April 29, 1999. Approximately 10,000 Falun Gong members engaged in a silent protest around Zhongnanhai, China's most important government building, in Tiananmen Square. The Chinese government was able to disperse them peacefully, but it had been caught off-guard. The protest had been organized in secret, and officials had not known it was going to occur.

The PRC perceived the structure of the Falun Gong movement as threatening. Falun Gong was apparently modeled after the CCP. It had a central committee with three lines of replacements for leaders who might get arrested in a government crackdown. It had a leadership structure in every province, with members organized into cells. A retired military general, Yu Changxin, had organized and led the protest around Zhongnanhai.[16] To the PRC, Falun Gong had both organized itself and acted like a political entity preparing to confront the national government.

In July 1999, the Chinese government labeled Falun Gong a cult and banned it. Falun Gong members continued to stage limited protests, and once they even hijacked public television to broadcast their own messages. To the PRC, these actions confirmed that Falun Gong was a political movement attempting to gain power. The Chinese government has continued to crack down on Falun Gong and imprison its leaders.[17]

Falun Gong is an example of a group that operated freely until some members acted in ways the Chinese government perceived as a threat, and then all members suffered the consequences. It is probable, if not certain, that most members of Falun Gong were not involved in any of the protests or other activities the Chinese government feared.

Christianity

The PRC counts 21 million Christians (both Catholics and Protestants) in China, and their numbers are growing quickly. The Center for the Study of Global Christianity in Massachusetts estimates that the number of unofficial Christians is closer to 70 million. Developing a precise figure is difficult because Christians do not correlate to a specific minority group captured in the PRC's census. The PRC has established official Protestant and Catholic churches and knows how many members they have, but the Chinese government also permits the existence of smaller unofficial churches. The Catholic churches are under more scrutiny, likely because of their link to the Pope and Rome.[18] The Protestant churches, including "house churches," tend to be nondenominational and are not highly regulated by the government.

The unofficial Protestant "house churches" tend to grow to the maximum capacity allowed by local law (usually 25 people) and then split into two or more churches to stay below the legal threshold. This keeps individual church populations small, so they do not threaten the government, and causes a steep increase in the number of churches. The Chinese government has recognized that Protestant churches do not pose an immediate threat to the CCP, probably because they have no organized leadership structure and do not question party rule.[19]

Not all Christians in the PRC have managed to steer clear of government crackdowns. Approximately 300 Christians are detained at any given time.

The government has sporadically raided unregistered Christian gatherings with more than 100 participants.[20] The Chinese government also targets individuals who try to organize larger groups. For example, the head of the Chinese House Church Alliance was expelled from Beijing before the 2008 Olympic Games. His group is receiving special attention from the Chinese government because it is trying to organize smaller, disparate groups into a larger, unified whole.[21]

Islam

China has approximately 20 million Muslims, and that number is growing. Ten of China's 55 official minority groups are Muslim. Muslims live in every part of China, and in many places they are relatively free to practice their religion and embrace Muslim culture—except in Xinjiang. Jackie Armijo, an expert on Islamic education in China, made this point in 2006:

> Over the past twenty years, throughout all of China (except for Xinjiang), mosques have organized classes in Arabic and Islamic studies for all members of their community, from three-year olds in pre-school programs, to eighty-year old [sic] retirees determined to study the Qur'an and learn about their faith in their twilight years. In addition to government-run Islamic colleges, communities have also established independent schools. According to government estimates there are now 35,000 mosques in China, 45,000 Muslim teachers, and 24,000 students studying in Islamic schools.[22]

In Xinjiang, however, the situation is different. Teaching Islam to children is forbidden.[23] Some parents choose to send their children to other parts of China where they can receive a Muslim education. Restrictions on religious clothing and appearance are sometimes enforced. Xinjiang's Uyghurs are the one Muslim group having trouble with the Chinese government, which has responded to the ETIM's attacks and threats by regarding Xinjiang's Muslims with increasing suspicion.

PROBLEMS WITH SEPARATISM

The PRC has zero tolerance for separatist movements. In addition to the Uyghur separatists in Xinjiang, the PRC is also concerned about separatism in Tibet and Taiwan. The permanent loss of any of these territories would be a blow to China's geopolitical power and national pride. In the PRC's view, the loss of any single territory could also motivate other separatist elements to redouble their efforts, creating a kind of domino effect.

For the Chinese government, suppressing separatism is a matter of national security. The PRC's rhetoric often suggests an artificial unity between different forms of separatism, referring to Tibetan and Taiwanese advocates alongside Uyghurs as if the three causes constituted a consolidated threat to China's territorial integrity. For example, the PRC's 2008 white paper on national defense stated, "Separatist forces working for 'Taiwan independence,' 'East Turkistan independence' and 'Tibet independence' pose threats to China's unity and security."[24]

Tibet

Tibetans seek independence from the PRC for several reasons, including Tibetan nationalism and the twin drives for religious freedom and ethnic survival. The Dalai Lama leads the Tibetan movement. He claims he only wants more autonomy for Tibet inside of China, but the Chinese government sees the Tibetan movement as a separatist campaign that threatens national sovereignty. In a March 1999 speech, the head of the Communist Party in Tibet said, "The struggle between us [the Chinese government] and the Dalai clique is not an issue of ethics, religion or human rights. . . . It's about maintaining national sovereignty and territorial integrity. . . . [We must] firmly stand guard and severely crack down on any separatist activities."[25]

The PRC has ruled Tibet since 1951. The Tibetans rebelled in March 1959. When they lost, the Dalai Lama was forced to flee Tibet and live in exile.[26] Since then, the Chinese government and the Dalai Lama have had only intermittent communication. Major unrest, including riots, occurred in 1988 and 2008.[27]

In an attempt to influence the future of this conflict, the Chinese government involved itself in the selection of the Panchen Lama, the number-two leader of Tibetan Buddhists.[28] Tibetan Buddhists believe the Dalai Lama and the Panchen Lama are reincarnated when they die. The surviving Lama typically selects the deceased Lama's successor, who accepts the rights, duties, and possessions of the deceased Lama. The first of the two religious figures to die during the PRC's rule was the tenth Panchen Lama, in 1989. The Dalai Lama chose his successor without the PRC's consent. The Dalai Lama's choice immediately disappeared, and the PRC replaced him with its own choice, who is not really accepted by the Tibetan people. The eleventh Panchen Lama has been educated by the Chinese government and is becoming a pro-Beijing spokesperson. The Panchen Lama recently began giving public interviews criticizing the Dalai Lama and accusing him of separatism. For example, in 2009 the Panchen Lama said, "For a long time the Dalai's separatist clique has ignore[d] the success of Tibet's development, plotted and planned to ruin Tibet's social stability and wantonly attacked the policies of the central government."[29]

Tibetan protests, riots, and rebellions have accelerated in recent years. In 2008 protests took place not only inside Tibet itself, but also in neighboring parts of China and at Chinese embassies around the world.

The Chinese government claims Tibetan activists have attacked 18 Chinese diplomatic missions.[30] The PRC heavily publicizes its version of the Tibet situation inside China. Some Tibetans report that when they travel in China, other Chinese citizens treat them as terrorist suspects. They say Han Chinese call them separatists and deny them hotel rooms.[31]

Like Xinjiang's Uyghurs, Tibetans fear for their ethnic and cultural survival. Tibetan advocates claim the Chinese government systematically moves Han Chinese into Tibet to dilute the Tibetan population (a claim Uyghur advocates also make about Xinjiang). The Chinese government denies the Tibetans' claim, saying Tibet's population is 2.87 million and 95 percent are Tibetans or other minorities. The PRC presents these statistics as proof it is not deliberately increasing the presence of Han Chinese in Tibet. Tibetans disagree with these figures and claim "greater Tibet" extends beyond the Tibetan Autonomous Region (TAR), which the PRC uses as the official definition of Tibetan territory. Ethnic Tibetans believe Tibet actually includes the TAR, Qinghai, part of Gansu, part of Sichuan, and part of Yunnan. This combined area is roughly twice the size of the TAR and makes up about 20 percent of Chinese territory.[32] Under this definition, Tibetans claim they now make up less than 50 percent of Tibet's population.[33]

Exact figures are impossible to determine, but evidence clearly indicates the proportion of non-Tibetans in "greater Tibet" has increased over the past 50 years. According to the PRC's statistics, the proportion of non-Tibetans in the TAR increased from 3.2 percent in 1964 to 5.9 percent in 2008.[34] In Qinghai, one of the provinces claimed by Tibet's government-in-exile, the minority population has decreased from 57.8 percent in 1995[35] to less than 50 percent in 2009.[36]

The Chinese government often links the separatist movements in Xinjiang and Tibet. Both are minority-dominated regions of China the PRC wants to continue to control, and both minorities have similar grievances against the PRC. The Chinese government sees the two issues as related in a strategic way. If either Tibet or Xinjiang achieved independence, then the other region would use that precedent to fuel its drive for secession from China.

Taiwan

When the Communists gained the upper hand in the Chinese Civil War, the Nationalists fled to Taiwan and set up a parallel government that endures to this day. The Communist PRC and the Nationalist Republic of China have a curious relationship; both believe in one China that includes Taiwan, and each believes it is the rightful government of that one China, but neither is willing to reopen hostilities. Although the PRC and Taiwan are de facto separate countries, Taiwan has never declared its independence.

The PRC has clearly stated that declaring independence would mean declaring war. A 2000 editorial in a PRC journal said the Chinese military would "spare no effort in a blood-soaked battle" to protect China's territorial integrity from the threat of Taiwanese separatism.[37] The PRC regards Taiwan as a renegade province that separated from the rest of China after World War II.

The United States has historically backed Taiwan. The consistent U.S. message is to urge Taiwan to refrain from declaring independence and urge China to refrain from forcing premature reunification.

The PRC perceives a link between separatism in Taiwan and separatism in Xinjiang. The PRC fears that an independent Taiwan would set the precedent that parts of China can break away from Beijing (and vice versa—a successful Uyghur separatist movement would show Taiwan that it could secede safely).

PRC COUNTERMEASURES TO DISSENT AND SEPARATISM

The PRC employs four key countermeasures to minimize the effects of dissent and separatist sentiment: media censorship, Internet censorship, surveillance, and protest law.

Media Censorship

Information is power, as the saying goes. The PRC does not want to lose control over the Chinese people, so it tries to restrict their access to information it deems potentially detrimental to state interests. The PRC censors television, radio, print, and digital media. As with other freedoms in China, the border between what is permitted and what is prohibited in the realm of mass communication is undefined and fluctuates over time. When individual journalists' work pushes the boundaries of the government's comfort level, the PRC often not only arrests the "violators" but also retracts freedoms it previously allowed.[38] As Carin Zissis of the Council on Foreign Relations writes, "The government's monitoring structure promotes an atmosphere of self-censorship; if published materials are deemed dangerous to state security after they appear in the media, the information can then be considered classified and journalists can be prosecuted."[39]

Government censorship can apply to any topic, from protest coverage to public health issues. For example, before the 2008 Olympic Games, the PRC issued a 21-point directive that prevented media from covering issues related to public health. This delayed the release of information about tainted milk powder, which led to additional deaths from contamination.[40]

Journalists in China are often harassed, arrested, and imprisoned for espionage, leaking state secrets, defamation, or other trumped-up charges.[41] In addition, the PRC sometimes openly threatens the foreign media. In January 2001, three people set themselves on fire in Tiananmen Square in a protest against Chinese government policies. The PRC threatened to bring homicide charges against foreign journalists who were present at the event and reported on it.[42]

Internet Censorship

The Chinese government spends vast amounts of money and manpower trying to control digital media with the so-called "Great Firewall of China," which blocks websites the PRC deems potentially damaging. The firewall is a combination of Western technology and approximately 30,000 Internet police.[43] The PRC has forged agreements with technology companies— including Microsoft, Yahoo, and Google—to help maintain control over the electronic information those in China can easily access and to punish any who try to circumvent state communication policies. For example, Yahoo provided the PRC with user data that helped prosecute a journalist who disseminated information in 2004 that the CCP wanted to keep secret.[44]

Most people in China know that the government limits the information they receive from official or public channels, so reports flow quickly via cell phones. For example, in the summer of 2004 false rumors that U.S. scientists had predicted an earthquake in the Xi'an area circulated via text message. The story did not appear on television or in print in China, but the average person assumed the government was censoring the news. For several days, people slept outside, away from high-rise buildings, to avoid being crushed.[45] The PRC has tried to assert some control over cell phone communication. In 2007, the government shut down text-messaging services in Xiamen to prevent people from joining an ongoing protest that was already 20,000 strong.[46]

Surveillance

The PRC deployed new surveillance tools in connection with the 2008 Olympics, spending more than $6.5 billion and installing more than 300,000 video cameras. This project, called "Grand Beijing Safeguard Sphere," used automated video facial recognition, biometrics matching, and large data-bases to try to spot known dissidents and separatists before they could act.[47]

The technology driving this program was mostly Western. The PRC reportedly purchased sophisticated tools from major companies such as IBM, General Electric, Honeywell, and United Technologies. This effort was part of a larger PRC project to bring video surveillance to China's 600 largest cities.[48]

The Chinese government routinely monitors protests, marches, and demonstrations. Video surveillance set up for the Olympics will almost certainly also be used to observe these events, allowing the Chinese government to respond quickly to any sign of public disorder.

Protest Law

One of the primary forms of dissent in the PRC is the protest. The Chinese government discourages protests but has not been able to eliminate them. Since 1989, when more than 100,000 protesters seeking economic and political change filled Tiananmen Square and drew international attention to a demonstration that ended with protesters' deaths, the PRC has been careful to stop demonstrations before they grow large or chaotic.[49]

The Tiananmen Square incident prompted the PRC to develop its current protest law. Michael Bristow of the BBC reports:

> That law—brought in shortly after the Tiananmen killings in 1989—requires applicants to provide a range of information about an intended protest. This includes the type of posters and slogans to be used, how many people intend to take part, and the names and addresses of protest organizers. A demonstration can be turned down if it could harm national sovereignty or unity, or even if the police suspect it will "undermine public order."[50]

By creating a specific law to govern protests, PRC officials criminalized all but the most benign, allowing themselves to arrest and imprison protesters legally. While one can never know PRC officials' exact intent, they likely assumed this law would act both as a deterrent to potential protesters and as broad legal justification for almost any action the government could take against them. For example, in 2005 the PRC sentenced 27 farmers who protested the confiscation of their fields to prison sentences of 2 to 15 years.[51]

The PRC's protest law has not succeeded in stopping demonstrations. In fact, protests have only increased overall, as the *Epoch Times* reported in 2006:

> In recent years, group protests in China have risen at a rate of at least 17% a year in response to land expropriation disputes, election embezzlement, state-owned enterprise reforms, environmental pollution, and denial of justice. Official records for 2005 put the number of protests involving more than 15 people at 87,000—an average of 241 group protests a day. Official Chinese websites state that group protests increased five-fold from 10,000 to 60,000 between 1994 and 2003. The number of people who attend group protests has also increased by 12 percent yearly, from 730,000 in 1994 to 3,070,000 in 2003. Protests with over 100 people increased four-fold from 1400 to 7000.[52]

However, the PRC did use its protest law to suppress dissent during the 2008 Beijing Olympics. The Chinese government went through the motions of setting up specially designated protest areas and allowing people to apply for protest permits. Nearly 150 people filed 77 different applications, and the government approved none of them.[53] The PRC stated that some of the applications were "illegal" and claimed all of the legal protesters' issues had been resolved by the time the Olympics began.[54] For example, Reuters reported that two elderly women whose homes had been destroyed to make way for Olympics-related construction were sentenced to "re-education through labor" for applying to protest. (The sentence was later rescinded.)[55]

As in the case of the two elderly women, protests need not be large to gain the attention of PRC authorities. One common method of individual protest that causes the Chinese government to react is self-immolation. In January 2001, five people set themselves on fire in Tiananmen Square. The Chinese government claimed they were members of Falun Gong. (Falun Gong leaders denied the claim.) This incident caused the Chinese government to set up new antiriot squads in each of the provincial capitals.[56]

Any protest in China registers as a significant form of dissent. In the PRC, a protest is no longer a simple expression of dissatisfaction but an act of defiance likely to incur repercussions from the state.

PRC RHETORIC ON UYGHUR "SPLITTISM," TERRORISM, AND THE ETIM

Xinjiang's form of separatism receives less foreign press coverage than Tibet's or Taiwan's, but it is equally important to the PRC. Chinese officials have coined their own English-language term, "splittism," to describe separatism, and they apply it to Uyghur independence advocates as follows:

> The national splittism we are discussing here has a particular meaning and strict definition. It refers to a reactionary trend of social thought that is aimed at creating national division and undermining the unification of the motherland, a reflection of the bourgeois conception of nationalities on the nationalities issue. This trend of social thought is essentially designed to oppose and subvert the people's socialist regime under the leadership of the CCP. It fundamentally negates the historical fact that Xinjiang is an inalienable part of the motherland's territory, and it negates the new type of socialist relations of equality, unity, mutual assistance and common prosperity among the various nationalities as well as the party's nationalities policy and a series of great achievements made by implementing this policy.[57]

The Chinese government routinely conflates political advocates with "splittists," or militant separatists, and militant separatists with hardened international terrorists. PRC officials have also begun to group "East Turkistan terrorists" with Tibetan and Taiwanese separatists in their public statements about threats to Chinese sovereignty. For example, in 2009 a Chinese government official stated that the Dalai Lama and his followers "continued to collude with such dregs as overseas democracy activists, 'Falungong elements' and 'Eastern Turkistan terrorists,' trying to form so-called 'united front work' to oppose the central government and split the motherland."[58] The PRC has not produced evidence to support allegations of this alliance. By alleging ties between the ETIM and other "East Turkistan terrorists," democracy activists, and Falun Gong practitioners, the PRC packages its problems with all three groups into the internationally accepted framework of the global war on terrorism.

Although the Uyghur separatist movement is centuries old, the "terrorist" label is relatively new. According to a 2005 report by Human Rights Watch and Human Rights in China, "Uighurs interviewed in the region point out that opponents to Chinese rule in the area have been given many labels over the last half-century; they were described by the state as feudal elements and as ethnic nationalists in the 1950s and 1960s, as counter-revolutionaries in the 1970s and 1980s, as separatists in the 1990s, and now, since 2001, as terrorists."[59]

The PRC has no formal definition of terrorism. The PRC modified its criminal code in 2001 to focus more specifically on terrorism, but the new code refers to "terrorist activities" without saying what they are. Chinese officials say they are working on the country's first antiterrorism legislation,[60] which will include a definition.[61] This legislation has been under discussion since 2007, and as of this writing there is no timetable for its completion.[62] With a one-party political system and state-controlled media, the PRC is particularly vulnerable to the pitfalls associated with the "we know it when we see it" approach to terrorism. The PRC can use the "terrorist" label as a tool to stigmatize dissenters, and the PRC permits no loyal opposition to challenge that characterization. In practice, the PRC either emphasizes or understates domestic terrorism as needed to advance the national agenda.

Similarly, the quantity and tone of media reports on the ETIM change with the global political climate. The Chinese government emphasizes ETIM activity and the general threat of Uyghur separatism when those emphases serve the state's interests more than silence on the subject. Shichor writes:

> When projecting an image of a loyal and trusted partner to the global, U.S.-led struggle against terrorism, the PRC tends to overestimate the threat of Uyghur separatism to China's regional stability and national security. However, when the Chinese are trying to raise investments from abroad and attract foreign businessmen, especially from Hong Kong, to become involved in Xinjiang's economy, those same leaders tend to underestimate the threat. . . . China's attitude toward Uyghur separatism and Islamic radicalism has changed over

time, reflecting this fundamental dilemma. Overlooking and understating Uyghur and Islamic activism would create an image of stability and tranquility that in turn would deprive Beijing of its ability to react firmly to a potential national and religious threat. On the other hand, overstating and underlining the explosive threat to Xinjiang would not only harm economic development and tourism, but would also expose the Chinese military and political weakness in dealing with these problems for so long.[63]

Except for a brief period in 1999, the PRC largely minimized the threats it faced in Xinjiang up until 9/11. Then, the PRC emphasized its domestic terrorism problem and the Al-Qaida-affiliated ETIM in particular until a year or so before the Beijing Olympics. After the Olympics were over, Chinese officials again emphasized Uyghur separatism in general and the ETIM in particular.

Until 9/11, the PRC generally minimized separatist incidents in Xinjiang, either preventing coverage of these incidents or downplaying them. (The exception is a 1999 announcement by Xinjiang's governor that thousands of terrorist incidents took place in the 1990s, including explosions, assassinations, and other violence.[64]) PRC officials considered a successful terrorist attack a weakness, and they sought to hide weaknesses in the Chinese government whenever possible. As late as September 2, 2001, a government official gave a speech indicating that everything in Xinjiang was peaceful.[65]

After 9/11, the PRC's approach to disseminating information about the ETIM and terrorist events in China changed again. Officials issued several statements cataloguing East Turkistan terrorist activity. The PRC began publicizing events that would have been downplayed or suppressed altogether before, including a number of incidents from the 1990s that had not previously been announced. The high-level officials who once stressed Xinjiang's stability and prosperity now made common cause with the United States by calling the PRC "also a victim of international terrorism."[66] At times, Chinese officials deployed this new key term broadly, applying it to crimes usually committed without a political agenda, such as robberies.[67]

Coverage changed yet again before the 2008 Olympics, when the PRC wanted to project strength and stability. For example, officials acknowledged that bus bombings on May 5 and July 21, 2008, were intentional, but inexplicably claimed they were not related to terrorism.[68] The PRC also minimized news coverage whenever possible. For example, Xinjiang police detained foreign journalists covering a series of bombs in Kuqa on August 10, 2008, and deleted the journalists' photos of the incident.[69] While the Chinese government advertised its raids against the ETIM during this period, it consistently denied that violence inside its borders was related to terrorism. The PRC attributed violent events to individuals lashing out over personal grievances. For example, when an explosion killed 19 people in Zhejiang

Province on May 17, 2008, the PRC explained that the culprit was a disgruntled gambler who had loaded his vehicle with explosives and was on his way to bomb a gambling house when he had a traffic accident.[70] This explanation seems improbable; the explosion was likely linked to some kind of domestic terrorism, even if it was not the work of the ETIM.

After the Olympics ended, the PRC again began emphasizing its domestic terrorism problem and the ETIM in particular. Its definition of terrorism seemingly expanded to apparently spontaneous unrest. For example, a Xinjiang official described the ethnic riots of July 2009 as "a typical terrorist attack."[71] In October 2008 the Chinese government issued a news release identifying the eight most-wanted ETIM terrorists, with photos and identification numbers. This was the first such news release in five years.

From 2001 through mid-2009, the PRC released four major statements identifying specific people and organizations as "East Turkistan terrorists." The first came in November 2001, the second in January 2002, the third in December 2003, and the fourth in October 2008. The earlier releases mentioned a variety of groups, but by 2008 the PRC was focusing on the ETIM, by then the most notorious militant group in China.

When the PRC does release information, as in these four statements, it is often questionable. In the words of China scholar Martin Wayne, "The information China either has or releases is contradictory at best, and some is so obviously inconsistent, incorrect, or falsified that it greatly weakens the case China is trying to make."[72] For example, the December 2003 statement contained a "most wanted" list of East Turkistan terrorists. Top on the list was Hasan Mahsum, who by the PRC's own admission was already dead. According to an official statement posted on the websites of PRC embassies, Chinese Foreign Ministry spokesman Liu Jianchao confirmed on October 24, 2003, that Mahsum had been shot to death by the Pakistani army on October 2, during a raid along the Afghan border.[73] The statement naming Mahsum as one of the 11 "most wanted" East Turkistan terrorists came out more than two months later, on December 15. About a week afterward, on December 24, the same Chinese Foreign Ministry spokesman announced Mahsum's October 2 death, as if for the first time.[74] Pakistan's military spokesman added that Chinese officials helped to identify Mahsum's body.[75] (A blogger who follows Uyghur issues noted that Xinhua initially published a story on the second announcement of Mahsum's death, then removed links to the story, saying it had been withdrawn because of its "sensitive nature."[76]) This rather confusing chain of events could have several explanations. Perhaps the simplest is miscommunication within the PRC's vast bureaucracy: Chinese officials preparing the "most wanted" list may not have been aware that Mahsum had been killed, and the December announcement of his death could have been an attempt to rectify that error without explaining it. Alternatively, PRC officials may not have been certain the individual killed in Pakistan was really Mahsum.

The October announcement of his death may have been premature and repeated in December, once officials had confirmed it more thoroughly. More ominously, the PRC could have deliberately withheld the news of Mahsum's death. His reported connection to Osama bin Laden and the Taliban was the primary link between the PRC's crackdown in Xinjiang and the U.S.-led global war on terrorism. Fearing Mahsum's death might also be the death of Western sympathy for Chinese policies in Xinjiang, the PRC may have inadvertently released the news in October, then quickly suppressed it (which would explain the lack of media coverage) until a more opportune time.

This is only one of several examples of PRC claims about Uyghur separatism and the ETIM that seem contradictory or implausible. As Shichor writes, "The bottom line is that Beijing has been trying to manipulate public opinion—at home and abroad—by exploiting the remoteness of Xinjiang as well as the cultural distance and the restricted information, to influence foreign governments (primarily the United States), international organizations (primarily the United Nations), various NGOs, the media and even some academics using the emerging and fashionable unity in the fight against 'terrorist threats.' "[77]

CONCLUSION

Over the past decade, the PRC has alternately downplayed and emphasized the threat of terrorism in Xinjiang as needed to advance the state's agenda. Beijing's primary objective is to maintain control of China's vast territory. To that end, Chinese officials have tried to control the information coming in and out of Xinjiang by censoring the news media and deploying the "Great Firewall of China" to regulate Internet use. In recent years the PRC has also increased its video surveillance capabilities and screened potential protesters to prohibit potentially damaging displays of dissent.

From Beijing's perspective, Uyghur separatists are only one of several groups that threaten state control. Others include Tibetan separatists, Taiwanese separatists, pro-democracy advocates, and religious activists.

The Chinese government is strong enough to repress any relatively small movement that challenges its rule, including the Uyghur separatist movement. However, Beijing could have difficulty combating either a large, well-organized movement or many simultaneous small movements scattered across China. In the PRC's view, the loss of any single territory could motivate other separatist elements to redouble their efforts, creating a kind of domino effect. Therefore, the PRC tries to prevent dissenting groups from growing large or organized enough to form a real alternative to the Communist Party. The PRC has zero tolerance for separatism.

Chinese policy and official rhetoric often elide key distinctions between the different groups and individuals Beijing perceives as threatening. For example,

Chinese officials have insinuated an unsubstantiated link between East Turkistani terrorists, Falun Gong activists, and the Dalai Lama in Tibet. (These three movements are distinct, and the notion of their cooperating to divide China is farfetched indeed.) The Chinese government also routinely conflates political advocates with "splittists," or militant separatists, and militant separatists with hardened international terrorists. For example, the "East Turkistani terrorists" purportedly conspiring with Falun Gong activists and the Dalai Lama could be either Uyghur political advocates or an actual terrorist group like the ETIM; Chinese officials would refer to both groups in the same way. Furthermore, if a few members of a group establish themselves as political challengers, Beijing is likely to treat the entire group as an enemy of the state, as it has with Falun Gong.

The PRC's tendencies to insinuate unity among different movements, equate political advocacy with militancy and even terrorism, and punish whole groups for a few individuals' actions present a policy dilemma for the United States. The U.S. government opposes terrorism and has committed itself to a protracted fight against Al-Qaida and Al-Qaida's allies. However, condemning the ETIM as one of those allies could have unintended consequences, since the PRC often fails to articulate a distinction between East Turkistani terrorists, Uyghur political activists, proponents of different causes, and unaffiliated individuals with no designs on state power. The next chapter will examine the U.S. approach to this sensitive issue.

6

―――∞∞∞――――

The ETIM and U.S. Policy

U.S. policy on the ETIM is controversial and complex—perhaps surprisingly so. The ETIM is a terrorist group that counts Al-Qaida as a key ally and targets one of the United States' counterterrorism partners. Based on those facts alone, the logical U.S. stance would be to condemn the ETIM in the strongest possible terms and contribute funding, expertise, or some other form of national security resources to an international effort to eradicate the group. However, in this case that straightforward approach could backfire. The PRC could interpret strong, public condemnation as U.S. approval for security crackdowns that would likely exacerbate tensions in Xinjiang.

The United States has taken a moderate approach, placing the ETIM on two terrorism blacklists—one for finance and one for immigration—and lobbying for its inclusion on a UN blacklist, but keeping the group off the State Department's high-profile list of FTOs.

Blacklists[1] formally designate a group as a terrorist organization. They aim to restrict group members' funding and mobility, especially across international borders. They raise the group's profile, particularly in the country or international organization that issues the designation. Finally, placement on a blacklist generally legitimates efforts to combat the group—a particularly potent consideration in the case of the ETIM, given the PRC's history of suppressing its dissidents. Reprisals nominally aimed at the ETIM could result in persecution of the entire Uyghur ethnic group in Xinjiang. Critics have accused the U.S. government of blacklisting the ETIM based on intelligence "spoon-fed" by the PRC.

This chapter reviews the acts and statements that qualify the ETIM as a terrorist group by any definition (except its own); explores why blacklisting the ETIM as a terrorist group was controversial; and concludes with a brief discussion on the future of the ETIM.

THE ETIM AS A TERRORIST GROUP

Blacklisting a group formally designates it as a terrorist organization. The specific criteria for placement vary from list to list, because the term "terrorism" has no universally accepted definition. U.S. federal law includes a number of slightly different versions.[2] The United Nations has never achieved international consensus on a legal definition, and so its Comprehensive Convention on International Terrorism has remained in the "draft" stage since 2000. However, most people intuitively grasp a difference between terrorism and other forms of violence. "Terrorism" connotes condemnation on moral as well as legal grounds. It differs from mere nationalism, separatism, or sedition in that it must include violence or the credible threat of violence. Terrorism also differs from insurgency, rebellion, militancy, revolution, insurrection, and guerilla warfare in that it targets innocents or "noncombatants." Terrorism excommunicates; a country, person, or group stigmatized as "terrorist" no longer belongs to the international community but opposes it.

Academic and government definitions of terrorism may differ in the details, but most include four key elements that characterize terrorism: (1) context, (2) target, (3) motivation, and (4) objective. No one element is sufficient to identify a violent act as a terrorist one; rather, it is the interplay between these four related elements that distinguishes the distinctive nature of terrorism. We assess that the ETIM qualifies as a terrorist group, despite its own objection to the term.[3]

Context. Terrorism occurs outside the framework of conventional military engagement. A terrorist attack or threat takes place either during peacetime or at a location other than a battlefield. For example, taking a military general prisoner is a legitimate act in wartime, provided the captors abide by international law. However, when the Italian Red Brigades abducted U.S. Gen. James L. Dozier in 1981, he was a hostage (not a prisoner), and the kidnapping was an act of terrorism (not war), because the United States was not engaged in hostilities at the time.

Although terrorism occurs outside the framework of conventional military engagement, conventional military forces can still commit terrorism. Examples include Adolf Hitler's genocide against the Jews in World War II and Idi Amin's reign of terror in Uganda. Acts like Hitler's and Amin's are sometimes called "state terrorism" because the more general term "terrorism" may connote a nonstate perpetrator.

Target. The targets of terrorism are innocent people or "noncombatants," chosen for their symbolic value more than for their effect on operational capability.

Generally speaking, noncombatants do not have a realistic chance to defend themselves, and their surrender does not guarantee their lives will be spared. For example, General Dozier was a noncombatant at the time of his abduction because he was in his apartment, off-duty. Although he was a high-ranking member of the U.S. military, his life (or death) and freedom (or captivity) were unlikely to affect the Red Brigades' operational environment in any significant way. Terrorists targeted General Dozier not for who he was, but for what he represented: the capitalist superpower backing Italy's government.

Targets may be symbolic because of their association with a particular country, religion, ethnicity, class, or other aspect of human identity, or because of their very randomness. Some definitions of terrorism differentiate between random and symbolic targets, but this is a false distinction; randomness is symbolic in itself. Random violence implies that anyone or anything may be next, signaling that the perpetrators' rage and destruction know no boundaries. Random violence delivers a psychological message as well as a physical blow.

Alex Schmid, former officer-in-charge of the United Nations' Terrorism Prevention Branch, describes the terrorist focus on symbolism by identifying two separate targets for a terrorist attack: the target of violence and the target of terror. The target of violence is the actual victim of the attack, and the target of terror is the social group "whose members' sense of security is purposively undermined" by the violence.[4] For example, insurgents in southern Thailand frequently attack Buddhist monks. The target of terror extends beyond the attacked monks, and even beyond monks in general, to encompass the entire Buddhist minority in southern Thailand. In the case of random violence, the target of terror could be the whole society in question.

In Schmid's formulation, the target of terror may then mobilize a secondary target of demands, usually a government, or target of attention, such as the mass public. This mobilization creates the practical or political imperative to respond to the terrorists, perhaps by complying with their wishes. Simply put, terrorists attack a smaller group of people to induce terror in a larger group, hoping the terrorized group will generate sufficient political will to change circumstances in the terrorists' favor.

This emphasis on symbolism and sequential targets does not mean terrorist acts have no immediate, practical consequences. On the contrary, the most devastating terrorist attacks have physical and economic dimensions as well as symbolic value. For example, 9/11 affected U.S. infrastructure and the national economy as well as the American psyche. Symbolism is not the only salient feature of terrorist target selection, but it is a critical and characteristic one that does not figure as prominently in other forms of violence.

Motivation. Terrorism is politically motivated. At its core is group conflict over power and resources (broadly defined); that is, the violence has a purpose beyond a private, personal agenda. Terrorism is "political" in the sense that the terrorist wants to affect a polity by changing the course of events in his community, country, or the world as a whole.

In a sense, the "politically motivated" dimension of terrorism is another way of expressing Schmid's idea about sequential targets. The violence is a means to an end—a way to terrorize a polity in order to manipulate policy makers—not an end in itself. Terrorism is political in the sense that its aims and consequences are communal, but it can be motivated by religious, economic, or social concerns, as well as by the struggles over authority commonly called "politics."

Objective. The immediate objective of terrorist violence or threats is to create fear, in the hope that fear will create political consequences, or useful targets of demands. (Some theorists argue whether the psychological effect of terrorism is more properly called fear, terror, intimidation, coercion, or a number of other, similar terms, but these distinctions are irrelevant outside academe.) The important point is that the effect of the act, not the act itself, is the true objective of terrorism. Attempts to define terrorism by referring to specific acts—hijackings, kidnappings, etc.—doom themselves to obsolescence. A rigorous definition of terrorism must be able to withstand the constant evolution of terrorist tactics and countermeasures, hence the focus on "Why?" instead of "What?"

Context, target, motivation, and objective seem to be the most critical, characteristic, and widely accepted elements of the definition of terrorism. Other, more formal definitions include additional details and nuances. For example, some stipulate that terrorist violence must be deliberate and premeditated, but both of these concepts are contained in the notions of motivation and objective. Others try to derive a definition by adapting the laws that govern fair conduct in war. Several years after formulating his previous definition of terrorism and its sequential targets, Schmid proposed defining terrorism as the peacetime equivalent of war crimes. While useful for the layman, this concept is problematic for the policy maker; as the war crimes expert Michael Scharf notes, "[T]he laws of war establish rights as well as obligations for those over whom they apply."[5] Equating terrorists with lawful combatants in war erodes the distinctions between the two, affording terrorists several privileges and protections, including the "combatant's privilege" of immunity from prosecution for certain common crimes and the right to prisoner-of-war status.

Based on its actions and statements through August 2009, the ETIM qualifies as a terrorist group by any reasonable definition. It launches and threatens premeditated attacks on noncombatants in an effort to create a climate of fear and coerce the Chinese state to accede to its political demands.

By its own admission, the ETIM has targeted noncombatants. The group continues to target unarmed civilians when it attacks buses, government offices, and businesses owned by Han Chinese. Even some of the military and police personnel the ETIM has attacked qualify as noncombatants, because they did not have a realistic chance to defend themselves. For example, in August 2008 the ETIM in Kashgar attacked a group of about 70 police during their morning exercises, killing 16 of them. The PRC immediately suspected ETIM involvement,[6] and the ETIM later claimed responsibility in the November 2008 issue of its magazine.[7]

The ETIM has also threatened broad groups of innocents. For example, a July 2008 online video declares, "Once again, we are warning that the mujahideen from the Turkestan Islamic Party will target all the participants in the Olympics as well as venues, sports facilities, and residential compounds. . . . If you wish to remain alive and intact, you must stay away from the Olympics, which will not go on peacefully as the Communist Chinese wish."[8] This statement goes beyond warning bystanders that they may become collateral damage in an offensive against the Chinese state. In this video, the ETIM specifically announces its intention to attack noncombatants—defenseless athletes, spectators, and residents—who are in no way responsible for the ETIM's grievances.

In both of these examples, the ETIM's targets have symbolic value. The police serve as a symbol of the PRC's security forces; killing them suggests to others in the military and law enforcement fields that they may be next. The PRC intended the 2008 Olympics to symbolize China's culture, prosperity, and strong standing in the international community. Attacking the Olympics in Beijing (which the ETIM did not actually do) would have damaged the PRC's global image, perhaps irreparably.

The ETIM's public declarations clearly tie its violence back to political objectives, as in this statement from August 1, 2008: "We, members of the Turkestan Islamic Party, have declared war against China. We oppose China's occupation of our homeland of East Turkestan, which is a part of the Islamic world."[9] The ETIM styles itself as a political entity as well as a militant force. The group refers to itself as a "party" and posted a "constitution" on its website. According to the ETIM's constitution, the group aims to establish a fundamentalist Muslim state in the Uyghur homeland, rule by sharia law, and eventually restore the Caliphate Turkey abolished in 1924.

Predictably, the ETIM rejects the "terrorist" label. In a January 2009 online video, an ETIM personality named Commander Seyfullah claims the ETIM is not a terrorist group. "Dear brothers, be well aware that the path we are asking you to follow is not 'terrorism' or barbaric or hegemonic work as the infidels have claimed with their poisonous tongues," Commander Seyfullah says. "But, it is the path of preciousness and glory exactly as Allah ordained for the believers. . . . It is the only path to rescue the Muslims of East Turkestan from the hands of the unjust invaders."[10] Yet the ETIM's own statements reveal its intent to create a powerful and pervasive climate of fear in order to achieve these aims. In the same video where Commander Seyfullah rejects the "terrorist" label, an ETIM member identified as Abdullah Mansur says, "Making preparations to fight these Atheist Communists is an obligation on every Muslim, and that includes scaring them, frightening them, and [also] causing horror in their hearts."[11] He could hardly have been more explicit about his group's desire to inflict terror.

BLACKLISTING THE ETIM

Calling a group "terrorist" is an act of rhetoric, but formally designating it as such by placing it on a blacklist is an act of national policy. A formal designation moves beyond rhetoric to practical and political consequences.

As of this writing, the United States has placed the ETIM on two of its three terrorism blacklists. The George W. Bush administration designated the ETIM on a finance blacklist and an immigration blacklist but left the group off the State Department's high-profile FTO list. At U.S. urging, the United Nations has also blacklisted the ETIM.

Current Blacklist Status

Finance Blacklist

The U.S. Treasury Department has blacklisted the ETIM itself and the group's current leader, Abdul Haq, freezing their assets and banning transactions with both entities. The ETIM is not believed to have a significant financial presence in the United States, so these measures were largely symbolic.[12]

The Treasury blacklist is officially called the Office of Foreign Assets Control Specially Designated Nationals and Blocked Persons list, less formally known as the "OFAC list" or the "SDN list." It was established by Executive Order 13224.

The Treasury Department added the ETIM/ETIP to the OFAC list on September 3, 2002, and added Abdul Haq several years later, on April 20, 2009. The news release for Abdul Haq's designation identifies him as the overall leader and commander of the ETIM and a member of Al-Qaida's Shura Council as of 2005. The release charges Haq with raising funds, recruiting ETIM members, and directing the group's military commander to attack Chinese cities, particularly those hosting the 2008 Olympics. The release also features a quote from the Treasury Department's Under Secretary for Terrorism and Financial Intelligence, who calls Haq a "brutal terrorist."[13]

Immigration Blacklist

The U.S. State Department placed the ETIM/ETIP on the Terrorist Exclusion List (TEL) on April 29, 2004. This list restricts terrorist immigration in much the same way the OFAC list restricts terrorist financing. It was established by 8 U.S. Code § 1182.

UN Blacklist

The United Nations designated the ETIM/ETIP a terrorist group under UN Security Council Resolutions 1267 and 1390 on September 11, 2002, at the behest of the U.S., Chinese, Afghan, and Kyrgyz delegations.[14] The UN designation requires all member states to freeze the ETIM's assets, ban its travel, and prohibit the transfer of any military equipment, technical advice, or training to the ETIM. The United Nations added "Islamic Party of Turkestan" and "Djamaat Turkistan" as alternative names for the group on October 3, 2008.[15]

The UN blacklist is notable for its title: "The Consolidated List Established and Maintained by the 1267 Committee with Respect to Al-Qaida, Usama bin Laden, and the Taliban and Other Individuals, Groups, Undertakings and Entities Associated with Them." The ETIM's presence on the UN list explicitly asserts an association between the ETIM and Al-Qaida or the Taliban.

On April 20, 2009, the United Nations also blacklisted ETIM leader Abdul Haq. Placing Haq on this list froze his assets, banned his travel, and subjected him to an arms embargo.

What's Missing?

The United States has not designated the ETIM an FTO, despite placing the group on the OFAC list, advocating for the UN blacklisting, and adding the ETIM to the TEL.

The State Department's FTO list is the most widely known of all the U.S. blacklists. It is an interagency vehicle for imposing financial and immigration sanctions on the listed groups, to include blocking assets, refusing visas, deporting members, and prosecuting supporters who provide funds. Furthermore, the list "publicly stigmatizes groups and provides a clear focal point for interagency cooperation on terrorist sanctions. . . . The FTO list has unique importance not only because of the specific measures undertaken to thwart the activities of designated groups but also because of the symbolic, public role it plays as a tool of U.S. counterterrorism policy,"[16] according to a 2003 Congressional Research Service report.

The State Department has obviously wrestled with what to call the ETIM and other groups that are not designated FTOs. From 2001 to 2006, the State Department's annual published report on terrorism[17] included not only a list of FTOs, but also a supplementary list variously titled "Other Terrorist Groups" (2001–2003), "Other Terrorist Organizations" (2004), or "Other Groups of Concern" (2005–2006). The criteria for and consequences of placement on each supplementary list are unclear. The ETIM made the supplementary list every year but 2001, when it was mentioned in the text of the report as "cause for concern." The 2007 and 2008 annual reports contain no such supplementary list, but they do mention the ETIM in their summaries of terrorism in China.

The State Department takes the lead in the FTO designation process.[18] FTOs must be foreign organizations whose actions meet the definition of "terrorism" in 22 U.S. Code § 2656f(d) or the definition of "terrorist activity" in 8 U.S. Code § 1182(a)(3)(b). In addition, groups on the FTO list "must threaten the security of U.S. nationals *or* the national security (national defense, foreign relations, *or* the economic interests) of the United States."[19]

A former State Department official told a congressional hearing in 2009 that the case against the ETIM was not strong enough to seek an FTO designation.[20]

Controversy and Consequences

The ETIM established itself as a genuinely threatening terrorist organization in 2008 and 2009—but the case was not so clear in 2002, when the United States first blacklisted the group. Before targeting the Beijing Olympics, and before collaborating with Al-Qaida's media shop, the ETIM was just an obscure militant group rankling the Communists in a remote part of Central Asia, with no apparent designs on Western interests. Open sources show no sign of U.S. concern before and immediately after 9/11. For example, a U.S. Pacific Command special report on Uyghur Muslim separatists from September 28, 2001, does not mention the ETIM and concludes that "no single identifiable group" is responsible for separatist violence in Xinjiang.[21] Similarly, a Congressional Research Service report on Uyghur separatism from December 17, 2001, contains no mention of the ETIM or any of its common aliases. Also in December 2001, the top U.S. envoy on counterterrorism noted publicly that although the United States had captured Uyghur fighters in Afghanistan, the Uyghurs' group (the ETIM) was not a designated terrorist organization. The envoy, Gen. Francis X. Taylor, added, "While these people are indeed involved in terrorist activities in Afghanistan . . . the legitimate economic and social issues that confront people in northwestern China are not necessarily counterterrorist issues."[22]

The 2002 U.S. blacklisting raised the ETIM from international obscurity to sudden prominence. With that prominence came controversy. Critics suggested the United States blacklisted the ETIM and pushed the United Nations to do the same as part of a quid pro quo arrangement with the PRC, using the ETIM as a scapegoat. Later analysis showed the American justifications for the UN blacklisting overstated the number of attacks and casualties for which the ETIM was responsible.[23] Ongoing debate about the ultimate fate of the Uyghurs detained at GTMO has kept the blacklisting controversy alive. In June 2009, a subcommittee of the U.S. House Foreign Affairs Committee launched a planned series of hearings on Uyghur issues.

These hearings included testimony on whether the ETIM should have been blacklisted and whether the organization even exists.

After 9/11, the United States sought international partners for what the George W. Bush administration called the "Global War on Terrorism." As a major world power, the PRC's cooperation or lack thereof would play a critical role in the success of this effort. For the PRC, the primary threat to national security was not Al-Qaida's brand of jihad but the nationalistic aspirations of ethnic and religious minorities in outlying parts of China's vast territory. Chinese and U.S. counterterrorism interests converged in the ETIM, a separatist group that shared Al-Qaida's ideology.

In January 2002, the PRC issued a 15-page report formally linking its fight against Uyghur separatism to the war on terrorism.[24] This report claimed that East Turkistan terrorist groups, including the ETIM, had launched attacks with Osama bin Laden's support since the 1990s.[25] The PRC and the United States began bilateral talks on counterterrorism.

In August 2002, Deputy Secretary of State Richard Armitage announced the United States would designate the ETIM a terrorist group under Executive Order 13224, which it did in September, placing the group on the OFAC list and freezing its assets. A few days later, the United States joined the PRC, Afghanistan, and Kyrgyzstan in asking the United Nations to add the ETIM to its funding blacklist as well. Later that same month, Chinese interrogators visited the Uyghurs detained at GTMO.

The timing of these events struck some observers as suspicious. As the Council on Foreign Relations noted, "The Bush administration's clampdown on the ETIM came as the United States sought to prevent a possible Chinese veto in any U.N. Security Council debate over Iraq, shortly after Chinese officials said they would tighten regulations on the export of missile-related technology, and before Chinese President Jiang Zemin's scheduled October 2002 visit to President Bush's Texas ranch."[26] In other words, the sudden U.S. push to brand the ETIM a terrorist group (well before the Olympic-themed online videos of 2008 raised the group's international profile) seemed to be part of a quid pro quo agreement that also involved the PRC's assent to the strategic direction of U.S. foreign policy—particularly the intent to intervene in Iraq. Other critics also accused the Bush administration of blacklisting the ETIM so Beijing would continue buying bonds used to finance the U.S. debt.[27]

In 2002, the ETIM was not even the most nefarious of the several militant groups agitating for an independent Xinjiang. "It was always a surprise to those of us who study this issue that ETIM itself was singled out," Xinjiang expert Dru Gladney told a congressional subcommittee.[28] Millward noted in 2004 that the East Turkistan Liberation Organization (ETLO) seemed to be "the main group to watch" based on events since 1997. He observed that the PRC had attributed several specific attacks to the ETLO, including arson, poisoning, and shootings, while the connections between violence in Xinjiang and other specific organizations were often vague at best.[29] (The United States has since declined to designate the ETLO or any of the other Uyghur groups the PRC considers terrorists.)

The day after the United Nations blacklisted the ETIM, the United States released a news statement with background on the group. Presumably this statement outlines the strongest unclassified evidence of the ETIM's terrorist activity the United States had at the time. The statement contains two dubious claims. One is almost certainly misquoted from the PRC's public statements, and the other is misleading at best.

The U.S. news statement contains figures on attacks, deaths, and injuries that match previous PRC statements almost verbatim, but with one important difference: the United States attributed to "elements of the ETIM" *all* the attacks, deaths, and injuries the PRC attributed to East Turkistan terrorism in general. Both the U.S. statement and PRC officials referred to more than 200 attacks committed from 1990 to 2001, killing 162 people and injuring more than 440 others. The U.S. news statement blamed all of these attacks on the ETIM. Previous PRC statements provided exactly the same figures for attacks, deaths, and injuries, but blamed only some of them on the ETIM. The PRC explicitly blamed other attacks, deaths, and injuries on different groups, such as the ETLO, and described some of the incidents without attributing them to a specific group.[30] The most likely explanation for this discrepancy is that the U.S. officials who generated the news statement simply misinterpreted and misquoted the previous PRC statements.

In part because of this confusion, critics have accused the Bush administration of promulgating intelligence "spoon-fed"[31] to the United States by the PRC. A former U.S. State Department official denied that charge, saying the United States corroborated Chinese intelligence independently. He added that the PRC also "provided reams and reams of information" on the ETLO and other groups, but the United States refused to blacklist these other groups because it could not corroborate the Chinese reporting.[32]

The most damning evidence of the ETIM's threat to American interests comes in the U.S. news statement's final paragraph. Other open-source information suggests this final paragraph is misleading. It reads as follows:

Although ETIM did not originally target U.S. nationals, there is evidence indicating that ETIM members have been taking steps to plan attacks against U.S. interests and nationals abroad, including the U.S. Embassy in Bishkek, Kyrgyzstan. On May 22, 2002, two suspected ETIM members were deported to China from Kyrgyzstan on the grounds that they were planning terrorist attacks. The Kyrgyz government stated that the two men were planning to target embassies in Bishkek as well as trade centers and public gathering places.

When the Kyrgyz government announced on May 23, 2002, that it had deported the two Uyghurs, it identified them as members of the "East Turkistan Liberation Front," not the ETIM. The Kyrgyz announcement accused the two Uyghurs of being involved in assassinations in Bishkek, killing the chairman of the Ittipak Uyghur Association and a member of a Chinese trade delegation, but not of plotting to attack the U.S. embassy.[33] U.S. diplomats in Beijing announced the ETIM affiliation and the plot against the U.S. embassy only later, in late August 2002,[34] after the two Uyghurs had been in Chinese custody for three months. When a journalist asked the Kyrgyz government about the embassy plot, the Kyrgyz foreign minister was cautious: "There were *some suspicions* that they *might* have been planning an attack against the U.S. Embassy" (emphasis added). One suspect was found with a map showing embassies in Bishkek.[35] Investigations and interrogations conducted after the two Uyghurs were deported to the PRC may have uncovered additional, as-yet-unreleased evidence that the Uyghurs belonged to the ETIM and planned to attack the U.S. embassy. However, when the Kyrgyz government deported the Uyghurs, it believed they belonged to a different group and accused them of a different crime.

U.S. officials maintain they reached their own conclusions about the ETIM and blacklisted the group "not as a concession to the PRC, but based on independent evidence that ETIM is linked to al-Qaeda and has engaged in deliberate acts of violence against unarmed civilians," said Assistant Secretary of State James Kelly in December 2002.[36]

Kelly's remark acknowledges the perception that the United States blacklisted the ETIM as part of a broader political agenda. The ETIM tried to capitalize on this perception years later, in a statement released on May 1, 2009. According to the ETIM's statement, "The American government announced last month that the Turkistan Islamic Party is a terrorist group, and will be punished by freezing its finances (money) in America. . . . It's mentioned in the statement that the American government kowtows in front of the Chinese government especially in the cases of Afghanistan and Pakistan, and that is the reason the Chinese government forced them to [make] these declarations."[37] Although the ETIM statement mentions the entire group's placement on the OFAC list, its reference to "last month," which would be April 2009, indicates the ETIM is probably actually reacting to Haq's blacklisting.

Uyghur nationalists were devastated by the U.S. blacklisting, sure it would stigmatize the entire Uyghur national project as "terrorism." For example, consider the diatribe written just after the OFAC blacklisting by Erkin Dolat, the editor-in-chief of the Uyghur Information Agency activist group:

> Now China can practically label any Uighur dissident a "terrorist" who has links to the East Turkestan Islamic Movement or other "terrorist" organizations. . . .
> The Uighur people understand, as longtime victims of the Great Game, that

politics is filthy, especially when a great power betrays an individual, group or even a state for its own national interest. This time, the Uighur people have seen how dirty it can get when the US sacrifices them for getting some short-term benefit from China. In the past, the Uighurs have seen the United States as the beacon of democracy and bulwark of human rights and freedom. The Uighurs have also considered the United States as the only power on Earth that can truly challenge and pressure China in terms of human rights and religious freedom. However, the US decision to include ETIM on its FTO list has proved that the opposite is sometimes also true.[38]

Indeed, Chinese officials were telling Uyghurs the Bush administration had "bought into the notion that Uighurs are terrorists," said then-U.S. Assistant Secretary of State for Human Rights Lorne Craner.[39] In an effort to neutralize the Chinese officials' claim, Craner delivered a speech at Xinjiang University in December 2002, stressing the importance of human rights and warning the PRC not to use counterterrorism as an excuse to suppress peaceful dissent.[40] (The speech, naturally, received only a fraction of the media coverage afforded the original blacklisting.)

Despite Craner's speech and similar U.S. statements, few doubt that Beijing used the war on terrorism to justify continued repression. A House resolution passed in September 2007 admits as much. H. Res. 497 reads in part, "The authorities of the People's Republic of China have manipulated the strategic objectives of the international war on terror to increase their cultural and religious oppression of the Muslim population residing in the Xinjiang Uyghur Autonomous Region."

The ETIM will likely remain on the U.S. OFAC list, the TEL, and the UN terrorism blacklist for the foreseeable future, in large part because of its attacks and statements in 2008 and 2009. Even if the United States did blacklist the ETIM as part of a quid pro quo arrangement with the PRC in 2002, and even if that arrangement were improper at the time, the ETIM's activities in 2008 cemented its identity as terrorist group. Furthermore, its statements in 2009 signaled firm alignment with Al-Qaida's jihadist ideology. Removing the ETIM from the U.S. funding and immigration blacklists now would be tantamount to explicit approval of the ETIM's tactics, undermining years of U.S. counterterrorism policy. It would create untold difficulties in U.S.-Chinese relations and likely embolden the ETIM to commit further acts of terror.

The United States persisted in leaving the ETIM off the State Department's high-profile FTO list even after the ETIM threatened the Olympics. This situation is unlikely to change unless the ETIM aligns itself with Al-Qaida operationally as well as ideologically by targeting U.S. interests. Some may argue that designating the ETIM a terrorist group under certain U.S. laws but not others suggests inconsistency or even incoherence in U.S. counterterrorism policy. However, a more publicly aggressive stance on the ETIM may not affect the group's operational capability and will likely exacerbate tensions in Xinjiang by emboldening the Chinese government to further suppress the minority Uighur population the ETIM claims to represent.

Placement on both the OFAC list and the TEL can have consequences comparable to the FTO designation.[41] In other words, the United States might not have much to gain by putting the ETIM on the FTO list. Placing the ETIM on the FTO list may also be a bargaining chip in more broad-based negotiations with the Chinese government, either now or in the future. The United States must weigh the costs and benefits of naming a group to the FTO list in light of other national interests. "Of course, the public attention and diplomatic leverage that goes along with being on the better-known FTO list is not equaled," acknowledges the Congressional Research Service in a 2003 report. "However, the point is that in terms of the results with respect to fighting an organization's activities, the U.S. sanctions regime is far more complicated than either being 'on' the list or 'off' the list would imply."[42]

In addition, the PRC may read the high-profile FTO designation as carte blanche to repress Uyghurs in Xinjiang. This would be a negative result from a counterterrorism as well as a human rights perspective. The ETIM feeds on Uyghur resentment of the Chinese government. Encouraging Beijing to develop ever more repressive policies toward its Uyghur minority in the name of counterterrorism would almost certainly broaden the ETIM's appeal and worsen the security situation in Xinjiang.

OUTLOOK

We assess that the ETIM (or at least a group much like it) will continue to carry out at least small-scale attacks in Xinjiang. We further assess that the ETIM's local support base will grow in proportion to the severity of the PRC's security measures. U.S. policy plays an indirect role in shaping the PRC's security posture in Xinjiang. The ETIM's ongoing relationship with Al-Qaida and other terrorist groups has the potential to enhance the ETIM's strategic and tactical capabilities.

The ETIM is only one of the most recent combatants in the centuries-old ethnic conflict over China's northwest territory. The essential components of this conflict—a clash between the Uyghur and Han cultures and a long-standing struggle for the region's resources—have changed little over time. Uyghur activists resent their subjugation to a distant capital and regard Beijing's governance as a sustained program of assimilation and exploitation. The ETIM and similar groups feed on this abiding resentment, which will likely endure unless Beijing's governance changes.

Substantial reform is highly unlikely as long as the PRC remains in power. The PRC's overriding objective is to maintain control over its vast territory, including its geopolitically, economically, and symbolically significant northwest frontier. Uyghur dissent, protest, and national ambition only lead the PRC to intensify its efforts to control Xinjiang even more tightly. From Beijing's perspective, a successful insurgency in Xinjiang would be not only a blow to national pride but also a potential catalyst for other ethnic and religious uprisings around the country.

The PRC will not give up Xinjiang, with its strategic location and rich natural resources. Nor will the Uyghur separatists abandon their claim to the territory. As circumstances stand today, the ETIM and other militant fringe elements of the broader Uyghur separatist movement are highly unlikely to lay down their arms and join the political fold. The ETIM has endured for nearly 20 years, despite the PRC's efforts to eradicate the group. Since the late 1990s, the ETIM has cultivated transnational ties that will help it survive the PRC's security measures. These ties include alliances with Al-Qaida and other terrorist groups, bases abroad, and an online presence that may help the ETIM circumvent the PRC's restrictions on separatist activity inside Xinjiang.

The true breadth and depth of separatist sentiment in general, and ETIM support in particular, are almost impossible to assess. However, even if the PRC eliminates the ETIM as we know it today, militant Uyghur separatists will likely reassemble essentially the same organization under another name.

We posit that while the ETIM itself represents no serious challenge to Beijing's power, the group may be able to provoke the PRC into harsh security crackdowns that abrogate human rights, exacerbate ethnic tensions, and precipitate further violence. The United States plays an indirect role in shaping the PRC's security posture in Xinjiang. Designating the ETIM as a terrorist group on two U.S. blacklists brought the previously obscure group instant international notoriety. On one hand, raising international awareness of the ETIM presumably enhanced efforts to combat the group. On the other hand, blacklisting the ETIM publicized the group and its cause in a way that the ETIM has come to embrace.

The ETIM's leadership is clearly aware of its U.S. blacklist status, as demonstrated by a 2009 video that mentioned the U.S. asset freeze. However, the blacklisting has little to no direct operational effect because the group has little to no presence in the United States. The real significance of U.S. policy on the ETIM is the message that policy sends to Beijing. Chinese officials will likely interpret harsh, public condemnation of the group as tacit approval to take any measures they deem necessary to crush the ETIM.

The ETIM's ongoing relationship with Al-Qaida and other terrorist groups has the potential to enhance the ETIM's strategic and tactical capabilities. Strategically, the ETIM has developed a propaganda arm affiliated with Al-Qaida's and perhaps even modeled on it. It has begun to court a different demographic by releasing certain statements in Arabic instead of in the Uyghur language. The ETIM has also apparently adopted the tactic of using female suicide bombers. The ETIM may have entered a new phase of organizational learning, observing other terrorist groups and implementing their successful strategies and tactics.

We see two key vulnerabilities in the ETIM's relationship with Al-Qaida. First, Al-Qaida focuses on fighting the United States and its allies, but the ETIM regards the Han Chinese as its primary enemy. In 2004, a man who identified himself as the ETIM's deputy emir told the *Wall Street Journal* about a conflict between the ETIM's focus on the PRC and Al-Qaida's belief that the mujahideen's "first duty is to free Palestine and the sacred Arab lands."[43] A 2008 ETIM video hinted that the group may be obliged to defend its focus on the PRC to other jihadis. This difference in priorities could evolve into a key fissure in the relationship between the ETIM and the Arab-centric global jihadi community. Second, as the ETIM cleaves more closely to Al-Qaida and the global jihadi community, it risks losing its appeal for militant Uyghurs who want an organization dedicated entirely to their particular struggle.

Cooperation with other holy warriors from all over the globe is among the ETIM's founding principles. This dedication to worldwide jihad is enshrined in the first paragraph of the group's constitution. The group is built for the global jihad. Al-Qaida's expertise, financial resources, and international footholds will likely help the ETIM weather the PRC's security crackdowns and remain a relatively constant force capable of conducting at least small-scale attacks in Xinjiang for many years to come.

Appendix A

—∞∞∞—

Uyghur Separatism Timeline

Events in italics took place outside Xinjiang. They are included to provide context for key developments in the history of Uyghur separatism.

1644	*The Qing dynasty captures Beijing, beginning 267 years of empire.*
1759	The Qing dynasty invades the territory now known as Xinjiang.
Circa 1813	*The Russian and British empires begin "The Great Game," a strategic rivalry for control of Central Asia.*
1839	*Great Britain and the Qing dynasty begin fighting the Opium Wars. The first Opium War ends in 1842; the second lasts from 1856 to 1860. Britain wins both wars decisively, forcing the Qing to legalize opium imports.*
Circa 1855–1873	*Muslims rebel against Qing rule in China's southern Yunnan Province.*
1862	Revolt breaks out in Shaanxi, spreading to Kansu and Xinjiang.
1867	Yaqub Beg proclaims himself the Khan of Eastern Turkistan. He goes on to expel the Qing from Xinjiang and establish the Kingdom of Kashgaria.
1877	Yaqub Beg dies; the Qing dynasty reconquers Xinjiang.

Circa 1880–1920	*The Jadidism movement based in Russia modernizes Muslim culture and education.*
1884	The Qing dynasty declares that the regions of Uyghuristan, Altishahr, Junggaria, and the Ili Valley are a province of China called Xinjiang.
1911	*The Qing dynasty falls.*
1914	*World War I begins.*
1917	*Revolution breaks out in Russia, ending centuries of czarist rule. Civil war follows.*
1918	*World War I ends.*
1922	*The Communists win Russia's civil war and establish the Union of Soviet Socialist Republics (USSR).*
1923	*Turkish nationalists establish the Republic of Turkey from the remnants of the Ottoman empire.*
1924	*Mustafa Kamal Atatürk abolishes the Caliphate.*
1927–1950	*Nationalists and Communists fight for control of China.*
1931	The Chinese government tries to interfere in the hereditary leadership of the eastern Xinjiang oasis of Hami, sparking a series of insurrections.
1933	First Eastern Turkistan Republic is established.
1934	First Eastern Turkistan Republic falls.
Circa 1937	*Soviet dictator Josef Stalin's purges reach Central Asia.*
1939	*World War II begins.*
1944	Ethnic riots break out in Yining.
1944	The Second Eastern Turkistan Republic is established.
1945	*World War II ends.*
1949	*China's Communists defeat the Nationalists and establish the People's Republic of China (PRC).*
1949	The Second Eastern Turkistan Republic falls. Uyghur leaders die in a plane crash on their way to meet with the Communist government in Beijing.
1950	The PRC launches the first in a series of incentives encouraging Han to migrate to Xinjiang.
1955	The PRC incorporates Xinjiang as the Xinjiang Uyghur Autonomous Region (XUAR).
1958	Mao launches the "Great Leap Forward" collectivization and industrialization campaign in Xinjiang.

Circa 1962	*Relations sour between the PRC and the USSR.*
1962	More than 60,000 Uyghurs and Kazakhs living in the PRC flee to the USSR.
1966	*Mao launches the "Cultural Revolution."*
Circa 1968	The East Turkistan People's Revolutionary Party advocates for an independent, secular, and Communist East Turkistan allied with the Soviet Union.
1976	*Mao dies. In the years that follow, Deng Xiaoping enacts broad political, social, and economic reform and opens Xinjiang to tourism and foreign trade.*
1989	Uyghurs riot in Urumqi over the publication of an anti-Muslim book.
1990	The PRC closes Xinjiang to foreigners. Uyghurs riot over government policies in Baren.
1991	*The USSR collapses.*
1995	Uyghurs demonstrate in Hotan over the arrest of a respected local cleric.
1996	The PRC launches the "Strike Hard, Maximum Pressure" campaign against crime and separatism.
1997	Uyghurs demonstrate in Yining over a government ban on a traditional social gathering known as the *mashrap*. Bus bombings in Urumqi coincide with Deng Xiaoping's memorial.
1999	The PRC launches the "Develop the Great Northwest" campaign.

Appendix B

———<small>∞∞∞</small>———

PRC News Releases
about the ETIM

TERRORIST ACTIVITIES PERPETRATED BY "EASTERN TURKISTAN" ORGANIZATIONS AND THEIR LINKS WITH OSAMA BIN LADEN AND THE TALIBAN[1]

November 29, 2001

I. Terrorist activities committed by "Eastern Turkistan" elements in and outside the Chinese territory

The "Eastern Turkistan" force has a total of over 40 organizations. They have engaged themselves in terrorist violence to varying degrees, both overtly and covertly. Among these organizations, eight openly advocate violence in their political platforms. They are: "Eastern Turkistan Islamic Resistance Movement" in Turkey; "Eastern Turkistan Liberation Organization", "Eastern Turkistan International Committee", "United Committee of Uygurs' Organizations" in central Asia, and "Central Asian Uygur Hezbollah" in Kazakhstan; "Turkistan Party" in Pakistan; "Eastern Turkistan Islamic Movement" in Afghanistan; and "Eastern Turkistan Youth League" in Switzerland.

1) Incidents of terrorist violence perpetrated by "Eastern Turkistan" elements over the past ten years in the Chinese territory mainly include:

On 5 April 1990, they killed and injured more than 100 civilians and soldiers in Barin Township of Kizilsu Kirgiz Autonomous Prefecture;

On 5 February 1991, the "Islamic Reformist Party" masterminded a bus explosion in Urumqi, killing and injuring over 20 people;

Between June and September 1993, the "Eastern Turkistan Democratic Islamic Party" carried out a series of bombings in southern Xinjiang, which led to more than deaths and injuries; [The number of deaths and injuries is apparently missing.]

On 15 July 1996, the "Eastern Turkistan Islamic Justice Party" engineered a prison rebellion in Xayar County, killing 15 people and a riot in Yining on 5 February 1997, which resulted in over 300 casualties;

On 25 February 1997, the "Eastern Turkistan National Solidarity Union" staged a horrendous bomb explosion incident in Urumqi which involved nearly 100 casualties, and in early 1998 the same group was responsible for 25 poisoning cases in southern Xinjiang, where over 40 people fell victim and four died;

In January 2001, Akbelbek Timur, an "Eastern Turkistan" terrorist who is now in custody, bought explosives in Kazakhstan and smuggled them into Xinjiang for attempted terrorist activities.

2) Incidents of terrorist violence's committed by "Eastern Turkistan" elements in recent years outside China mainly include:

In February 1997, "Eastern Turkistan" terrorists opened fire on the Chinese Embassy in Turkey, assaulted the Chinese Consulate-General in Istanbul, and burned Chinese national flags;

On 5 March 1998, terrorists of the "Eastern Turkistan National Center" carried out bomb attacks on the Chinese Consulate-General in Istanbul;

In November 1999 and August 2000, the "Eastern Turkistan" elements were involved in the armed insurgence and invasion led by the "Uzbek Islamic Movement" into the southern regions of Uzbekistan and Kyrgyzstan respectively;

In May 2000, terrorists of the "Uygur Liberation Organization" set fire to the Chinese Commodities Market in Bishkek and murdered one person from China's Xinjiang, who was sent to Kyrgyzstan to investigate the case;

On 28 September, terrorists under the command of the "Uygur Liberation Organization" killed two Kazkh policemen in Alma-Ata;

In May 2001, terrorists of the "Uygur Youth Association of Kazakhstan" robbed in Alma-Ata a bank vehicle that carried banknotes.

II. The Relationship Between the "Eastern Turkistan" Terrorists and the Taliban in Afghanistan and Osama bin Laden

Osama bin Laden and the Taliban in Afghanistan have provided the "Eastern Turkistan" terrorist organizations with equipment and financial resources and trained their personnel. The basic facts are as follows:

1) The "Eastern Turkistan Islamic Movement" (hereinafter referred to as ETIM) is a major component of the terrorist network headed by Osama bin Laden. Hasan Mahsum, the ETIM ringleader, is hiding in Kabul, Afghanistan, and carries an Afghanistan passport issued by the Taliban. Osama bin Laden demanded that the ETIM stir up turmoil in the near future in the three Central Asian countries, namely, Uzbekistan, Tajikistan and Kyrgyzstan, and then stage an organized infiltration into China's Xinjiang. The "Turkistan Army" under the ETIM fights in combat for the Taliban in Afghanistan. This "Army" has a special "China Battalion" with about 320 terrorists form Xinjiang. The battalion is under the direct command of Hasan Mahsum's deputy Kabar.

2) The armed elements of the ETIM received training in terrorist training camps in Afghanistan's Kabul, Mazar-i-Sharif, Kunduz, Vardak, Kandahar, Herat, Shibarghan and other places. Some of these camps are directly under the control of Osama bin Laden and the Taliban and some are military bases of the "Uzbek Islamic Movement". The "Central Asian Uygur Hezbollah" is said to have a 1000-strong armed force and have training bases in Afghanistan. The "Uygur National Army" received battle training in July and August 1999 in the Taliban bases in Afghanistan. They practiced conventional weapons

with live ammunition and learned the Taliban guerilla warfare tactics and terrorist skills such as assassination, explosion and poison-doping. After their training, the "Eastern Turkistan" elements have fought in combats in Afghanistan, Chechnya, and Uzbekistan, or returned to Xinjiang for terrorist and violent activities.

3) In early 1999, Osama bin Laden met with Hasan Mahsum, the ETIM ring-leader, and undertook to offer him financial assistance. Since October 2000, Osama bin Laden and the Taliban have provided the ETIM with 300,000 U.S. dollars in various ways, and undertook to cover all the expenses of the ETIM activities for the year of 2001. The activities of the "Central Asian Uygur Hezbollah" are also partially financed by Osama bin Laden.

"EAST TURKISTAN" TERRORIST FORCES CANNOT GET AWAY WITH IMPUNITY[2]

January 21, 2002

Terrorism is a big public hazard in the world today, posing an enormous threat to the peace, security, and order of the international society.

Over a long period of time—especially since the 1990s—the "East Turkistan" forces inside and outside Chinese territory have planned and organized a series of violent incidents in the Xinjiang Uygur Autonomous Region of China and some other countries, including explosions, assassinations, arsons, poisonings, and assaults, with the objective of founding a so-called state of "East Turkistan." These terrorist incidents have seriously jeopardized the lives and property of people of all ethnic groups as well as social stability in China, and even threatened the security and stability of related countries and regions.

Then how did the "East Turkistan" issue come about? What terrorist activities have the "East Turkistan" forces engaged in?

I

The term "East Turkistan" first appeared at the end of the 19th century. Here, "stan" means "place" or "region." However, "East Turkistan" is not merely a geographical concept, but a political concept first put forward by old colonialists with the aim of dismembering China.

Originally, the term "Turks" referred to people of an ancient nomadic tribe. In the fifth century, the Turks wandered about the region of the Altay

Mountains. From the mid-sixth century to the mid-eighth century, they appeared frequently on the grasslands of north China, and conducted exchanges with people in China's Central Plains during the Western Wei (535–557), Sui (581–618) and Tang (618–907) dynasties, through various channels and at many levels. In 552, the Turks founded a khanate, which, at the height of its prosperity, ruled quite a vast area. In the Sui and early Tang dynasties, the Turks became a major force in north China. Later, they split into eastern and western branches, which engaged in constant struggles for dominance of the khanate. In the mid-eighth century, the eastern and western khanates of the Turks declined and went out of existence one after the other, and their descendants gradually merged with other ethnic groups. After the 11th century, the "Turks" mentioned in foreign history books embraced all the ethnic groups who spoke the Turkic language, which is a branch of the Altay language family. At the end of the 19th century, some people proposed to unite all the ethnic groups speaking the Turkic language from the Strait of Bosporus to the Altay Mountains to form a political state. In fact, throughout history there has never been a unified country consisting of all the Turkic-speaking peoples, despite claims to the contrary.

To split Xinjiang from China and bring it under their domination, some of the old colonialists gave Xinjiang the name "East Turkistan" (correspondingly, they called the countries in Central Asia "West Turkistan"), fabricating the fallacy that Xinjiang was the home of "Eastern Turks."

After the establishment of a frontier command headquarters (duhufu) in the Western Region by the Han Dynasty in 60 B.C., Xinjiang became a part of Chinese territory. From that time on, the central government has never ceased jurisdiction over Xinjiang. But in the beginning of the 20th century, a handful of fanatical Xinjiang separatists and extremist religious elements fabricated the myth of "East Turkistan" in light of the sophistries and fallacies created by the old colonialists. They claimed that " 'East Turkistan' had been an independent state since ancient times," and that the ethnic group in that state had a history of nearly 10,000 years. They incited all ethnic groups speaking the Turkic language and believing in Islam to unite to form a state featuring the "integration of religion and politics." They denied the historical fact that all China's ethnic groups have joined their efforts to create the great motherland, and called for "opposition to all ethnic groups other than the Turks," and for the elimination of "pagans."

Since the formation of the "East Turkistan" theory, separatists of every description have conducted activities in the name of "East Turkistan," in an attempt to set up a political state called "East Turkistan."

From the early 20th century to the late 1940s, the "East Turkistan" forces instigated riots on many occasions with the connivance and support of foreign forces. In November 1933, Sabit Damolla and others founded the so-called "East Turkistan Islamic State" in Kashi—an attempt of the separatists at putting their separatist theory into practice. But, thanks to the opposition of the people of all ethnic groups in Xinjiang, it collapsed within three months.

Since the peaceful liberation of Xinjiang, the people of all ethnic groups have united as one, worked hard and built their fine homeland with joint efforts. Xinjiang's society is stable, its economy has kept developing, the local people's living standard has rapidly improved, and the situation as a whole is good. But the "East Turkistan" forces, not to be reconciled to their failure and in defiance of the will of the people of all ethnic groups, have been on the lookout for every opportunity to conduct splittist and sabotage activities with the backing of international anti-China forces.

In the 1990s, under the influence of extremism, separatism and international terrorism, part of the "East Turkistan" forces inside and outside Chinese territory turned to splittist and sabotage activities with terrorist violence as the main means, even brazenly declaring that terrorist violence is the only way to achieve their aims. The programs of the "East Turkistan Islamic Party" and of the "East Turkistan Opposition Party" seized by the police clearly point out that they will "take the road of armed struggle," and "conduct various terrorist activities in densely populated regions." In the booklet What Is the Hope for Our Independence compiled by them, they openly declare that they will create a terrorist atmosphere at kindergartens, hospitals and schools at any cost. The "East Turkistan" terrorists have engineered a series of bloody terrorist incidents, leaving many blood-soaked chapters in the historical annals.

II

Incomplete statistics show that from 1990 to 2001, the "East Turkistan" terrorist forces inside and outside Chinese territory were responsible for over 200 terrorist incidents in Xinjiang, resulting in the deaths of 162 people of all ethnic groups, including grass-roots officials and religious personnel, and injuries to more than 440 people. The main terrorist incidents include:

1. Explosions

Like most terrorist groups in the world, the "East Turkistan" terrorists are keen on directing explosions at innocent people, in order to create an atmosphere of terror and to extend their influence.

On February 28, 1991, an explosion engineered by the "East Turkistan" terrorist organization at a video theater of a bus terminal in Kuqa County, Aksu Prefecture, Xinjiang, caused the death of one person and injuries to 13 others. On the same day, the terrorists also planted a bomb at a private store in the county seat, which, fortunately, did not explode.

On February 5, 1992, while the Chinese people were celebrating the Chinese New Year, the Spring Festival, the terrorists blew up two buses (Buses No. 52 and No. 30) in Urumqi, the regional capital of Xinjiang, killing three people and injuring 23 others. Two other bombs they planted—one at a cinema and the other in a residential building—were discovered before they could explode, and defused.

From June 17 to September 5, 1993, the "East Turkistan" terrorist organization was responsible for ten explosions at department stores, markets, hotels and places for cultural activities in the southern part of Xinjiang, causing two deaths and 36 injuries. Among them, the June 17 explosion at the office building of an agricultural machinery company in Kashi demolished the building, killed two people and injured seven others. The August 1 explosion at the video theater of the Foreign Trade Company in Shache County, Kashi Prefecture, injured 15 people, and the August 19 explosion in front of the Cultural Palace in the city of Hotan injured six people.

On February 25, 1997, directing its terrorist activities to the capital of Xinjiang again, the "East Turkistan" terrorist organization blew up three buses (Buses No. 2, No. 10 and No. 44) in Urumqi. Nine people died and 68 others were seriously injured in the incidents, among whom were people of the ethnic Uygur, Hui, Kirgiz and Han origins. Between February 22 and March 30, 1998, the "East Turkistan" terrorist organization set off a succession of six explosions in Yecheng County, Kashi Prefecture, injuring three people and causing a natural gas pipeline to explode and start a big fire. The direct economic losses came to over one million yuan.

Early in the morning of April 7, 1998, the same terrorist organization engineered eight explosions one after another at places such as the homes of a director of the Public Security Bureau of Yecheng County, a vice-chairman of the Yecheng County Committee of the Chinese People's Political Consultative Conference (CPPCC) and a deputy commissioner of Kashi Prefecture. The explosions injured eight people.

2. Assassinations

To sabotage national unity and create an atmosphere of terror, the terrorists have targeted their attacks at officials, ordinary people and patriotic religious personages of the Uygur ethnic group, as well as the ethnic Han people, killing them as "pagans."

On August 24, 1993, two "East Turkistan" terrorists stabbed and seriously injured Abliz Damolla, an executive committee member of the CPPCC Yecheng County Committee in Kashi Prefecture and imam of the Great Mosque there.

On March 22, 1996, two armed and masked terrorists broke into the home of Hakimsidiq Haji, vice-chairman of the Islamic Association of Xinhe County, Aksu Prefecture, and assistant imam of a mosque, and shot him dead.

Early in the morning of April 29, 1996, a dozen armed-to-the-teeth terrorists broke into the homes of Qavul Toqa, a member of the CPPCC National Committee and deputy to the Xinjiang Uygur Autonomous Region People's Congress at Qunas Village of Alaqagha Township in Kuqa County, and three local Uygur grassroots officials, creating bloody terrorist incidents by means of explosion, shooting and stabbing. The terrorists threw two bombs into Qavul Toqa's home, seriously injuring him and his wife. Avul Toqa, Qavul Toqa's younger brother, was stabbed to death with seven wounds, and his wife was first stabbed then shot to death. Anvar Qavul, Qavul Toqa's son, died of nine stab wounds and a shot to the head, and his wife died of eight stab wounds and two shots to the head. Javup Muhammatman, a village official, received serious stab wounds.

The "East Turkistan" terrorist organization plotted the assassination of Arunhan Aji, executive committee member of the Islamic Association of China, vice-chairman of the CPPCC Xinjiang Regional Committee and chairman of the Kashi Islamic Association, on May 12, 1996. Early on the morning of that day, Arunhan Aji and his son were on their way to the Aitga Mosque to worship when four terrorists attacked them. Both of them were seriously injured, Arunhan Aji with 21 stab wounds and his son with 13 stab wounds.

Early in the morning of March 23, 1997, a gang of terrorists, led by Tursun Turdi, gatecrashed into the home of Omarjan, manager of the Jinyinchuan Reclamation Area of Aksu Prefecture, killing him and his wife. Early in the morning of July 3 of the same year, the same gang stormed into the home of Turdi Niyaz, a village official of Bashereq Township in Avat County, killing him and his wife.

Early in the morning of November 6, 1997, a terrorist group headed by Muhammat Tursun, at the order of the "East Turkistan" organization abroad, shot and killed Yunus Sidiq Damolla, a member of the Islamic

Association of China and of the Islamic Association of Xinjiang, chairman of the Islamic Association of Aksu and imam of the Mosque of Baicheng County, while he was on his way to the mosque to worship. On January 27, 1998, the same terrorists shot and killed Abliz Haji, executive committee member of the CPPCC Yecheng County Committee and imam of the county's Great Mosque, while he was on his way to the mosque to worship.

On June 4, 1997, four terrorists broke into the home of Muhammat Rozi Muhammat, an official of Huangdi Village of Aqik Township in Moyu County, Hotan Prefecture, and killed him with 11 stab wounds.

On August 23, 1999, a dozen of terrorists led by Yasin Muhammat broke into the home of Hudaberdi Tohti, political instructor of the police station of Bosikem Township in Zepu County, Kashi Prefecture, killing Hudaberdi Tohti with 38 stab wounds and his son with a shot to the head. Then the terrorists set Tohti's home on fire, causing serious burns to his wife.

On February 3, 2001, a gang of terrorists broke into the home of Muhammatjan Yaqup, an official at the People's Court of Shufu County, Kashi Prefecture, killing him with 38 stab wounds.

3. Attacks on Police and Government Institutions

On August 27, 1996, six terrorists in combat fatigues drove to the office building of the Jangilas Township People's Government, Yecheng County, where they cut the telephone lines and killed a deputy head of the township and a policeman on duty. Afterwards, they kidnapped three security men and one waterworks tender in a village of the same township, and later killed them in the desert 10 kilometers away.

Early in the morning of October 24, 1999, terrorists attacked the police station in Saili Township, Zepu County, with guns, machetes, incendiary bottles and grenades. They shot one member of a local security guard dead and wounded another, wounded a policeman and killed a criminal suspect in custody. After that, they burned ten rooms, one jeep and three motor-bikes belonging to the police station.

4. Crimes of Poison and Arson

From January 30 to February 18, 1998, members of the "East Turkistan Liberation Organization" were responsible for 23 poisoning cases in Kashi City. One innocent person died as a result, and four others suffered serious effects. In addition, thousands of domestic animals died or suffered badly.

On May 23, 1998, members of the "East Turkistan Liberation Organization" who had sneaked into Xinjiang after receiving special training abroad, committed 15 cases of arson with some 40 chemical comb rents in the busiest areas of Urumqi, such as the Hued Plaza, Damien, the Hetman Road Clothing Materials Wholesale Market, the Changchun Hotel Wholesale Market, the Hongshan Timber Market, the Urumqi Hotel, and the Business and Trade Center. They threatened to "make Urumqi a sea of fire and cause losses of hundreds of millions of yuan." Thanks to prompt action by the authorities, no serious damage was caused.

On October 11, 1999, three terrorists put three ignition devices in cotton heaps at the cotton purchasing station of the Hotan City Cotton and Hemp Company. One of them exploded, causing the loss of two tons of cotton. The other two devices were removed in time.

5. Establishing Secret Training Bases and Raising Money to Buy and Manufacture Arms and Ammunition

In order to train hardcore members and enlarge their organization, the "East Turkistan" terrorist forces secretly established training bases in Xinjiang, mainly in remote parts of the region. In 1990, the "Shock Brigade of the Islamic Reformist Party" established a base to train terrorists in the remote Basheriq Township, Yecheng County. Three training classes were run there, with more than 60 terrorists having been trained, mainly in the theory of religious extremism and terrorism, explosion, assassination and other terrorist skills, and physical strength. Most of the trainees later participated in the major terrorist activities, such as explosions, assassinations and robberies, from 1991 to 1993 in various parts of Xinjiang.

In February 1998, Hasan Mahsum, ringleader of the "East Turkistan Islamic Movement" abroad, sent scores of terrorists into China. They established about a dozen training bases in Xinjiang and inland regions and trained more than 150 terrorists in 15 training classes. In addition, they set up large numbers of training stations in scattered areas, each of them composed of three to five members, and some of them being also workshops for making weapons, ammunition and explosive devices. The Xinjiang police uncovered many of these underground training stations and workshops, and confiscated large numbers of antitank grenades, hand-grenades, detonators, guns and ammunition.

On December 30, 1999, the police discovered an underground hideout in Poskam Township, Zepu County. In this hideout, which was 3 meters from the ground and measured 3 meters long, 2 meters wide and 1.7 meters high, they found tools for making explosive devices, such as electric drills and electric welding machines, as well as blueprints and antitank grenades.

On February 25, 2000, the police arrested seven terrorists in the No. 3 Village, Kachung Township, Shache County, and discovered a tunnel leading to an underground bunker beneath the house of one of them, which was equipped with ventilation devices and water supply and sewage systems. The tunnel was 7 meters long and 2.5 meters high and the bunker was 12 meters long, 3.8 meters wide and 2 meters high. The police seized 38 antitank grenades, 22 electric detonators, 18 explosive devices, 17 kilograms of explosive charges and more than 20 fuses from the bunker.

In August 2001, police discovered a four-meter-deep tunnel under the house of a terrorist in Seriqsoghet Village, Uzun Township, Kuqa County, and confiscated 61 explosive devices from the tunnel, which also contained various kinds of equipment for making arms and ammunition.

6. Plotting and Organizing Disturbances and Riots, and Creating an Atmosphere of Terror

In order to create an atmosphere of tension and fear, and extend its political influence, the "East Turkistan" terrorist forces plotted and organized riots and disturbances many times, by engaging in terrorist acts of beating, smashing, looting, arson and murder, which seriously endangered social stability, people's lives and property.

On April 5, 1990, a group of terrorists, aided and abetted by the "East Turkistan Islamic Party," created a grave terrorist incident in Barin Township, Akto County, Xinjiang. They brazenly preached a "holy war," the "elimination of pagans" and the setting up of an "East Turkistan Republic." The terrorists tried to put pressure on the government by taking ten persons hostage, demolished two cars at a traffic junction and killed six policemen. They shot at the besieged government functionaries with submachine guns and pistols, and threw explosives and hand-grenades at them.

From February 5 to 8, 1997, the "East Turkistan Islamic Party of Allah" and some other terrorist organizations perpetrated the Yining Incident, a serious riot during which the terrorists shouted slogans calling for the establishment of an "Islamic Kingdom." They attacked innocent people, destroyed stores and burned and otherwise damaged cars and buses. During this incident seven innocent people were killed, more than 200 people were injured, more than 30 vehicles were damaged and two private houses were burned down. The terrorists attacked a young couple on their way home, knifing the wife to death after disfiguring her and severely injuring the husband. A staff member of a township cultural station was stabbed to death and then thrown into a fire.

Besides engaging in terrorist violence within China's borders, the "East Turkistan" terrorist forces have also been involved in violent incidents beyond the borders.

In March 1997, "East Turkistan" terrorists opened fire at the Chinese embassy in Turkey, and attacked the Chinese consulate-general in Istanbul, burning the Chinese national flag flying there.

On March 5, 1998, they launched a bomb attack against the Chinese consulate-general in Istanbul.

In March 2000, Nighmet Bosakof, president of the Kyrgyzstan "Uygur Youth Alliance," was shot dead in front of his house by members of a terrorist organization named the "East Turkistan Liberation Organization" because he had refused to cooperate with them.

In May 2000, members of the "Uygur Liberation Organization" beyond the boundaries extorted US$100,000 as ransom after kidnapping a Xinjiang businessman, murdered his nephew, and set the Bishket Market of Chinese Commodities on fire. On May 25, 2000, terrorists attacked the work team of the Xinjiang People's Government which went to Kyrgyzstan to deal with the above case, causing one death and two injuries. The culprits then fled to Kazakhstan, killing two Kazakhstan policemen who were searching for them in Alma-Ata in September the same year.

The ironclad details of these bloody facts are irrefutable proof of the nature of the "East Turkistan" forces as a terrorist organization that does not flinch from taking violent measures to kill the innocent and harm society so as to achieve the goal of splitting the motherland.

III

There is plenty of evidence to show that most of the terrorist and other violent incidents which have occurred in Xinjiang were directly plotted and engineered by the "East Turkistan" organization beyond China's borders, with the collusion of a handful of people within the borders.

The 15 cases of arson caused by chemical comburents in Urumqi, the regional capital of Xinjiang, in May 1998 were plotted and carried out by members of the "East Turkistan Liberation Organization" from beyond China's borders who had slipped into Xinjiang.

In February 1998, dozens of members of the "East Turkistan Islamic Movement" who had received special training in Afghanistan sneaked into Xinjiang and inland provinces and cities, and established 15 secret cells to offer technical training in explosives to 150 terrorists from various regions. They purchased a large amount of chemical raw materials to secretly produce explosives and other devices, according to the formula supplied by the terrorist organization beyond China's borders. In September 1998, in one search operation alone the Xinjiang police seized more than 300 trunks of over 20 varieties of chemical raw materials, totaling six tons, for producing explosives in the warehouse of the Urumqi North Railway Station.

In 1998, a gang led by Hogaxim Qasim from Hotan County and Muhammatjan Huxir from Bole City, both in Xinjiang, went to Afghanistan to join the "Islamic Holy Warriors," an "East Turkistan" terrorist organization, and received special training in shooting, demolition and assassination. In December the same year, they were secretly sent back to Xinjiang to establish organizations, recruit members, raise funds, collect arms and ammunition, and organize terrorist and other violent activities.

Organized and plotted by terrorists dispatched by the "East Turkistan Islamic Movement" outside China in 1999, terrorists in Hotan established an underground organization, which set up dozens of secret cells in seven counties and cities of the Hotan area for terrorist training and production of explosives and other arms and ammunition. The antitank grenades seized from them by the police alone totaled over 4,500, along with 98 guns of various types and tools for producing guns and explosives.

The "East Turkistan" terrorists also smuggled arms into China with the collusion of people both within and beyond the country's borders to arm fellow terrorists in China. On April 6, 1998, the Chinese customs and frontier checkpost at the Qorghas land port discovered six pistols, one folding submachinegun, over 19,000 bullets and more than 90 antitank grenades in a sheep wool container. The culprits confessed that they had acted under the orders of the "East Turkistan International Committee" and the "East Turkistan Liberation Organization" outside China, and had smuggled arms and ammunition into China 17 times.

The "East Turkistan" terrorists are closely connected with international terrorist forces.

The "East Turkistan" terrorist organization based in South Asia has the unstinting support of Osama bin Laden, and is an important part of his terrorist forces. The "East Turkistan Islamic Movement" headed by Hasan Mahsum is supported and directed by bin Laden. Since the formation of the "East Turkistan Islamic Movement," bin Laden has schemed with the heads of the Central and West Asian terrorist organizations many times to help the "East Turkistan" terrorist forces in Xinjiang launch a "holy war," with the aim of setting up a theocratic "Islam state" in Xinjiang.

The terrorist forces led by bin Laden have given much financial and material aid to the "East Turkistan" terrorists. In early 1999, bin Laden met with the ringleader of the "East Turkistan Islamic Movement," asking him to "coordinate every move with the 'Uzbekistan Islamic Liberation Movement' and the Taliban," while promising financial aid. In February 2001, the bin Laden terrorists and Taliban leaders met at Kandahar to discuss the training of "East Turkistan" terrorists. They decided to allocate a fabulous sum of money for training the "East Turkistan" terrorists and promised to bear the funds for their operations in 2001. Moreover, the bin Laden terrorists, the Taliban and the "Uzbekistan Islamic Liberation Movement" have offered a great deal of arms and ammunition, means of transportation and telecommunication equipment to the "East Turkistan" terrorists.

Bin Laden's group has also directly trained personnel for the "East Turkistan" forces. Hasan Mahsum chose some criminals, religious extremists and national separatists both from home and abroad for training at bin Laden's terrorists training camps in Afghanistan, at Kandahar, Mazari Sharif, and other places. After the training, some of the key "East Turkistan" members were secretly sent back to China to set up terrorist organizations, and planned and carried out terrorist activities; some joined the Taliban armed forces in Afghanistan, some joined the Chechen terrorists in Russia and some took part in terrorist activities in Central Asia. In August 1999, "East Turkistan" terrorists bore a part in kidnapping four Japanese scientists and senior local officers of the Kyrgyzstan Ministry of Internal Affairs in south Kyrgyzstan, and held them hostage, and in August 2000, they took part in the invasion of Uzbekistan and the mountain area of south Kyrgyzstan, attacking local government forces of the two countries.

Most of the explosions, assassinations and other terrorist incidents that have taken place in Xinjiang in recent years are related to these organizations. So far, the Chinese police have arrested over 100 terrorists who had sneaked into Xinjiang after being trained in terrorist training bases in Afghanistan and other countries. The police of some other nations have also extradited or transferred to China a dozen or so "East Turkistan" terrorists they captured.

As the appeal for international cooperation in curbing terrorism is becoming increasingly stronger following the "September 11" terrorist attacks in the United States, the "East Turkistan" forces that bear evident marks of terrorism have found themselves in an extremely embarrassing situation. While they are distressed by the destruction of the bin Laden terrorist forces and Taliban terrorist training bases by US missiles, they cannot but "take the initiative" to express their support for the US military retaliation, attempting to distance themselves from the bin Laden terrorist forces. To erase their terrorist marks and conceal their label as a terrorist organization, they have demanded that their members not publish radical remarks for the time being, in order to avoid being linked with terrorist organizations by the countries in which they are located. The terrorist organizations in South Asia lost no time in conducting a secret strategic shift, evacuating their members in Afghanistan to the surrounding South and Central Asian and Middle East regions to preserve and accumulate their strength. Meanwhile, the "East Turkistan" terrorist forces have employed the tactic of mounting attacks as a means of defense. Once again, under the banner of protecting "human rights," "religious freedom" and "the interests of ethnic minorities," they claim that the Chinese government "has taken the opportunity to crack down on ethnic minorities," in an attempt to mislead the public and deceive international opinion, and thus dodge the international crackdown on terrorism.

IV

To achieve their aim of splitting China, in recent years the handful of the "East Turkistan" terrorists within and outside the territory of China have carried out a series of sabotage activities by means of terrorism and violence. It is only natural that this has been firmly opposed by people of all ethnic groups in China, including the Uygur people in Xinjiang. In order to protect the lives and property and common interests of the people of various ethnic groups, maintain the stability of China's Xinjiang and the surrounding regions, safeguard national unity, social stability and the smooth progress of the modernization drive, the Chinese government has resolutely cracked down on the violent activities of the "East Turkistan" terrorist forces in accordance with the law. However, the Chinese government targets only a few core members and criminals who have schemed, directed and participated in violent terrorist incidents. Toward the majority of the people involved, who have been hoodwinked into bearing a part in some of the activities of the "East Turkistan" terrorist organization, the Chinese government adopts the attitude of educating and helping them, and welcomes them back to the true path. The ethnic groups in Xinjiang have always had the glorious tradition of loving and safeguarding national unity, and Islam is a peace-loving religion. The Chinese government's crackdown on the "East Turkistan" terrorist forces is not directed at any particular ethnic group or any particular religion, but at criminal activities of violence and terrorism, in order to better protect the common interests of the country's various ethnic groups and safeguard normal religious activities. All the people in the country, including the people of all ethnic groups in Xinjiang, have given wholehearted support to the Chinese government's policies. Over the past few years, the situation in Xinjiang has been stable, and the people's peaceful living and working environments have been effectively safeguarded. The people there have been living and working in peace and contentment.

After the September 11 incident, terrorist activities have become discredited worldwide and the "East Turkistan" terrorists in Xinjiang have gone underground temporarily. The situation in Xinjiang is stable, and the people there live and work as usual. The Chinese government has not taken advantage of any opportunity to institute "suppression," nor does it deem it necessary to do so. It is obvious that the "East Turkistan" terrorist organizations are brazenly peddling rumors out of ulterior motives.

China's Xinjiang Uygur Autonomous Region exercises regional ethnic autonomy, and carries out the policies of ethnic equality and freedom of religion. It fully respects and protects the various rights of ethnic minorities and the citizen's freedom of religious belief. With the wholehearted support of the people all over the country and the common endeavors of the people of all ethnic groups in Xinjiang, the various undertakings in Xinjiang have advanced by leaps and bounds. The people of different ethnic groups, the various religions, and religious believers and non-believers respect each other and treat each other equally, co-exist in peace and harmony, and pursue common development. The region presents a scene of prosperity. Although there are still a handful of "East Turkistan" terrorists both at home and abroad, it is impossible for them to fundamentally affect Xinjiang's excellent situation, in which the society is stable, the people of all ethnic groups are united, the various undertakings are making progress and people's lives are constantly improving.

The Chinese government opposes terrorism in any form; at the same time it opposes the application of double standards concerning the anti-terrorism issue. Any tolerance or indulgence toward the "East Turkistan" terrorist forces will not harm China and the Chinese people alone. Today, as the international community becomes more clearly and deeply aware of the harm brought about by terrorism, we hope that all peace-loving people throughout the world, regardless of ethnic status or religious belief, region or country, political or social system, will fully recognize the nature of the "East Turkistan" terrorist forces and the serious harm caused by them, see through all their disguises, and jointly crack down on their terrorist activities, leaving not a single opportunity for them to exploit to their advantage.

FIRST BATCH OF "EASTERN TURKISTAN" TERRORIST GROUPS, INDIVIDUALS IDENTIFIED[3]

December 15, 2003

Beijing, Dec. 15 (Xinhua)—China's Ministry of Public Security on Monday publicized a list of the first batch of identified "Eastern Turkistan" terrorist organizations and 11 members of the groups.

The following is its full text:

Contents

List of the first batch of identified "Eastern Turkistan" terrorist organizations

I. The Eastern Turkistan Islamic Movement (ETIM)

II. The Eastern Turkistan Liberation Organization (ETLO)

III. The World Uyghur Youth Congress (WUYC)

IV. The East Turkistan Information Center (ETIC)

List of the First Batch of Identified "Eastern Turkistan" Terrorists

I. Hasan Mahsum

II. Muhanmetemin Hazret

III. Dolqun Isa

IV. Abudujelili Kalakash

V. Abudukadir Yapuquan

VI. Abudumijit Muhammatkelim

VII. Abudula Kariaji

VIII. Abulimit Turxun

IX. Hudaberdi Haxerbik

X. Yasen Muhammat

XI. Atahan Abuduhani

List of the first batch of identified "Eastern Turkistan" terrorist organizations

I. The Eastern Turkistan Islamic Movement (ETIM)

The Eastern Turkistan Islamic Movement (ETIM), also called the Eastern Turkistan Islamic Party, Allah Party or the Eastern Turkistan National Revolution Association, is one of the most dangerous terrorist organizations among "Eastern Turkistan" terrorist forces. It acts for the aim of splitting China by means of terror and establishing a theocratic "Eastern Turkistan Islamic State" in Xinjiang, northwest China. In 1993, Muhanmmed Tuhit and Abudu Rehmen, both natives of Hotan, Xinjiang, along with other "Eastern Turkistan" activists, founded the ETIM. But the organization disintegrated late that year. In 1997, Hasan Mahsum and Abudukadir Yapuquan ganged up with other "Eastern Turkistan" activists to restore this organization. On September 11, 2002, the ETIM was put on the list of global terrorist organizations by the United Nations.

1. Major acts of terrorism performed by the ETIM

In recent years, the ETIM has established bases outside China to train terrorists, and has constantly sent agents to sneak into the Chinese territory to mastermind and guide terrorist and sabotage activities.

In early 1998, the ETIM dispatched Usiman Yimit, Memet Reman and 10 other terrorists to carry out acts of terrors in China. They set up more than 10 secretive training grounds, where over 150 terrorists were trained. Memet Reman, a key leading member of this terrorist ring, purchased 301 boxes of raw chemical materials in more than 20 varieties, which weighed 6 tons and cost 102,000 yuan (12,290 dollars), in Urumqi, capital of Xinjiang. The terrorists planned to make explosives with these materials and use them for large-scale bomb blasts and assassinations across the region.

Between early 1998 and the end of 1999, the ETIM ordered the Hotan Kulex terror gang to set up several secret lairs in Hotan Prefecture, southwest Xinjiang, to produce explosives and train terrorists. The gang manufactured more than 5,000 hand grenades and detonation devices, and gradually developed into an outfit of more than 1,000 members. It was responsible for the December 14 terrorist killings in Moyu County of Hotan Prefecture in 1999, the February 4 robbery and murder case in Urumqi the same year, and other acts of terror, which in all claimed the lives of six innocent people and caused heavy property losses.

In one of their terrorist attacks launched in Xinhe County of Xinjiang, ETIM members shot dead a policeman on June 18, 1999.

To date, Chinese police have seized 98 guns of all varieties, more than 4,500 hand grenades and a large cache of swords and knives, detonation devices and raw explosive materials that belong to the ETIM and its subordinates.

2. Chief leader of the ETIM

Hasan Mahsum, also known as Ashan Sumut, Abdu Mohammad, or Hasang Zunduluohe on foreign soils, male, of the Uyghur ethnic group, was born in 1964. A native of Shule (Kunixar) County, Kashi Prefecture in Xinjiang, Hasan Mahsum was arrested in October 1993 by the Chinese police on a charge of performing acts of terror, and the judiciary ruled Hasan Mahsum receive three years of reeducation through labor. In 1997, he fled China and has since stayed in terrorist training camps in Afghanistan to coach terrorists, and has plotted a series of bloody terrorist attacks in Xinjiang.

3. Major sources of funds and personnel of the ETIM

The funding of the ETIM mainly comes from the Al-Qaeda [Al-Qa'ida] outfit of Usama Bin Laden. The group also makes money through drug trafficking, arms smuggling, kidnapping, blackmailing, robbery and other organized crimes. The ETIM mainly picks its recruits from separatists, convicted criminals and terrorists who have run away from Xinjiang, and offers them secret training for terrorist missions.

4. Relations between the ETIM and other global terrorist organizations

The ETIM is closely linked to Usama Bin Ladin's Al-Qaeda outfit, and has got an all-out support from the Taliban regime of Afghanistan and the Al-Qaeda in its training of armed personnel and terrorists. The ETIM sends its members to training bases of the Taliban forces and the Al-Qaeda outfit for military training, and then dispatches them back to Xinjiang, China, to form terrorist groups and conduct terrorist activities like bomb blasts, assassinations and poisoning.

II. The Eastern Turkistan Liberation Organization (ETLO)

The Eastern Turkistan Liberation Organization (ETLO), also known as the Eastern Turkistan National Party, is one of the most dangerous terrorist organizations among "Eastern Turkistan" terrorist forces. It acts for the aim of founding an "Eastern Turkistan" state in Xinjiang, China, by means of violence and terror. The ETLO was founded in Turkey with its headquarters in Istanbul. The founder of the ETLO is Muhanmetemin Hazret, and its main leaders include Umer Kanat, Dolqun Isa and Ubul Kasimu.

1. Major acts of terrorism performed by the ETLO

After its founding, the ETLO has conducted a series of violent terrorist crimes in China and across Central Asia, with some South and West Asian countries as the base camp for terrorist training and Central Asia as the forward position and bridgehead for terrorist operations.

On April 6, 1998, Muhanmetemin Hazret directed his ETLO members to smuggle 6 military pistols, 1 submachine gun, over 19,000 bullets, 92 hand grenades, 45 grenade fuses, 2 bottles of tube-shape explosives, 4 boxes of casket-shape explosives and 100 detonators into China via the Horgos Port in Xinjiang.

On May 23, 1998, ETLO agents committed arson in a series of cases in Urumqi, capital city of Xinjiang.

Between May and June 1998, Askar Tuhti, Ahmet, Balamjan Ahmet and some other ETLO members launched bomb attacks in the state of Oshskaya, Kirghizstan.

In 1999, the Internal Affairs Department of Alma-Ata, Kazakhstan, cracked a major criminal case, in which four Uyghurs were murdered with their bodies cut into pieces in June 1998. Investigations showed that it was Abulimit Turxun, a chieftain of the ETLO, who had committed the murder to prevent possible information leakage by two ETLO members attempting to quit the terrorist group. The Kazak police who captured ETLO members in Alma-Ata also found the organization's detailed plans for plane hijacking and jailbreaks in a notebook they seized.

In May 2000, the Xinjiang Regional People's Government sent officials to help investigate a blaze at the "Tur Bazaar" in Bishkek City, Kirghizstan. On May 25, terrorists sent by the ETLO shot at the officials, killing the Foreign Affairs Office director of the Kyrgyz Autonomous Prefecture of Kizilsu,

Xinjiang, on the spot and injuring a deputy chief of the prefecture's Public Security Bureau. The terrorists then escaped to Kazakhstan, where they murdered two local police on duty in Alma-Ata in September the same year.

On May 18, 2000, members of the ETLO conducted an armed robbery of the Alma-Ata World Bank in Kazakhstan, but were later captured by the Kazak police. In December 2001, Lahmatula Yusubof and Muhtedin, both members of a Kazak extremist organization, were arrested by the Kazakhstan internal affairs department on charges of robbery, illegal possession of arms and murder. The two confessed that since 1997, they had been involved in several acts of terror masterminded by the ETLO.

In September 2001, the ETLO assigned Abulat Tursun and Ahmet (alias Parhat) to smuggle large quantities of arms and ammunition into China. The arsenal, purchased overseas, included 5 mini-submachine guns, 7 India-made handguns, over 1,000 submachine gun bullets and more than 400 handgun bullets. The two then entered China from the Zham Port in Tibet, southwest China, in an attempt to carry out sabotage activities on the Chinese soil. On February 19, 2003, the Chinese police uncovered the terrorist group they had developed.

On June 29, 2002, Arken Yakuf and Rahmutulla Islayil, both members of the ETLO, murdered Chinese diplomat Wang Jianping in Bishkek, Kirghizstan. The local police found at the their residence handguns they had used in the killing along with some grenades, which had been accepted as hard evidence by the local judiciary.

2. Chief leader of the ETLO

Muhanmetemin Hazret, or Mamtimin Hazrat in Uyghur, male, of the Uyghur ethnic group, was born in 1950. A native of Moyu County, Hotan Prefecture in Xinjiang, and a college graduate, Muhanmetemin Hazret used to work for the Xinjiang Film Studio until he fled to Turkey in 1989. He founded the ETLO in 1996 and has since mustered a large number of violent terrorists to attend training on terror in regions like Chechenya of Russia. He is behind a series of violent terrorist crimes in China and across Central Asia.

3. Major sources of funds and personnel of the ETLO

The funding of the ETLO mainly comes from armed robbery, drug trafficking and arms smuggling, as well as gift money given by the Al-Qaeda outfit. It mainly recruits young Xinjiang Uyghurs under the age of 30 in Central Asia, and convicted criminals and violent terrorists who escaped from

Xinjiang. It provides religious, military and physical training to prepare them for terrorist activities.

4. Relations between the ETLO and other global terrorist organizations

Under the support of Taliban, the ETLO has sent its new recruits, all youths from Xinjiang, to some training camps in Afghanistan, where they are first brainwashed with religious extremist ideas and then receive military training. In 1998, Osama Bin Laden provided the ETLO and the Eastern Turkistan Islamic Movement with funds up to several million US dollars, helping them spread religious extremism and carry out terrorist activities. Under the reign of the Taliban regime, the ETLO was allowed to run special military training camps at Mazari Sharif and Khost, Afghanistan.

In 1999, when armed forces of the Islamic Movement of Uzbekistan invaded the southern part of Kirghizstan, Muhanmetemin Hazret provided a financial assistance of 600,000 US dollars, one third of which was for the training of "Eastern Turkistan" terrorists who joined in the military operations of the Islamic Movement of Uzbekistan.

In 1997, the ETLO sent its members to fight in Chechenya, a move the Chechen rebels repaid with a generous supply of weapons and ammunition and military coaches.

Most diehard members of the ETLO are also key figures in the Eastern Turkistan Islamic Movement (ETIM) terrorist organization. For example, Abulimit Turxun, former head of the ETLO Kazakhstan branch, is also head of an Islamic suicide squad under the ETIM. Arken Yakuf and Rahmutulla Islayil, the two murderers who killed Chinese diplomat Wang Jianping in Kirghizstan on June 29, 2002, are members of both the ETIM and the ETLO. From March 19 to March 22, 1998, the two terrorist organizations met in Bishkek and signed a joint declaration, announcing the decision to jointly establish a so-called league of "The Eastern Turkistan Union of Jihad".

III. The World Uyghur Youth Congress (WUYC)

The World Uyghur Youth Congress (WUYC), also known as the International Uyghur Youths League, the World Uyghur Youths League, or International Eastern Turkistan Youths Congress, is jointly founded by a band of Uyghurs who have fled abroad from Xinjiang, China, and decedents of Xinjiang people living abroad. It is a terrorist organization aiming at splitting Xinjiang from China. The First WUYC was held in Munich, Germany, in November 1996.

1. Major acts of terrorism performed by the WUYC

Major leading members and subordinate groupings of the WUYC have been active in performing violent acts of terrorism. The former chairman of the WUYC, Dolqun Isa, have organized criminal gangs in Xinjiang, creating incidents of theft, robbery and explosion, among others. He has also played an active role in terrorist activities. As vice president of the Eastern Turkistan Liberation Organization at present, Dolqun Isa assists the terrorist organization's leader, Muhanmetemin Hazret, in collaborating with other terrorist groups outside China to engage in violent terrorist activities. He also oversees the operations of the organization's branch in Germany. The first chairman of the WUYC, Umer Kanat, and chairman of the Eastern Turkistan National Freedom Center, Enwar Yusuf, are responsible for the United States branch of the Eastern Turkistan Liberation Organization. The Eastern Turkistan Youths League (launched in Istanbul, Turkey, in March 1993, and later moving to Switzerland and becoming part of the WUYC) clearly advocates in its charter "the development of strong and powerful underground forces to overthrow the existing Chinese regime and realize the independence of Xinjiang". The WUYC has, since its founding, formulated action plans to assassinate Party, government and military leaders of the Xinjiang Uyghur Autonomous Region, destroy railways and bridges, initiate terrorist explosions, attack Chinese agencies stationed abroad, and create armed disturbances at the border areas between China and India, Tajikistan and Afghanistan. In 1993, the WUYC masterminded and implemented two explosions in Xinjiang, one in the office building of the Kashi Agricultural Machinery Company and the other in a video lounge in Shache County, which left two persons dead and 22 others injured.

2. Chief leader of the WUYC

Dolqun Isa, or Dolkun Aisa in Uyghur, male, of the Uyghur ethnic group, was born on September 2, 1967. A native of Aksu City in Xinjiang, China, and a senior high school graduate, Dolqun Isa later absconded to Turkey and assumed the post of vice president of the Eastern Turkistan Liberation Organization. He became chairman of the executive committee of the WUYC in November 1996, and held the position of WUYC chairman for three consecutive terms afterwards. In November 2002, he served as vice chairman of the preparatory committee of the Eastern Turkistan Uyghur Congress. When in Xinjiang, Dolqun Isa formed a gang with lawbreakers to commit theft, robbery and other crimes and carry out explosions and other terrorist activities. In addition, he spares no efforts to advertise terrorist ideas and support acts of terror of all kinds.

3. Major sources of funds and personnel of the WUYC

The WUYC mainly resorts to theft, robbery or other criminal means for funding. It also receives financial aid from other international terrorist organizations. Most of its recruits are Uyghur youths living outside China.

4. Relations between the WUYC and other terrorist organizations

The WUYC is closely tied to other terrorist organizations. Its subordinate grouping, the Eastern Turkistan Youths League, maintains a close relationship with organizations in West Asia engaging in violence. It has asked these organizations many times for help in purchasing arms and explosives. The WUYC also keeps cooperative relations with other "Eastern Turkistan" terrorist organizations. In convening the Third WUYC, it got support from the Eastern Turkistan Liberation Organization, and Muhanmetemin Hazret, leader of the Eastern Turkistan Liberation Organization, has always served as an aegis for Dolqun Isa.

The WUYC also energetically helps "Eastern Turkistan" terrorists. In 2002, Dolqun Isa, in collaboration with Ahmat Tuhit, sent people to Alma-Ata, Kazakhstan, to take Muhammat Wupur, a terrorist, to a training camp at the border between Afghanistan and Uzbekistan, and later transfer him to Germany to seek "asylum".

The WUYC and terrorist organizations like the Eastern Turkistan Liberation Organization and the Eastern Turkistan Islamic Movement support each other, and they are interrelated. Abudu Salam, head of the law department of the first session of the WUYC, is concurrently an assistant to vice chairman of the Eastern Turkistan Islamic Movement. The key members of the WUYC also take important posts in the Eastern Turkistan Liberation Organization. After the Sept. 11 terrorist attacks against the United States, Hasan Mahsum, head of the Eastern Turkistan Islamic Movement, tried to draw close to the WUYC led by Dolqun Isa for help in whitewashing the notoriety of the Eastern Turkistan Islamic Movement as a terrorist organization. The WUYC also actively collaborates with other international terrorist organizations.

IV. The East Turkistan Information Center (ETIC)

The East Turkistan Information Center (ETIC), also known as East Turkistan Liaison Center, was founded in Munich, Germany, in June 1996 by a band of separatists of Xinjiang origin residing in the European country. It is a terrorist organization aiming at developing networks inside China, masterminding and carrying out violent acts of terrorism, and inciting religious extremism and "Jihad".

1. Major acts of terrorism performed by the ETIC

The ETIC has long been using various media, especially the Internet, for its propaganda on terrorism, extremism and separatism. In the articles the organization published, including "Is There Hope for Our Independence" and "To Win Independence or to Die", the ETIC openly advertises religious extremist ideas and advocates "Jihad" by means of violence and terror. It calls on Muslims in the Chinese territory to employ explosives and poisons to create terrorist incidents targeted at kindergartens and schools of the Han people and government establishments, and attack the Chinese armed forces, in an attempt to "achieve our goals by reaching the high tide of such campaigns."

The ETIC is active in supporting "Eastern Turkistan" terrorism, extremism and separatism, and provides shelter for terrorists. It has sent secret information via the Internet to "Eastern Turkistan" activists inside China on how to make poisons and explosives. The organization has masterminded and directed destructive terrorist activities targeted at petroleum pipelines, natural gas pipelines, railways and other large civilian infrastructure facilities in China. In March 2003, the ETIC plotted explosions along the railway between Lanzhou of Gansu Province and Hami of Xinjiang.

2. Chief leader of the ETIC

Born in 1960, Abudujelili Kalakash, or Abduljelil Karakash or Abdujelil Karikax in Uyghur, male, of the Uyghur ethnic group, is a native of Moyu County in Hotan Prefecture, Xinjiang. He is concurrently vice chairman of the Eastern Turkistan National Congress and ETIC president. After the February 5 Incident of Yining in Xinjiang in 1997, he encouraged "Eastern Turkistan" activists in China to continue such terrorist activities, claiming "the larger scale an incident of the sort is launched on, the better the result it will produce." In April 1999, he collaborated with Muhanmetemin Hazret, leader of the Eastern Turkistan Liberation Organization, and others in mapping out plans for terrorist activities in Africa, an area no "Eastern Turkistan" organizations and Uyghurs have set foot in, with focus placed on bomb attacks against Chinese embassies there. After the September 11 Incident, Abudujelili Kalakash met secretly with Abudukadir Yapuquan, vice chairman of the Eastern Turkistan Islamic Movement, and other, to discuss future plans. In late June 2002, he secretly transmitted to "Eastern Turkistan" activists in China through the Internet information on how to make poisons and explosives in preparation for acts of violence and terror.

3. Personnel and major sources of funds of the ETIC

Abudujelili Kalakash is the founder and first president of the East Turkistan Information Center. The major members of the ETIC are divided into two groups. One is composed of staff workers in the public identity of journalists and publishers. There are 30 staff members at the ETIC headquarters, including 8 full-time workers, and 40 journalists and publishers operating in 18 countries. The other group consists of the so-called secret information providers hired inside and outside China, who are in fact fugitive convicts wanted by the Chinese police and "Eastern Turkistan" terrorists trained outside China.

Abudujelili Kalakash uses diversified channels to raise funds for hiring staff, building and maintaining the website and financing secret agents. On October 16, 1999, the first session of the 2nd Eastern Turkistan National Congress delegated to Abudujelili Kalakash the right to raise funds in the name of the congress. The funding also comes from regular donations offered by merchants of Xinjiang origin in Turkey and Saudi Arabia and other ethnic separatist organizations, donations from Xinjiang merchants doing businesses outside China, and capital provided by the Eastern Turkistan Liberation Organization.

4. Relations between the ETIC and other international terrorist organizations

ETIC President Abudujelili Kalakash also serves as vice chairman of the World Uyghur Youths Congress, an "Eastern Turkistan" terrorist organization. After 1998, he joined the Eastern Turkistan Liberation Organization headed by Muhanmetemin Hazret, and has since played an active role in the organization's terrorist activities targeted at Xinjiang.

List of the First Batch of Identified "Eastern Turkistan" Terrorists

I. Hasan Mahsum

1. Brief account of Hasan Mahsum

Hasan Mahsum, or Hesen Mehsum in Uyghur (also known as Ashan Sumut or Hasang Zunduluohe), male, of the Uyghur ethnic group, was born in 1964. A native of 5th Team of 12th Village of Alaf Township in Shule (Kunixar) County, Kashi Prefecture of Xinjiang, China, the former peasant with primary school education now heads the Eastern Turkistan Islamic Movement terrorist organization. Currently, he concentrates his activities mainly in some South Asian counties and regions. The Chinese police has requested the Interpol to issue a red notice targeting him.

2. Major activities of Hasan Mahsum

Hasan Mahsum was detained by the Chinese police for instigating and engaging in acts of violence and terror in 1993, and the judiciary ruled he receive reeducation through labor for a term of three years. He fled abroad in 1997.

Once outside China, Hasan Mahsum gathered together a band of Xinjiang religious extremists to form and serve as chairman of the Eastern Turkistan Islamic Movement terrorist organization, which advocates the establishment of the so-called Eastern Turkistan Islamic State in Xinjiang by means of "Jihad". In September 1998, he moved the headquarters of the terrorist organization to Kabul, Afghanistan. Under the sponsorship of Bin Laden's Al-Qaeda outfit, the Taliban regime and the Islamic Movement of Uzbekistan, Hasan Mahsum set up several training camps, raised funds and recruited members. He organized physical and military training for more than 600 violent terrorists, and masterminded and directed several terrorist incidents in Xinjiang.

In 1998, Hasan Mahsum sent Usiman Yimit, Memet Reman and other 10 violent terrorists to China to carry out violent terrorist acts. They set up a dozen secret training camps and trained more than 150 terrorists. Memet Reman, a diehard member of the group, went to Urumqi, capital of Xinjiang, and purchased over 20 kinds of chemical materials to make explosives in an attempt to launch large-scale bomb blasts and assassinations in Xinjiang. The chemical materials he bought, cased in 301 boxes and weighing 6 tons, cost 102,000 yuan (12,290 US dollars).

Between early 1998 and the end of 1999, Hasan Mahsum exercised direct leadership of the Kulex Gang in Hotan Prefecture, southwest Xinjiang. During that time, the terrorist gang set up several underground explosives-production workshops in the prefecture, trained personnel, produced more than 5,000 hand grenades and other explosive devices, and recruited more than 1,000 members. The gang was responsible for a murder of violent terrorist nature in Moyu County of Hotan on December 14, 1999, and robbery and murder cases on February 4 the same year in Urumqi, which in all claimed the lives of 6 innocent people and caused heavy property losses.

After the September 11 Incident, Hasan Mahsum has continued plotting and carrying out terrorist activities.

II. Muhanmetemin Hazret

1. Brief account of Muhanmetemin Hazret

Muhanmetemin Hazret, or Mamtimin Hazrat in Uyghur, male, of the Uyghur ethnic group, was born in 1950. A native of Moyu County in Hotan Prefecture, Xinjiang, China, the college graduate worked for the Xinjiang Film Studio until he fled to Turkey in 1989. He currently heads the Eastern Turkistan Liberation Organization terrorist organization and mainly operates in West and Central Asia. The Chinese police has requested the Interpol to issue a red notice targeting him.

2. Major activities of Muhanmetemin Hazret

Muhanmetemin Hazret established the Eastern Turkistan Liberation Organization in 1996 and claimed president of the terrorist group. Since then, he has mustered a large number of violent terrorists and trained them in Chechnya of Russia, before sending them to the Chinese territory in batches to carry out acts of violence and terror. To extend the sphere of activities of the Eastern Turkistan Liberation Organization, he has set up branches in Central Asian nations like Kazakhstan and Kirghizstan. He is behind a series of robberies and murders in the two countries in the last few years, which were aimed at raising fund to support the terrorist organization.

In 1998, Muhanmetemin Hazret dispatched his members to smuggle arms and ammunition into China in preparation for acts of violence and terror. In February 1998, Muhanmetemin Hazret sent Hemit and a dozen other terrorists to Yining City and Yining County in Xinjiang, where they held six training courses for over 20 terrorists. Muhanmetemin Hazret also assigned them to fetch smuggled arms and ammunition and work out a list of persons to be assassinated.

On April 6, 1998, Muhanmetemin Hazret directed his followers to smuggle 6 Soviet-made military pistols, 1 submachine gun, over 19, 000 bullets, 92 hand grenades, 45 grenade fuses, 2 bottles of tube-shape explosives, 4 boxes of casket-shape explosives and 1 package of 100 detonators into China via the Horgos Port.

On May 23, 1998, Muhanmetemin Hazret sent Ayat and other terrorists to Urumqi, where they committed arson in 15 cases, causing deaths and enormous property losses to the local people.

In the summer of 1999, Muhanmetemin Hazret dispatched four of his followers under the disguise of tourists to Xinjiang to look for hiding places for terrorists in large numbers. They studied and mapped the terrain of Baicheng County and the area along the Tarim River.

On March 28, 2000, Muhanmetemin Hazret sent personnel to Bishkek, capital of Kirghizstan, where they shot dead Nihmet Bosakef, chairman of the Uyghur Youths League.

In May 2000, the Xinjiang Regional People's Government sent officials to help investigate a blaze at the "Tur Bazaar" in Bishkek. On May 25, terrorists assigned by Muhanmetemin Hazret shot dead the Foreign Affairs Office director of the Kyrgyz Autonomous Prefecture of Kizilsu, Xinjiang, and injured a deputy chief of the prefecture's Public Security Bureau. The gunmen then fled to Kazakhstan, where they murdered two local police on duty in the Kazak capital of Alma-Ata in September of the same year.

In June, Muhanmetemin Hazret directed his subordinates Arken Yakuf and Rahmutulla Islayil to murder Wang Jianping, a diplomat of the Chinese Embassy to Kirghizstan.

On January 29, 2003, Muhanmetemin Hazret claimed in an interview with Radio Free Asia: "It is inevitable that we have to establish a military organization to show our determination on the issue of Eastern Turkistan to our enemies and friends."

On February 19, 2003, Chinese police uncovered in the northern province of Hebei a terrorist group organized by Abulat Tursun, a terrorist dispatched by Muhanmetemin Hazret. Abulat confessed that he had smuggled 5 mini-submachine guns, 7 pistols and more than 1, 400 bullets into Xinjiang in an attempt to carry out terrorist activities.

III. Dolqun Isa

1. Brief account of Dolqun Isa

Dolqun Isa, or Dolkun Aisa in Uyghur, male, of the Uyghur ethnic group, was born on September 2, 1967. A native of Aksu City, Xinjiang, China, the senior high school graduate is one of the key members of the Eastern Turkistan Liberation Organization and has been head of the World Uyghur Youths Congress terrorist organization for many years. Dolqun Isa is now the target of an Interpol red notice (File No. 40684/97; Control No. A-539/10-1997). He currently concentrates his activities mainly in Germany.

2. Major activities of Dolqun Isa

After he fled to Turkey, Dolqun Isa became vice president of the Eastern
Turkistan Liberation Organization. In 1994, he organized the Eastern Turkistan
Students Union and served as chairman and concurrently chief editor of
the Eastern Turkistan Youth newspaper. In 1996, he moved to Germany and
joined the Eastern Turkistan Union in Europe. In November 1996, he assumed
the post of chairman of the executive committee of the World Uyghur Youths
Congress and acted as chairman of the terrorist organization for three terms
in succession. In November 2002, he resigned the chairmanship and became
vice chairman of the preparatory committee of the Eastern Turkistan Uyghur
Congress.

When in Xinjiang, Dolqun Isa formed a gang with several convicted criminals to commit burglary, robbery and other crime and participated in masterminding a series of bomb blasts in Xinhe County. Since he fled abroad,
he has organized and participated in all sorts of terrorist activities launched
by the Eastern Turkistan Liberation Organization. At a gathering to mark
the 10th anniversary of the so-called December 12 student movement of
Xinjiang in Ankara, Turkey, on December 14, 1995, Dolqun Isa claimed,
"The uprising against the Chinese tyranny in Hotan Prefecture was organized by us."

IV. Abudujelili Kalakash

1. Brief account of Abudujelili Kalakash

Abudujelili Kalakash, or Abduljelil Karakash or Abdujelil Karikax in Uyghur,
male, of the Uyghur ethnic group, and born in 1960, is a native of Moyu
County in Hotan Prefecture, Xinjiang, China. He heads the East Turkistan
Information Center terrorist organization and is a key member of the World
Uyghur Youths Congress, another terrorist organization. Abudujelili Kalakash
now operates in Germany most of the time. The Chinese police has requested
the Interpol to issue a red notice targeting him.

2. Major activities of Abudujelili Kalakash

Abudujelili Kalakash settled down in Munich, Germany, in 1987. In 1996,
he established the East Turkistan Information Center and was elected vice
chairman of the First International Uyghur Youths Congress the same year.
He became vice chairman of the Eastern Turkistan National Congress in
1999, and is now president of the East Turkistan Information Center, vice
chairman of the German-Uyghur Friendship Association, anchorman of

Voice of Uyghur, chief editor of The Sparkle weekly and Eastern Turkistan Youth newspaper, and concurrently vice chairman of the Eastern Turkistan National Congress.

Abudujelili Kalakash stands for putting pressure on the Chinese government by means of terror and force. After the February 5 Incident in Yining of Xinjiang occurred in 1997, which involved acts of beating, smashing, burning and killing, Abudujelili Kalakash encouraged "Eastern Turkistan" activists in the Chinese territory, claiming that "the larger scale an incident of the sort is launched on, the better the result it will produce." He also contacted terrorist organizations in the Middle East and asked them to help train Uyghurs for acts of violence and terror. In April 1999, Abudujelili Kalakash reached a consensus with Mantimin Hazrat, leader of the Eastern Turkistan Liberation Organization, and other diehard terrorists on spreading terrorism. They decided to carry out terrorist activities in Africa, an area no "Eastern Turkistan" organizations and Uyghurs had set foot in at that time, and planned a series of bomb attacks against Chinese embassies there. In May 2001, his East Turkistan Information Center sent a message of threat to a Hong Kong trade delegation, in an attempt to force the delegation to cancel its business tour of Xinjiang. After the September 11 Incident, Abudujelili Kalakash met secretly with Abudukadir Yapuquan, vice chairman of the Eastern Turkistan Islamic Movement, and other terrorists, to discuss future action plans. In late June 2002, he constantly used the Internet to teach "Eastern Turkistan" activists in the Chinese territory how to make poisons and explosives in preparations for acts of violence and terror. In November 2002, he claimed "Eastern Turkistan" terrorist organizations "could arouse worldwide attention only when they destroy China's economy through 'Jihad.'" Between January and March 2003, Abudujelili Kalakash contacted with Silam Asan (male, Uyghur, native of Kashi, Xinjiang), a terrorist in the Chinese territory, via the Internet, and they plotted explosions on the railway between Lanzhou of Gansu Province and Hami of Xinjiang. On March 14, 2003, Chinese police uncovered the case. Silam Asan and his accomplice Memet Abula Abuliz both confessed that they were conducting violent terrorist activities under the direction of Abudujelili Kalakash.

V. Abudukadir Yapuquan

1. Brief account of Abudukadir Yapuquan

Abudukadir Yapuquan (original name Yabudukader Emit), or Abdukadir Uapqan in Uyghur, male, of the Uyghur ethnic group, was born in 1958. A native of Uapqan Township, Shufu County, Kashi Prefecture of Xinjiang, China, the junior high school graduate fled abroad in 1997 together with

Hasan Mahsum. Abudukadir Yapuquan is a key member of the Eastern Turkistan Islamic Movement terrorist organization, and now mainly operates in West and South Asia. The Chinese police has requested the Interpol to issue a red notice targeting him.

2. Major activities of Abudukadir Yapuquan

After he fled abroad, Abudukadir Yapuquan and Hasan Mahsum organized the Eastern Turkistan Islamic Movement terrorist organization and served as vice chairman, advocating establishing an "Eastern Turkistan Islamic State" in Xinjiang through "Jihad". Afterwards, Abudukadir Yapuquan set up training camps in Afghanistan to train terrorists. In 1998, he dispatched and directed Usiman Yimit, a diehard member of the terror group, and some others to enter the Chinese territory to raise funds, recruit personnel, and manufacture homemade arms and explosive devices in Xinjiang. The Chinese police uncovered the case, and Usiman Yimit confessed that he had committed acts of violence and terror under the direction of Abudukadir Yapuquan and Abudula Kariaji. Abudukadir Yapuquan is also responsible for organizing and implementing a series of robberies and murders such as the December 14 Case in Moyu County of Hotan Prefecture in 1999 and the February 4 Case in Urumqi, which resulted in deaths and injuries of innocent people. In 2001, Abudukadir Yapuquan took advantage of the pilgrimage to Mecca and led over 50 violent terrorists, who had been trained in Afghanistan, to Saudi Arabia to raise funds and preach the ideas of "Jihad" and the establishment of an independent "Eastern Turkistan Islamic State". Since the United Nations puts the Eastern Turkistan Islamic Movement on the list of international terrorist organizations, Abudukadir Yapuquan has mainly hidden in West and South Asia, engaging in terrorist activities.

VI. Abudumijit Muhammatkelim

1. Brief account of Abudumijit Muhammatkelim

Abudumijit Muhammatkelim (Abdumijit Mamatkrim in Uyghur), also known as Zibibulla, male, of the Uyghur ethnic group, was born in September 1967. A native of Shufu County of Kashi Prefecture, Xinjiang, China, the junior high school graduate has organized and masterminded several cases of gun killing, robbery and explosion. He fled abroad in July 1996 holding a false passport. Abudumijit Muhammatkelim is a key member of the Eastern Turkistan Islamic Movement terrorist organization and a target of the Interpol's red notice (File No. 40679/97; Control No. A-543/10-1997). He operates mainly in West and South Asia at present.

2. Major activities of Abudumijit Muhammatkelim

From 1991 to 1994, Abudumijit Muhammatkelim participated in a number of theft and robbery cases in Xinjiang. In January 1992, he masterminded a failed explosion in Akto County of Xinjiang and harbored a prime culprit of the case and a handgun. In December 1994, Abudumijit Muhammatkelim organized a terrorist group with himself as the head, which plotted acts of violence and terror with purchased and homemade weapons and ammunition. He directed his followers to commit a robbery on February 10, 1996, in Onsu County of Xinjiang, which involved the gun killing of two policemen and a herdsman. Under his instruction, Yasin Molla Memet and a dozen other followers in the Chinese territory broke into the homes of Kawul Tika and three other villagers in Kunas Village of Alahag Township, Kuqa County, Xinjiang, on April 29, 1996, killing four villagers and injured three others with explosives, guns and knives. On May 12 the same year, Abudumijit Muhammatkelim directed Abudulla and two other terrorists in an operation in Kashi City, Xinjiang, where the three chopped at religious personnel Arunhan Haji (vice chairman of the Xinjiang Uyghur Autonomous Region and head of Atigar Mosque) and his son Anwar with knives, leaving the father and son in severe injury.

Abudumijit Muhammatkelim joined the Eastern Turkistan Islamic Movement in 1997 and is one of the chiefs of the terrorist organization mainly responsible for personnel training and exterior liaison.

VII. Abudula Kariaji

1. Brief account of Abudula Kariaji

Abudula Kariaji, formerly named Abudulla Dawut, or Abdulla Kariaji in Uyghur, male, of the Uyghur ethnic group, was born in December 1969. A native of Shache County of Kashi Prefecture, Xinjiang, China, the junior high school graduate is a key member of the Eastern Turkistan Islamic Movement terrorist organization. Abudula Kariaji now concentrates on activities mainly in some South Asian countries. The Chinese police has requested the Interpol to issue a red notice targeting him.

2. Major activities of Abudula Kariaji

Abudula Kariaji fled to Afghanistan and received training for acts of violence and terror in 1995. He later joined the Eastern Turkistan Islamic Movement and served as vice chairman.

Abudula Kariaji has engaged in acts of violence and terror outside China for a long time, organizing military and physical training for a large number of terrorists in bases the terrorist group sets up outside China, and participating in masterminding and directing terrorist activities within the Chinese territory.

In 1998, Abudula Kariaji dispatched Usiman Yimit and other diehard members of the Eastern Turkistan Islamic Movement to sneak into China and directed them to raise funds, recruit members and made weapons and explosive devices in Xinjiang. The Chinese police uncovered the case and Usiman Yimit confessed his involvement in terrorist activities under the instructions of Abudukadir Yapuquan and Abudula Kariaji. In September 2001, Abudula Kariaji assigned Mutalip Abudu Rahman and other terrorists to enter China to recruit members and smuggle them to Afghanistan to join terrorist organizations via Nepal. The Chinese police unearthed the case and Mutalip Abudu Rahman confessed his involvement in violence and terrorism under the direction of Abudula Kariaji.

VIII. Abulimit Turxun

1. Brief account of Abulimit Turxun

Abulimit Turxun, or Ablimit Tursun in Uyghur, male, of the Uyghur ethnic group, was born in May 1964. A native of Urumqi City, Xinjiang, China, Abulimit Turxun is a key member of the Eastern Turkistan Liberation Organization terrorist organization. The Chinese police has requested the Interpol to issue a red notice targeting him.

2. Major activities of Abulimit Turxun

In 1997, Abulimit Turxun fled abroad and joined the Eastern Turkistan Liberation Organization headed by Muhanmetemin Hazret in Kazakhstan. He smuggled weapons into China on April 6, 1998, and was also responsible for a series of violent criminal cases including robbery, homicide and attack against police in Kazakhstan and Kirghizstan. In early 1998, Abulimit Turxun mustered Ayat Mahmut and other terrorists in Alma-Ata City of Kazakhstan for terrorist training. In early May 1998, he sent Ayat Mahmut and other terrorists into China, where they made more than 40 chemical combustible devices and used them in 15 consecutive cases of arson in some big stores and wholesale markets in Urumqi, capital of Xinjiang, on May 23, causing heavy economic losses. The Chinese police cracked the case and Ayat Mahmut confessed his involvement in the terrorist activities under the direction of Abulimit Turxun.

During a fund-raising campaign in Alma-Ata in June 1998, Abulimit Turxun killed four Uyghurs and dismembered their bodies, just to prevent possible information leak by two members of the Eastern Turkistan Liberation Organization, who intended to quit the terrorist group after an internal conflict.

IX. Hudaberdi Haxerbik

1. Brief account of Hudaberdi Haxerbik

Hudaberdi Haxerbik, or Hudabardiy Hacerbak in Uyghur, male, of the Uyghur ethnic group, was born in August 1970. A native of the 1st Team of Memeyar Village, the Hui Autonomous Township of Yuqunweng in Yining County, Xinjiang, China, Hudaberdi Haxerbik is a key member of the Eastern Turkistan Liberation Organization terrorist group. The Chinese police has requested the Interpol to issue a red notice targeting him.

2. Major activities of Hudaberdi Haxerbik

Hudaberdi Haxerbik has actively engaged in acts of violence and terror since he joined the terror ring headed by Ibulayin Ismayil in Yining City in August 1996 and another terrorist gang led by Hemit Muhanmed in April 1997. The Chinese police destroyed the two gangs, and both Ibulayin Ismayil and Hemit Muhanmed testified to Hudaberdi Haxerbik's active role in plotting and conducting terrorist activities.

On April 6, 1998, Hudaberdi Haxerbik, assigned by the Eastern Turkistan Liberation Organization, smuggled large quantities of arms and ammunition, hand grenades and explosive devices into China through the land port of Horgos in preparation for terrorist activities. He fled with a gun after the operation was foiled.

X. Yasen Muhammat

1. Brief account of Yasen Muhammat

Yasen Muhammat, or Yasen Mammat in Uyghur, alias Yasen Kari, male, married, of the Uyghur ethnic group, was born in 1964. He is a native of the 6th Team of 11th Village in Boskem Town, Zepu County of Xinjiang, China, and a junior high school graduate. The Chinese police has requested the Interpol to issue a red notice targeting him.

2. Major activities of Yasen Muhammat

In 1996, Yasen Muhammat organized and trained terrorists. In October 1998, he and Ahet Yimin and other fugitive terrorists began organizing and plotting acts of violence and terror, while making guns and ammunition, explosive devices and knives in large quantities.

On August 23 1999, Yasen Muhammat, Ahet Yimin and three other terrorists broke into the home of police officer Hudaberd in Boskem Township of Zepu County and shot dead the policeman and his son Aiez (a teacher of the township high school). In an attempt to murder Chinese policemen on October 21, 1999, Yasen Muhammat and Balat Alifu and other accomplices shot dead Tursun Kader, a driver who parked his vehicle in front of the police station in Gulbah Town, Zepu County, and injured Abudukader Muhamed, a township government employee. On October 24, 1999, Yasen Muhammat, Muhanmed Tursun Kari and other accomplices stole into the compound of Seli Township police station, bringing with them homemade guns, explosive devices and knives. They shot dead security assistant Altawula, injured police officer Wang Yazhou and security assistant Muhmed Yizemu, and killed Mehmut Yidelis, a criminal suspect of theft detained in the station for questioning, before they set fire to 10 office rooms, one jeep and three motorcycles of the police station.

XI. Atahan Abuduhani

1. Brief account of Atahan Abuduhani

Atahan Abuduhani, or Atahan Abduheni in Uyghur, male, of the Uyghur ethnic group, was born in May 1964. A native of the 3rd Team of 9th Village in Luoke Town, Yecheng County of Xinjiang, China, and a primary school graduate, he is a target of the Interpol's red notice (File No. 40682/97; Control No. A-551/10-1997). Currently, Atahan Abuduhani mainly concentrates on activities in Central Asia.

2. Major activities of Atahan Abuduhani

Atahan Abuduhani fled abroad in December 1984, and accepted the Islamic extremist thoughts and kept close contact with "Eastern Turkistan" organizations outside China. In August 1991, Atahan Abuduhani smuggled 7 handguns and 180 bullets into China. With the arms, his accomplices robbed a security van belonging to the Shayar County branch of the Agricultural Bank of China in Xinjiang on November 13 that year, causing heavy life and property losses. The Chinese police cracked the case and seized major culprits Yidelis and Yimit Talifu, who confessed that it was Atahan Abuduhani who provided them with the arms for terrorist activities. In September 1991, customs officers at the Susit Port of Pakistan seized 3 handguns and 300 bullets Atahan Abuduhani was trying to smuggle into China. Despite the failure, Atahan Abuduhani has made several attempts to smuggle arms into China afterwards.

CHINA IDENTIFIES ALLEGED "EASTERN TURKISTAN" TERRORISTS[4]

October 21, 2008

BEIJING, Oct. 21 (Xinhua)—China's Ministry of Public Security on Tuesday published the identities of eight alleged terrorists connected to the East Turkistan Islamic Movement (ETIM), which has been identified by the United Nations as a terrorist organization.

Following are their names and the charges against them:

I. Memetiming Memeti, born in Oct. 10, 1971, and formerly named Memetiming Aximu. A Chinese citizen, he is also known as Abuduhake, Memetiming Qekeman, Muhelisi, Saifuding.

With primary school education, Memetiming Memeti is head of the ETIM. His Identity number is 653225197110100533.

Charges against him include:

1. Participating in and leading the terrorist organization

In March 1998, Memetiming Memeti illegally exited China and joined the ETIM terrorist organization in a south Asian country. He then became a military trainer in the organization's training camp.

In November 2003, he became head of the ETIM after its former head Hasan Mahsum was shot dead. He raised funds, recruited terrorists and continued to develop the terrorist organization. He organized physical and military training for dozens of terrorists, and led the ETIM members to continue their violent terrorist activities.

In January, he issued an order to conduct terrorist attack specifically targeting the Beijing Olympic Games.

2. Recruiting members for the terrorist organization

For a long time, Memetiming Memeti has been sending key members of the ETIM to a certain Middle East country to spread separatism and extremism among Chinese people residing there, and trying to persuade them to join the ETIM.

In 2006, he sent a key ETIM member, Abdushukur, to a south Asian country to persuade young people there to join the terrorist organization by giving financial aid and spreading extremism.

Beginning 2007, he was very active in recruiting new members, and sent them to undergo training in physical endurance, firearms, military tactics and making explosives and poisons. Their purpose was to sabotage the Beijing Olympics in particular.

3. Inciting terrorist activities

In 2004, Memetiming Memeti organized the production of propaganda discs about the terrorist activities of ETIM former head Hasan Mahsum, and distributed them in China.

In January 2005, via the ETIM website, he called on the "Xinjiang Uygur people" to support and help the ETIM, and urged "all the Xinjiang muslims" to take part in "jihad".

In June 2008, he appeared in a video in which terrorism threats were made, which was broadcast on the ETIM website as well as the world's largest video-sharing website. He warned "all the athletes and audience prepared to take part in the Beijing Olympic Games" that "all strength has been concentrated" and "action has been in the implementation phase". He threatened to "give the Chinese government the deadliest strike by the simplest means" and "turn the year 2008 into China's year of condolence".

4. Masterminding, plotting and implementing terrorist activities

In August 2004, Memetiming Memeti ordered ETIM terrorists to blast a "Chinese club" in a south Asian nation.

Since August 2007, he and other leaders of the organization have sent a dozen terrorists to China as well as to Middle East and west Asian countries through illegal channels for anti-Olympic activities.

Under his guidance, trained terrorists sneaked into China's Xinjiang and other areas, set up terrorist groups, raised funds and bought chemical raw materials for making explosives and poisons, and purchased vehicles for terrorist attacks. They planned to sabotage the Olympic Games by conducting terrorist attacks within the Chinese territory before the Games opened.

Memetiming Memeti also sent dozens of terrorist teams to some Middle East and west Asian countries to raise funds and buy explosive materials for terrorist attacks against Chinese targets outside Chinese territory.

II. Emeti Yakuf, also know as Aibu Abudureheman and Saifula, was born on March 14, 1965.

He is a Chinese national with the official identity number of 65312719 6503140336. He is accused of being a key member of the ETIM, which is recognized by the United Nations as a terrorist group.

Charges against him include:

1. In November 1996, Emeti Yakuf illegally exited China for a South Asian country, joined the ETIM there and received terrorism training. In September 1998, he became a key member of the terrorist group. Since 2001, he has acted as ETIM military commander, in charge of recruiting new members, organizing terrorism training, as well as planning and carrying out terrorist attacks.

2. Since 2001, Emeti Yakuf, directed by another ETIM leader Memetiming Memeti, has recruited people with extremist ideologies in a Middle East country. Since the end of 2007, he ordered ETIM members to enter Chinese territory to prepare terrorist attacks against the Beijing Olympics.

3. Emeti Yakuf organized terrorism training camps in a South Asian country, training dozens of extremists in military and terrorist skills. Those trainees were sent to countries in the Middle East and West Asia. Dozens of terrorists were trained for seven months by Emeti Yakuf to learn how to make explosives and poison.

4. Since 2007, Emeti Yakuf has spread extremist philosophy and terrorism propaganda within China. In June 2008, Emeti Yakuf released an video statement on the ETIM website and a popular video website to stir up so-called "holy war" against the Beijing Olympics, threatening to attack Chinese government employees, service people, police, as well as politicians from Western countries, athletes and spectators, who were in Beijing for the Olympics. They even threatened to use biological and chemical weapons during the Olympic Games.

5. In January 2008, Emeti Yakuf worked out a detailed plan of terrorist attacks against the Beijing Olympics. Since August 2007, Emeti Yakuf has sent more than 10 terrorists to China and other countries to find opportunities to initiate explosions. Emeti Yakuf disseminated manuals and formulas on making explosives and poisons. Emeti Yakuf organized funding for ETIM terrorist groups worth hundreds of thousands yuan. Since 2008, Emeti Yakuf has issued several directives to his followers to conduct terrorist activities targeted at the Beijing Olympics.

III. Memetituersun Yiming, also known as Abuduaini, was born in1974. He is a Chinese national with ID number 65302119740830003X. With technical secondary school education, he is one of the key members of the ETIM.

Charges against him include:

1. Participating and supervising the terrorist organization

Memetituersun Yiming fled China and joined the ETIM in 1999. He received terrorist training in an East Asian country and became the bodyguard and driver for ETIM former head Hasan Mahsum. He then became responsible for the organization's logistics and fund-raising.

2. Recruiting members and collecting funds for the ETIM

For a long time, he took orders from his supervisor Emeri Yakufand by advocating extremist and secessionist ideas to encourage people in west Asia to join his organizations, and collect and raise funds for terrorist activities.

He also plotted and organized terrorist attacks targeting the Beijing Olympics. In the first half of 2008, he went to a west Asian country and organized more than 10 ETIM members to launch terrorist attacks, and tested bombs, and prepared to enter China illegally to carry out his activities. He also attempted to use explosives in terrorist attacks on targets both inside and outside China.

IV. Memetituersun Abuduhalike, also known as Metusun Abuduhalike, Ansarui or Naijimuding, was born in 1976. He is a Chinese national with ID card number 6532221976060144576 and a middle school education. He is one of the key members of the ETIM.

Charges against him include:

1. Participating in and supervising a terrorist organization

He illegally went abroad in May 1996, and joined the ETIM in 1997 when he began to receive terrorist training. After Hasan Mahsum was shot dead in November 2003, he became a key member of the ETIM, and was responsible for the organization's website maintenance and computer management.

2. Making videos of terrorist threats

In June and July, he made video footage of terrorist attacks against the Beijing Olympics for Memetiming Memeti and Emeti Yakuf, and broadcast them on a major video-sharing website. The video encouraged terrorists to launch attacks on targets in China, to achieve the goal of creating an atmosphere of terror and spreading the influence of terrorism.

3. Inciting terrorist activities

For a long time, Memetituersun Abuduhalike advocated extremist and violent terrorist ideology among extremists in China, taught them how to make poison and explosives and other methods for terrorist attacks, and encouraged them to launch terrorist attacks in the country. With his propaganda and incitement, extremists in Xinjiang formed terrorist groups and committed violent attacks against government organizations, police and the public before and during the Beijing Olympics.

4. Providing funds for terrorist activities.

Since April 2007, Memetituersun Abuduhalike took orders from Emeti Yahuf and sent large sums of money through financial organizations to support the activities of terrorist groups in China, the Middle East and west Asia, to help them purchase raw materials for making explosives and poisons, to buy vehicles and rent houses, in preparation for terrorist attacks.

V. Xiamisidingaihemaiti Abudumijiti, also known as Saiyide, was born in 1972, a Chinese national, with college education. His ID number is 653101 197211020819. He was identified by the United Nations as a core member of the ETIM.

Charges against him include:

1. Xiamisidingaihemaiti Abudumijiti illegally exited China in 1999 and joined the ETIM in a south Asian country in May 2006. In October 1999, he received specialized training in the terrorist training camp, including using weapons and making bombs, and became a core member of ETIM.

2. In December 2007, Xiamisidingaihemaiti Abudumijiti was dispatched by ETIM head Memetiming Memeti to a Middle East country, where he preached separatism and extremism among local Chinese, induced people who believed in extremism to join the terrorist organization, and built up a terrorist group to launch attacks abroad.

3. From December 2007 to June 2008, Xiamisidingaihemaiti Abudumijiti raised money for terrorist attacks in the Middle East country. He purchased large amounts of chemicals for making bombs, and focused on a supermarket where many Chinese business people assembled as the attack target. He planned to blow up the supermarket before the opening of Beijing Olympics.

VI. Aikemilai Wumaierjiang, was born in 1977, a Chinese national with junior high school education. His ID card number is 654126197706010012. He was identified by the United Nations as an ETIM member and a core member of the terrorist branch built up by Xiamisidingaihemaiti Abudumijiti.

Charges against him include:

1. Aikemilai Wumaierjiang illegally exited China in 2006. In December 2007, Xiamisidingaihemaiti Abudumijiti encouraged him to joining ETIM.

2. He assisted Xiamisidingaihemaiti Abudumijiti in the conspiracy to bomb a supermarket where Chinese business people assembled before the opening of Beijing Olympics.

VII. Yakuf Memeti, also known as Abudujilili Aimaiti, Abudula or Punjab, was born in 1976, a Chinese national with vocational secondary school education. His ID number is 652927760128101, and passport code is P.2631544. He is a key member of the terrorist group East Turkistan Islamic Movement.

Charges against him include:

1. Participating in terrorist groups

Memeti fled China in 1999 and joined the ETIM in a south Asian country where he received physical training, and instruction on using weapons and making explosive devices for six months in 2007.

2. Implementing terrorist activities

In July 2008, Yakuf Memeti received orders from ETIM military commander Aimaiti Yakuf in a south Asian country, and planned to sneak into China for a suicide attack targeting the Beijing Olympics. He also accepted a secret task assigned by ETIM head Memetiming Memeti and gathered information on Chinese companies and neighborhoods in a south Asian country. With local informants' help, he located a large oil refinery as target, but his attempts failed due to strict security.

VIII. Tuersun Toheti

Tuersun Toheti, also known as Mubaixier or Nurula, was born in 1975. A Chinese national, his ID number is 653125750620041. He finished senior high school and is a key member of the ETIM.

Charges against him include:

1. Participating in a terrorist organization

In August 1999, Tuersun Toheti joined the ETIM in a south Asian country and received training in terrorism skills. In 2002, he was designated to central and west Asian regions.

2. Implementing terrorist activities

In June 2008, Tuersun Toheti saw an ETIM terror threat video when he was in a west Asian country and contacted the organization's military commander Aimaiti Yakuf and key members like Memetituersun Abuduhalike in the hope of getting details of the terror plan. He also requested Aimaiti Yakuf send him chemical formulas of explosives as soon as possible.

In July of 2008, Tuersun Toheti organized a terrorist team with the organizations and prepared for terror attacks. They were actively involved in raising money, buying raw materials to make explosives and testing explosions, conspiring to attack Chinese targets during the Beijing Olympics.

Appendix C

―∞∞∞―

ETIM Member Biographies

ACTIVE ETIM MEMBERS

Abdul Haq al-Turkistani[1]

AKA: Abdelhaqq al-Turkestani, Abdul Haq Turkistani, Amir Abdul Haq, Shaykh Abdulhak, Abdul Haq, Abdul Heq, Abd Al-Haq, Abdulheq, Abuduhake, Abdul Saimaiti, Jundallah, Maimaiti Iman, Maimaitiming MaiMaiti, Maiumaitimin Maimaiti, Memetiming Memeti, Memetiming Qekeman, Memetiming Aximu, Muhammad Ahmed Khaliq, Muhelisi, Qerman, Saifuding
Date of Birth: October 10, 1971
Place of Birth: Chele County, Khuttan Area, Xinjiang
Gender: Male
Identity Number: 653225197110100533
Role: Overall emir
Location: Unknown, but likely the Waziristan area of Pakistan's Federally Administered Tribal Areas (FATA)
Notes: The ETIM's Shura Council selected Abdul Haq al-Turkistani to lead the organization after Hasan Mahsum died. Before this promotion, Abdul Haq al-Turkistani led the ETIM's Military Affairs Division.[2]

Several of the GTMO Uyghurs reported that the person running the day-to-day operations of their training camp in 2001 was Abdul Haq.[3]

The U.S. government added Abdul Haq al-Turkistani to its finance blacklist on April 20, 2009. Several previously unpublished aliases appeared on this list, which suggests the U.S. government obtained them from nonpublic sources.

Abu Khaled Saifallah[4]

AKA: Emeti Yakuf, Aibu Abudureheman, Commander Seyfullah, Commander Saifallah, Komutan Seyfullah, Saifula, Seyfullah
Date of Birth: March 14, 1965
Gender: Male
Identity Number: 653127196503140336[5]
Role: Head of the Military Affairs Division
Location: Unknown, but likely Waziristan
Notes: "Saifallah" means "sword of God" in Arabic. The Chinese government outlined specific charges against Saifallah in 2008, saying he is "in charge of recruiting new members, organizing terrorism training, as well as planning and carrying out terrorist attacks."[6]

Abu Khaled Saifallah appeared in ETIM videos threatening the Olympics.[7] He also wrote an article in the ETIM's magazine.[8]

Abudula Kariaji[9]

AKA: Abdulla Kariaji, Abudulla Dawut
Date of Birth: December 1969
Place of Birth: Shache County, Kashgar Prefecture, Xinjiang
Gender: Male
Role: Deputy emir
Location: Unknown, but he is believed to move about freely
Notes: China identified Kariaji as the ETIM's deputy emir in December 2003.[10] Kariaji himself reportedly admitted to being the deputy emir in a 2004 interview with the *Wall Street Journal*.[11] The Chinese government outlined several specific charges against Kariaji in 2003, accusing him of "participating in, masterminding, and directing terrorist activities within the Chinese territory."[12]

Abu Ja'afar al-Mansour[13]

AKA: Abdullah Mansur, Abdullah Mansour[14]
Gender: Male
Role: Part of the ETIM's Religious Education Division[15]
Location: Unknown, but likely Waziristan
Notes: Abu Ja'afar al-Mansour appeared in ETIM videos[16] and wrote an article in the ETIM's magazine.[17]

Abu Umar al-Farouq[18]

Gender: Male
Role: Member
Location: Unknown, but likely Waziristan
Notes: Abu Umar al-Farouq wrote an article in the ETIM's magazine.

Shaykh Bashir[19]

Gender: Male
Location: Unknown, but likely Waziristan
Notes: Shaykh Bashir was the spokesman in an ETIM video titled, "Why Are We Fighting China?"

Memetituersun Yiming[20]

AKA: Abuduaini
Date of Birth: 1974
Gender: Male
Identity Number: 65302119740830003X
Role: Member in charge of logistics and fund-raising
Notes: Memetituersun Yiming was Hasan Mahsum's bodyguard and driver. He now reports to Abu Khaled Saifallah.

In 2008, the PRC claimed Memetituersun Yiming belonged to the ETIM and charged him with planning attacks against the 2008 Olympics.

Memetituersun Abuduhalike[21]

AKA: Metusun Abuduhalike, Ansarui, Naijimuding
Date of Birth: 1976
Gender: Male
Identity Number: 6532221976060144576
Role: Responsible for website and computer management
Notes: In 2008, the PRC claimed Memetituersun Abuduhalike belonged to the ETIM and accused him of providing funds, encouraging terrorist attacks, advocating extremist ideology, and teaching others how to make poisons and explosives.

Xiamisidingaihemaiti Abudumijiti[22]

AKA: Saiyide
Date of Birth: 1972
Gender: Male

Identity Number: 653101197211020819
Notes: In 2008, the PRC claimed Xiamisidingaihemaiti Abudumijiti belonged to the ETIM and accused him of recruiting, raising funds, and procuring weapons. He reports to Abdul Haq.

Aikemilai Wumaierjiang[23]

Date of Birth: 1977
Gender: Male
Identity Number: 654126197706010012
Notes: In 2008, the PRC claimed Aikemilai Wumaierjiang belonged to the ETIM and accused him of attempted terrorist activities. He works with Xiamisidingaihemaiti Abudumijiti.

Yakuf Memeti[24]

AKA: Abudujilili Aimaiti, Abudula, Punjab
Date of Birth: 1976
Gender: Male
Identity Number: 652927760128101
Passport Number: P.2631544
Notes: In 2008, the PRC claimed Yakuf Memeti belonged to the ETIM and accused him of attempted terrorist activities. He reports to Abu Khaled Saifallah.

Tuersun Toheti[25]

AKA: Mubaixier, Nurula
Date of Birth: 1975
Gender: Male
Identity Number: 653125750620041
Notes: In 2008, the PRC claimed Tuersun Toheti belonged to the ETIM and accused him of planning bombings, procuring weapons, and raising funds. He reports to Abu Khaled Saifallah and Memetituersun Abuduhalike.

Abudukadir Yapuquan[26]

AKA: Yabudukader Emit, Abudukadeer Yafuquan
Date of Birth: 1958
Place of Birth: Uapqan Township, Shufu County, Kashgar Prefecture, Xinjiang
Gender: Male
Role: Helped re-establish the ETIM in 1997

Notes: Abudukadir Yapuquan was with Hasan Mahsum in 1997 when Mahsum re-established the ETIM.[27] In 2003, the PRC identified Abudukadir Yapuquan as an ETIM member.[28]

Abudumijit Muhammatkelim[29]

AKA: Zibibulla, Abdumijit Mamatkrim
Date of Birth: September 1967
Place of Birth: Shufu County, Kashgar Prefecture, Xinjiang
Gender: Male
Role: Responsible for personnel training and exterior liaison
Notes: In 2003, the PRC claimed Abudumijit Muhammatkelim belonged to the ETIM and charged him with bombings, murder, and robbery. The PRC indicated an INTERPOL red notice had been issued for him. INTERPOL's website notes that the objective of a red notice is "to seek the arrest or provisional arrest of wanted persons with a view to extradition."[30]

Abdushukur[31]

Gender: Male
Role: Recruiter
Notes: In 2008, the PRC claimed Abdushukur belonged to the ETIM. He reports to Abdul Haq and was sent to an unspecified south Asian country to provide financial aid in order recruit ETIM members.

Muhammat Tursun[32]

Gender: Male
Role: Cell leader
Notes: The PRC claimed Muhammat Tursun led a group that assassinated imams in 1997.

Usiman Yimit[33]

Gender: Male
Role: Member
Notes: In 2002, the PRC claimed Usiman Yimit belonged to the ETIM. He allegedly helped set up more than 10 training camps, where more than 150 people received terrorist training. In 1998, Usiman Yimit also allegedly helped purchase 301 boxes of raw chemical materials and planned to build explosives from them, then use the explosives for large-scale bombings and assassinations across Xinjiang. He reports to Abudula Kariaji.

Memet Reman[34]

Gender: Male
Role: Member
Notes: In 2002, the PRC claimed Memet Reman belonged to the ETIM.
In 1998, he allegedly helped set up more than 10 training camps, where more
than 150 people received terrorist training. Memet Reman also allegedly
helped purchase 301 boxes of raw chemical materials and planned to build
explosives from them, then use the explosives for large-scale bombings and
assassinations across Xinjiang.

Abdulla Salim[35]

AKA: Abu Salam
Gender: Male
Role: Recruiter
Location: Pakistan (as of 2001)
Notes: Abdulla Salim referred at least two of the GTMO Uyghurs (Abu Bakr
Qasim and Adel Abdulhehim) to a training camp in Afghanistan.

Abdul Kareem[36]

Gender: Male
Place of Birth: Koshar, Xinjiang
Role: Leader of breakaway ETIM faction
Notes: Abdul Kareem ran a breakaway faction of the ETIM known as the
Islamic Party of Reformation (*Hizbul Islah Al-Islami*) that was responsible
for several bombings between 1989 and 1990.[37] He was imprisoned by the
Chinese government in 1990 and was released in 2005. In 2008, the ETIM's
website claimed he had been released from prison and was now living,
teaching, and doing business in Koshar.[38]

ETIM MEMBERS DETAINED IN CHINA

Turdi Guzalinur[39]

Gender: Female
Role: Member
Notes: Turdi Guzalinur smuggled flammable liquids onto a flight from
Urumqi to Beijing in an effort to crash an airplane in 2008.

Hailiqiemu Abulizi[40]

Gender: Female
Date of Birth: Circa 1993

Role: Member
Notes: Hailiqiemu Abulizi was captured on August 10, 2008, in Kuqa, Xinjiang. She was injured when the bomb she was about to throw blew up prematurely.

Aji Muhammat[41]

Gender: Male
Role: Member and plot leader
Notes: Aji Muhammad was arrested in 2008 for leading a plot against the 2008 Olympics.

Abdurahman Azat[42]

Gender: Male
Role: Member
Notes: Abdurahman Azat was arrested for participating in an August 4, 2008, attack that killed 16 police who were exercising early in the morning.

Kurbanjan Hemit[43]

Gender: Male
Role: Member
Notes: Abdurahman Azat was arrested for participating in an August 4, 2008, attack that killed 16 police who were exercising early in the morning.

Ismail Kadir[44]

Gender: Male
Role: Third-highest-ranking leader
Notes: Ismail Kadir was arrested by Pakistani authorities and handed over to the PRC in March 2002. He was reportedly the third-highest-ranking ETIM leader at the time.

Sidike Hasimu[45]

Gender: Male
Role: Member
Notes: Sidike Hasimu was arrested in 1999 in possession of explosive chemicals. He trained in Jalalabad, Afghanistan.

Mutalifu Hasimu[46]

AKA: Mutalif Kasim, Mutalib Hasim
Place of Birth: Kashgar, Xinjiang

Gender: Male
Role: Member
Notes: Mutalifu Hasimu was sent to Xinjiang by Hasan Mahsum in 1999 to raise funds, procure weapons, and locate a map of the border between Afghanistan and China.

Huseyin Celil[47]

Date of Birth: Circa 1970
Gender: Male
Citizenship: Born a Chinese citizen; granted Canadian citizenship in 2001, but China does not recognize dual citizenship
Role: ETIM and ETLO member responsible for liaison between the two groups
Status: Sentenced to life in prison in China
Notes: Huseyin Celil was reportedly responsible for an alliance between the ETIM and ETLO in 1998. He reported to Hasan Mahsum. He was extradited from Uzbekistan to China in 2006.

Mutalip Abudu Rahman[48]

Gender: Male
Role: Recruiter
Notes: In 2001, Mutalip Abudu Rahman was sent from Afghanistan to China to recruit ETIM members to send back to Afghanistan. He reported to Abudula Kariaji.

DECEASED ETIM MEMBERS
Dia Uddin bin Yousef[49]

AKA: Dhiya-ud-deen bin Yousef, Dia' ud Deen b. Yusuf, Dia Uddin, Dia' ud Deen
Place of Birth: Kashgar, Xinjiang
Gender: Male
Notes: Dia Uddin bin Yousef re-established the ETIM in the late 1980s. He was killed leading the 1990 Baren Rebellion.

Hasan Mahsum[50]

AKA: Hasan Makhdoom, Hesen Mexsum, Hasan "Jundullah" Makhdoom, Hasan Sumuti, Ashan Sumut, Aishan Maihesumu, Hasang Zunduluohe, Abu Muhammad al-Turkistani
Date of Birth: 1964

Place of Birth: Alaf Township in Shule (Kunixar) County, Kashgar Prefecture, Xinjiang[51]
Gender: Male
Notes: Hasan Mahsum is a former emir of the ETIM. He studied Islam in a school founded by Abdul Hakeem, one of the scholars who started the original ETIM in 1940. Mahsum was detained in the 1990 Baren Rebellion and imprisoned several times. He became more militant in prison, and he re-established the ETIM in 1997.[52]

Mahsum led the ETIM from 1997 to 2003, when he was killed in an Al-Qaida stronghold in Pakistan.[53] He traveled abroad to solicit support for the ETIM, met with Osama bin Laden several times, and set up training camps in Afghanistan.[54]

Shaheed Abdul Wahhab[55]

Gender: Male
Place of Birth: Kashgar, Xinjiang
Notes: Abdul Wahhab left China in 1997 to train with the ETIM. He was detained and delayed in Russia but arrived at an unspecified ETIM camp in 2000. According to the ETIM's website, he later "took part in an operation in which he was martyred," or killed. ("Shaheed" means "martyr" in Arabic.)

Ismail Semed[56]

Gender: Male
Notes: Ismail Semed was deported from Pakistan to China in 2003 and executed on February 8, 2007, for "attempting to split the motherland" and "possessing firearms and explosives."

Zaiyiding Yusupu[57]

AKA: Zeydin Yusuf
Gender: Male
Notes: Zaiyiding Yusupu commanded the Baren Rebellion and died in the fighting on April 6, 1990.

Usama al-Turki[58]

Gender: Male
Notes: Usama al-Turki participated in an ETIM martyr video titled "Pidayi Usama." ("Pidayi" is a Uyghur word for a loyal volunteer, or someone willing to sacrifice his life.) Martyr videos are recorded before someone either goes into battle or commits a suicide attack. They are released after the person's death.

Shaheed Idris bin Omar[59]

AKA: Shaheed Idris B. Omar
Place of Birth: Kashgar, Xinjiang
Notes: Idris bin Omar studied Islam under Abdul Hakeem, one of the founders of the original ETIM. Bin Omar later joined Abdul Kareem's breakaway ETIM faction, the Islamic Party of Reformation (*Hizbul Islah Al-Islami*). This group was responsible for bombings in 1989 and 1990. Bin Omar was executed by the Chinese government in 1995.

UYGHURS DETAINED AT GTMO

Abdu Helil Mamut[60]

AKA: Abdul Helil Mamut, Abd Al Nasir, Abdul Nasser, Khaleel Mamut
Gender: Male
Internment Serial Number (ISN): 278
Role: Recruit who was training in the ETIM camp
Status: Released
Location: Bermuda
Notes: Abdu Helil Mamut arrived at the ETIM training camp in Tora Bora via Pakistan in June 2001. He was captured at a mosque in Pakistan after fleeing U.S. air strikes on Tora Bora.

Abdul Ghappar Abdul Rahman[61]

AKA: Abd al Ghatar Abd al Rahman
Gender: Male
ISN: 281
Role: Recruit who was training in the ETIM camp
Status: Ruled a "noncombatant," but remains in U.S. custody
Location: GTMO
Notes: Abdul Ghappar Abdul Rahman arrived at the ETIM training camp via Pakistan from Kyrgyzstan in June 2001. He was captured at a mosque in Pakistan after fleeing U.S. air strikes on Tora Bora. He admitted to knowing Abdul Haq, whom he had seen at the ETIM camp.

Abdul Razak[62]

AKA: Abdur Razakah, Abdal Razak Qadir
Gender: Male
ISN: 219
Role: Claimed he only delivered food to the ETIM camp
Status: Released

Location: Bermuda
Notes: Abdul Razak arrived at the ETIM training camp via Uzbekistan. He was captured at a mosque in Pakistan after fleeing U.S. air strikes on Tora Bora.

Abdul Semet[63]

AKA: Enam Abdulahat, Salahidin Abdulahat, Abd al Samad Abd al Ahad
Gender: Male
ISN: 295
Role: Recruit who was training in the ETIM camp
Status: Ruled a "noncombatant," but remains in U.S. custody
Location: GTMO
Notes: Abdul Semet arrived at the ETIM training camp via Pakistan in August 2001. He was captured at a mosque in Pakistan after fleeing U.S. air strikes on Tora Bora. He admitted to knowing Abdul Haq, whom he had seen at the ETIM camp.

Abu Bakr Qasim[64]

AKA: Abu Bakker Qassim
Gender: Male
ISN: 283
Role: Recruit who was training in the ETIM camp
Status: Released
Location: Albania
Notes: Abu Bakr Qasim arrived at the ETIM training camp via Pakistan from Kyrgyzstan in July 2001. He was captured at a mosque in Pakistan after fleeing U.S. air strikes on Tora Bora. He heard of the ETIM camp from an individual named Abu Salam, in Pakistan. (We have no further information on Abu Salam.)

Adel Abdulhehim[65]

AKA: Muhammad Qadir
Gender: Male
ISN: 293
Role: Recruit who was training in the ETIM camp
Status: Released
Location: Albania
Notes: Adel Abdulhehim arrived at the ETIM training camp via Pakistan from Kyrgyzstan in June 2001. He was captured at a mosque in Pakistan after fleeing U.S. air strikes on Tora Bora. He admitted to knowing Abdul Haq and Hasan Mahsum, whom he had seen at the ETIM camp.

Adel Noori[66]

Gender: Male
ISN: 584
Role: Member
Status: Ruled a "noncombatant," but remains in U.S. custody
Location: GTMO
Notes: Adel Noori was wanted by the PRC for participating in the 1990 Baren Rebellion. He stayed in an ETIM-run safe house in Kabul, Afghanistan, from July 26, 2001, until he fled the U.S.-led attack on Afghanistan. He was arrested in Lahore, Pakistan, with two Arabs. All three were wearing burkas, a loose garment usually worn by women.

Ahmad Tourson[67]

Gender: Male
ISN: 201
Role: Member
Status: Ruled a "noncombatant," but remains in U.S. custody
Location: GTMO
Notes: Ahmad Tourson was captured in Mazar-e-Sharif by Northern Alliance troops.

Ahmed Adil[68]

AKA: Ahnad Adil
Gender: Male
ISN: 260
Role: Recruit who was training in the ETIM camp
Status: Released
Location: Bermuda
Notes: Ahmed Adil arrived at the ETIM training camp via Pakistan in October 2001. He was captured at a mosque in Pakistan after fleeing U.S. air strikes on Tora Bora.

Ahmed Mohamed[69]

AKA: Hammad Memet, Ahmed Mohammed, Ahmad Muhamman Yaqub
Gender: Male
ISN: 328
Role: Recruit who was training in the ETIM camp
Status: Ruled a "noncombatant," but remains in U.S. custody
Location: GTMO
Notes: Ahmed Mohamed arrived at the ETIM training camp via Pakistan in November 2000. He was captured at a mosque in Pakistan after fleeing

U.S. air strikes on Tora Bora. He admitted to knowing Abdul Haq, whom he had seen at the ETIM camp.

Akhdar Qasem[70]

AKA: Akhdar Qasem Basit, Akhadar Qasem
Gender: Male
ISN: 276
Role: Recruit who was training in the ETIM camp
Status: Released
Location: Albania
Notes: Akhdar Qasem arrived at the ETIM training camp via Pakistan from Kyrgyzstan in August 2001. He was captured at a mosque in Pakistan after fleeing U.S. air strikes on Tora Bora. He admitted to knowing Abdul Haq, whom he had seen at the ETIM camp.

Arkin Mahmud[71]

AKA: Arkina Mahmud
Gender: Male
ISN: 103
Role: Member
Status: Ruled a "noncombatant," but remains in U.S. custody
Location: GTMO
Notes: Arkin Mahmud was captured in Mazar-e-Sharif by Northern Alliance troops.

Bahtiyar Mahnut[72]

AKA: Sadir Sabit
Gender: Male
ISN: 277
Role: Recruit who was training in the ETIM camp
Status: Ruled a "noncombatant," but remains in U.S. custody
Location: GTMO
Notes: Bahtiyar Mahnut arrived at the ETIM training camp via Pakistan in June 2001. He was captured at a mosque in Pakistan after fleeing U.S. air strikes on Tora Bora. He admitted to knowing both Abdul Haq and Hasan Mahsum, whom he had seen at the ETIM camp.

Dawut Abdurehim[73]

AKA: Sabit Khan Yassin, Thabid
Gender: Male

ISN: 289
Role: Recruit who was training in the ETIM camp
Status: Ruled a "noncombatant," but remains in U.S. custody
Location: GTMO
Notes: Dawut Abdurehim arrived at the ETIM training camp via Pakistan from Kyrgyzstan in June 2001. He was captured at a mosque in Pakistan after fleeing U.S. air strikes on Tora Bora.

Haji Mohammed Ayub[74]

AKA: Ayoob Haji Mohammed
Gender: Male
ISN: 279
Role: Recruit who was training in the ETIM camp
Status: Released
Location: Albania
Notes: Haji Mohammed Ayub arrived at the ETIM training camp in October 2001. He was captured at a mosque in Pakistan after fleeing U.S. air strikes on Tora Bora.

Hassan Anvar[75]

AKA: Ali Mohammed
Gender: Male
ISN: 250
Role: Recruit who was training in the ETIM camp
Status: Ruled a "noncombatant," but remains in U.S. custody
Location: GTMO
Notes: Hassan Anvar arrived at the ETIM training camp in September 2001.

Huzaifa Parhat[76]

AKA: Hozaifa Parhat, Ablikim Turahun
Gender: Male
ISN: 320
Role: Recruit who was training in the ETIM camp
Status: Released
Location: Bermuda
Notes: Huzaifa Parhat arrived at the ETIM training camp via Pakistan from Kazakhstan in May 2001. He was captured at a mosque in Pakistan after fleeing U.S. air strikes on Tora Bora. He admitted to knowing both Abdul Haq and Hasan Mahsum, whom he had seen at the ETIM camp.

Abdullah Abdulqadirakhum[77]

AKA: Jalal Jalaldin, Abdulla Abdulqadir, Jallal Abin Abd al Rahman
Gender: Male
ISN: 285
Role: Recruit who was training in the ETIM camp
Status: Released
Location: Bermuda
Notes: Abdullah Abdulqadirakhum arrived at the ETIM training camp via Pakistan from Kyrgyzstan in July 2001. He was captured at a mosque in Pakistan after fleeing U.S. air strikes on Tora Bora. He admitted to knowing both Abdul Haq and Hasan Mahsum, whom he had seen at the ETIM camp.

Nag Mohammed[78]

AKA: Edham Mamet, Najmedeen Mohammed
Gender: Male
ISN: 102
Role: Member
Status: Ruled a "noncombatant," but remains in U.S. custody
Location: GTMO
Notes: Nag Mohammed was captured in Mazar-e-Sharif. He admitted to being an ETIM member but claimed he did not know the ETIM was considered a terrorist organization.

Sabir Osman[79]

AKA: Hajiakbar Abdulghupur, Hajiakbar Abdul Ghupur
Gender: Male
ISN: 282
Role: Recruit who was training in the ETIM camp
Status: Ruled a "noncombatant," but remains in U.S. custody
Location: GTMO
Notes: Sabir Osman arrived at the ETIM training camp via Pakistan from Kyrgyzstan in July 2001. He was captured at a mosque in Pakistan after fleeing U.S. air strikes on Tora Bora. He admitted to knowing Abdul Haq, whom he had seen at the ETIM camp.

Saidullah Khalik[80]

AKA: Khalid Ali
Gender: Male
ISN: 280

Role: Recruit who was training in the ETIM camp
Status: Ruled a "noncombatant," but remains in U.S. custody
Location: GTMO
Notes: Saidullah Khalik arrived at the ETIM training camp in May 2001. He was captured at a mosque in Pakistan after fleeing U.S. air strikes on Tora Bora.

Yusef Abbas[81]

AKA: Abdul Sabour, Abd al Sabr Abd al Hamid Uthman, Abdu Supur
Gender: Male
ISN: 275
Role: Recruit who was training in the ETIM camp
Status: Ruled a "noncombatant," but remains in U.S. custody
Location: GTMO
Notes: Yusef Abbas arrived at the ETIM training camp via Pakistan from Kyrgyzstan in August 2001. He was captured at a mosque in Pakistan after fleeing U.S. air strikes on Tora Bora. He admitted to knowing "Abdul Maxum," whom he had seen at the ETIM camp. We assess that "Abdul Maxum" is an alias for Hasan Mahsum.

Notes

CHAPTER 1

1. This account synthesizes information presented in the following news articles: Richard Lloyd Parry, "Renewed Bomb Attacks Kill Five in China," *Times Online*, August 10, 2008, http://www.timesonline.co.uk/tol/news/world/asia/article4495365.ece (accessed August 20, 2009); Parry, "Female Suicide Bombers in Uighur Separatist War in Xinjiang Province," *Times Online*, August 11, 2008, http://www.timesonline.co.uk/tol/news/world/asia/article4507446.ece (accessed September 12, 2009); Xinhua, "Serial Explosions Kill Two in China's Remote Xinjiang," August 10, 2008, http://english.people.com.cn/90001/90776/90882/6470889.html (accessed February 1, 2009); Jim Yardley, "Police in Western China Kill 5 Suspected Militants After Bombing Attack," *The New York Times*, August 9, 2008; Yardley, "New Spasm of Violence in Western China as 11 Die in Wave of Bombings," *The New York Times*, August 11, 2008, http://www.nytimes.com/2008/08/11/world/asia/11xinjiang.html?pagewanted=print (accessed March 8, 2009); *China Daily*, "Blasts Rock Xinjiang, Guard Killed," August 11, 2008, http://www.chinadaily.com.cn/china/2008-08/11/content_6923306.htm (accessed October 24, 2009); William Foreman, "Bombing Spree Exposes Ethnic Divisions in China," *USA Today*, August 12, 2008, http://www.usatoday.com/news/world/2008-08-11-2286247682_x.htm (accessed October 24, 2009); Foreman, "City in China's West Locks Down After Bombings," Associated Press, published in the *Washington Post*, August 10, 2008, http://www.washingtonpost.com/wp-dyn/content/article/2008/08/10/AR2008081000455.html (accessed October 24, 2009); Agence France-Presse, "Police Attacked in China's Muslim Northwest," *Straits Times*, n.d., http://www.straitstimes.com/Breaking%2BNews/World/Story/STIStory_266584.html (accessed October 24, 2009); Malcolm Moore, "China Beefs Up Security in Kuqa After New Terror Attack," *Telegraph*, August 10, 2008, http://www.telegraph.co.uk/news/worldnews/asia/china/2533765/China-beefs-up-security-in-Kuqa-after-new-terror-attack.html (accessed October 24, 2009); Simon Elegant, "A China Threat from Pakistan?" *Time*, July 27,

2008, http://www.time.com/time/world/article/0,8599,1831216,00.html (accessed October 24, 2009); Xinhua News Agency, "Civilian Dies from Injuries in Xinjiang Bombing Attack," August 11, 2008, http://news.xinhuanet.com/english/2008-08/11/content _9179895.htm (accessed October 24, 2009); Stephanie Ho, "Muslim Separatists Blamed for Blasts in China's Far Western Xinjian Region," August 10, 2008, http://www.globalsecurity .org/security/library/news/2008/08/sec-080810-voa01.htm (accessed October 24, 2009).

2. Abdullah Mansur [Islam Awazi], "The Enemy Is Terrified by Our Operations," November 2008, http://www.nefafoundation.org/miscellaneous/nefa_tipenemyterrified 0809.pdf (accessed August 23, 2009).

3. The ETIM/ETIP/TIP/IPT's notable leaders include former emir Dia Uddin bin Yousef, former emir Hasan Mahsum, and present-day emir Abdul Haq al-Turkistani. This group still exists today. The ETIPA was founded by Alerken Abula in 1993; the PRC executed Abula in 2001 and claimed to have crushed his group. The PRC's 2002 statement " 'East Turkistan' Terrorist Forces Cannot Get Away with Impunity" distinguishes between the two similar-sounding groups, blaming the ETIP for the Baren Rebellion of 1990 and the ETIPA for the unrest in Yining in 1997. For more on the ETIPA, see Agence France-Presse, "Uygur Terror Group Smashed in Raids," *Hong Kong iMail*, January 23, 2001, http://www.hartford-hwp.com/archives/55/459.html (accessed August 19, 2009).

4. Turkistan Islamic Party [Islam Awazi], "Jihad Lands: Turkestan," n.d., http:// tipislamyultuzi.com/mazmun/summary/summary.html (accessed April 21, 2008).

5. Ibid.; Turkestan Islamic Party [Islam Awazi], "Steadfastness and Preparations for Jihad in the Cause of Allah," trans. Nine Eleven/Finding Answers (NEFA) TerrorWatch subscription service, January 20, 2009, http://www.nefafoundation.org/miscellaneous/ FeaturedDocs/nefatip0409-4.pdf (accessed August 19, 2009).

6. STRATFOR, "China: The Evolution of ETIM," May 13, 2008, http://www.stratfor .com/analysis/china_evolution_etim (accessed August 19, 2009).

7. The name "Islamic Party of Turkistan" can be confusing. A number of news reports associate this name with the Islamic Movement of Uzbekistan (IMU), saying the IMU changed its name in 2001 to reflect an expanded focus on Kazakhstan, Kyrgyzstan, Tajikistan, Turkmenistan, and Xinjiang as well as Uzbekistan. The IMU's spokesman flatly denied these reports. As in the case of the ETIM/ETIP, most Westerners continued to call the Uzbek group by its former name. For more on the IMU's alleged name change, see B. Raman, "Jihadi Terrorism in Central Asia: An Update," *International Terrorism Monitor*, Paper No. 1691, February 1, 2006, http://www.saag.org/common/uploaded _files/paper1691.html (accessed August 18, 2009), and Bruce Pannier, "Central Asia: IMU Leader Says Group's Goal Is 'Return of Islam,'" Radio Free Europe/Radio Liberty, June 6, 2001, http://www.idsa.in/publications/stratcomments/JagannathPanda110507 .htm (accessed February 1, 2009). Even though the ETIM and the IMU reportedly changed their names to the "Islamic Party of Turkistan" within a year of each other, operate in neighboring areas, and allegedly coordinate their activities, we assess that the ETIM and the IMU are different organizations with separate leadership and distinct (but complementary) ethno-nationalist aims.

8. For an example of this usage, see Yitzhak Shichor, "Virtual Transnationalism: Uygur Communities in Europe and the Quest for Eastern Turkestan Independence," in *Muslim Networks and Transnational Communities in and Across Europe*, ed. Stefano Allievi and Jørgen S. Nielsen (Leiden, Netherlands: Koninklijke, 2003), 284.

9. Ibid., 281.

10. Justin Rudelson, *Oasis Identities: Uyghur Nationalism Along China's Silk Road* (New York: Columbia University Press, 1997), 5–6; James A. Millward and Peter C. Perdue, "Political and Cultural History of the Xinjiang Region through the Late Nineteenth Century," in *Xinjiang: China's Muslim Borderland*, ed. S. Frederick Starr (Armonk, NY: M.E. Sharpe, 2004), 40.

11. The Chinese Nationalists had identified only five Chinese *minzu*, or peoples. The Nationalists considered all the Muslims in China, including the Uyghurs, to be a single people. See Dru C. Gladney, "The Chinese Program of Development and Control, 1978–2001," in Starr, *Xinjiang*, 104.

12. Graham E. Fuller and S. Frederick Starr, *The Xinjiang Problem* (Washington, DC: Central Asia–Caucasus Institute, 2003), 6.

13. Millward and Perdue, "Political and Cultural History," 27.

14. Graham E. Fuller and Jonathan N. Lipman, "Islam in Xinjiang," in Starr, *Xinjiang*, 328.

15. Gladney, "The Chinese Program," 103.

16. Rudelson, *Oasis Identities*, 7.

17. Fuller and Lipman, "Islam in Xinjiang," 321.

18. Millward and Perdue, "Political and Cultural History," 40.

19. Ibid., 42. Millward and Purdue note that both Han and Uyghurs sometimes resolve this apparent inconsistency by arguing that the Karakhanids ruling in Kashgar were linked to the prediaspora Uyghur house of khans.

20. Michael Dillon, "Uyghur Separatism and Nationalism in Xinjiang," in *Conflict, Terrorism and the Media in Asia*, ed. Benjamin Cole (New York: Routledge, 2006), 101–102.

21. Testimony of Dru C. Gladney, "Exploring the Nature of Uighur Nationalism: Freedom Fighters or Terrorists?" Hearing before the International Organizations, Human Rights, and Oversight Subcommittee.

22. Statistics Bureau of Xinjiang Uygur Autonomous Region, *Xinjiang Statistical Yearbook*. This publication is a generally reliable source for information on Xinjiang's demography, and leading China scholars cite it routinely. The 2008 *Xinjiang Statistical Yearbook* states that 9,650,629 Uyghurs lived in Xinjiang as of 2007.

23. Developing a precise figure for the Uyghur diaspora is practically impossible. In 2003, the Xinjiang expert Yitzhak Shichor estimated the Uyghur diaspora at just under 486,000 ("Virtual Transnationalism"); by 2009, he estimated that up to 600,000 Uyghurs live outside China ("The Uyghurs and China: Lost and Found Nation," June 7, 2009, http://www.opendemocracy.net/article/the-uighurs-and-china-lost-and-found-nation, accessed August 16, 2009). The World Uyghur Congress estimates on its website that 500,000 Uyghurs live in "West Turkistan," with another 75,000 Uyghurs living in Pakistan, Afghanistan, Saudi Arabia, Europe, and the United States.

24. The estimate of 500 Uyghurs in Munich comes from a WUC official; see Sebastian Fischer, "Uighur Exiles in Munich: 'The Reality Is Far Worse than Television Pictures Suggest,' " *Spiegel Online International*, July 9, 2009, http://www.spiegel.de/international/world/0,1518,635249,00.html (accessed August 16, 2009), and Yannick Pasquet, "Munich Fights to Welcome the Uighurs of Guantanamo," Agence France-Presse, March 17, 2009, http://www.infoweb.newsbank.com/. Just after Xinjiang's ethnic riots in July 2009, an anonymous Chinese diplomat told China's *Global Times* that almost 700 Uyghurs worked for the WUC in Munich, but this figure seems unrealistically high.

25. Owen Lattimore, *Pivot of Asia: Sinkiang and the Inner Asian Frontiers of China and Russia* (Boston: Little, Brown, 1950), 3, 222.

26. Xinhua News Agency, "China's Western Provinces Lead by Some Economic Measures," March 26, 2008, http://www.highbeam.com/doc/1P2-15587656.html (accessed August 2, 2009).

27. AsiaPulse News, "China 2009 Cotton Planting Area Down 12 Pct in 2009: Assoc," May 20, 2009, http://www.highbeam.com/doc/1G1-200160264.html (accessed August 2, 2009).

28. Xinhua News Agency, "China's Xinjiang Sees 48 Mln Tons of Oil and Gas Output in 2008," February 2, 2009, http://www.highbeam.com/doc/1G1-192957597.html (accessed August 2, 2009).

29. Ibid.

30. China Internet Information Center, "Xinjiang: The Call of the West," 2004, http://www.china.org.cn/english/en-xj/5.htm (accessed August 2, 2009).

31. China Mining Association, "China's Xinjiang Coal Reserves Adds 18.98 Billion Tons," May 8, 2008, http://www.chinamining.org/News/2008-05-08/1210233199d 13585.html (accessed August 2, 2009).

32. AsiaPulse News, "Gold Reserves in China's Xinjiang Region Estimated to Be 9 Mln Tons," March 8, 2001, http://www.highbeam.com/doc/1G1-71353999.html (accessed August 2, 2009).

33. Fuller and Lipman, "Islam in Xinjiang," 327.

34. People's Republic of China, Information Office of the State Council, "History and Development of Xinjiang," white paper, May 26, 2003, http://www.china.org.cn/e-white/20030526/index.htm (accessed March 31, 2009).

35. People's Republic of China, Information Office of the State Council, "Regional Autonomy for Ethnic Minorities in China," white paper, February 2005, http://www.bjreview.com.cn/nation/txt/2009-05/27/content_197768.htm (accessed August 3, 2009).

36. This distinguishes Mao's ethnic autonomy policy from Stalin's. Stalin offered the republics of the Soviet Union the right to secede, which they did in 1991. However, exercising that right under Stalin's regime would have meant certain death.

37. People's Republic of China, Information Office of the State Council, "Regional Autonomy."

38. People's Republic of China, Permanent Mission of the People's Republic of China to the UN, "Terrorist Activities Perpetrated by 'Eastern Turkistan' Organizations and Their Links with Osama bin Laden and the Taliban," November 29, 2001, http://www.china-un.org/eng/zt/fk/t28937.htm (accessed August 23, 2009); People's Republic of China, Information Office of the State Council, " 'East Turkistan' Terrorist Forces Cannot Get Away with Impunity," news release, January 21, 2002, http://www.china-un.ch/eng/rqrd/jzzdh/t85075.htm (accessed April 20, 2009).

39. James Millward, "Violent Separatism in Xinjiang: A Critical Assessment," in *Policy Studies* 6 (Washington, DC: East-West Center, 2004): 19, 26.

40. *Encyclopædia Britannica* Online, s.v. "Turkistan" (accessed August 12, 2009, at http://www.britannica.com/EBchecked/topic/610093/Turkistan).

41. Dewardric L. McNeal, "China's Relations with Asian States and Problems with Terrorism," Congressional Research Service, CRS Report for Congress, December 17, 2001, 8, https://www.policyarchive.org/handle/10207/1315 (accessed April 26, 2009).

42. Hashir Wahidi, "East Turkistan or Uyghuristan?" trans. Erkin Sidick, January 7, 1998, http://www.uyghuramerican.org/articles/38/1/East-Turkistan-Or-Uyghuristan/East-Turkistan-Or-Uyghuristan.html (accessed August 4, 2009).

43. Christian Tyler, *Wild West China: The Taming of Xinjiang* (New Brunswick, NJ: Rutgers University Press, 2004), 232.

44. Gaye Christofferson, "Islam and Ethnic Minorities in Central Asia: The Uyghurs," in *Islam, Oil, and Geopolitics: Central Asia After September 11*, ed. Elizabeth Van Wie Davis and Roiuben Azizan (Lanham, MD: Rowman & Littlefield, 2006), 56.

45. Ibid.

46. Turkistan Islamic Party, "Apparent Full Text of Turkistan Islamic Party Constitution," n.d., trans. Open Source Center, January 29, 2008, CPP20080129480002.

47. U.S. Department of the Treasury, Office of Public Affairs, "Press Statement on the UN Designation of the Eastern Turkistan Islamic Movement," news release, September 12, 2002, http://www.treas.gov/press/releases/po3415.hem (accessed August 15, 2009).

48. Dru C. Gladney, "Responses to Chinese Rule: Patterns of Cooperation and Opposition," in Starr, *Xinjiang*, 375.

49. Yitzhak Shichor, "Fact and Fiction: A Chinese Documentary on Eastern Turkestan Terrorism," *China and Eurasia Forum Quarterly* 4, no. 2 (2006): 90–91, http://www.silk roadstudies.org/new/docs/CEF/Quarterly/May_2006/Shichor.pdf (accessed April 24, 2009).

50. As of August 2009, blocked sites included Blogger, YouTube, Facebook, and Twitter. Josephine McDermott, "The Battle to Scale the Great Firewall of China," *Telegraph*, August 5, 2009, http://www.telegraph.co.uk/expat/5976173/The-battle-to -scale-the-Great-Firewall-of-China.html (accessed August 15, 2009).

51. Fuller and Lipman, "Islam in Xinjiang," 347.

52. Millward, "Violent Separatism," 28.

53. Yitzhak Shichor, "Blow Up: Internal and External Challenges of Uyghur Separatism and Islamic Radicalism to Chinese Rule in Xinjiang," *Asian Affairs* 32, no. 2 (2005): 131, http://vnweb.hwwilsonweb.com/hww/Journals/index.jhtml.

54. Rudelson, *Oasis Identities*, 14–15.

55. Human Rights Watch and Human Rights in China, "Devastating Blows: Religious Repression of Uighurs in Xinjiang" (a Human Rights in China special report), *Human Rights Watch* 17, no. 2(c) (April 2005): 101–105. http://www.hrw.org/en/reports/20025/ 04/11/devastating-blows (accessed April 24, 2009). These pages contain an English translation of two PRC regulations that define almost any information on religious or ethnic affairs as a "state secret."

56. Ibid., 6, 66, 73.

57. Fuller and Lipman, "Islam in Xinjiang," 347.

58. Shichor, "Fact and Fiction," 102.

59. Millward, "Violent Separatism," 13.

60. U.S. Department of the Treasury, Office of Public Affairs, "Press Statement."

61. People's Republic of China, Information Office of the State Council, " 'East Turkistan' Terrorist Forces."

CHAPTER 2

1. Stanley W. Toops, "The Demography of Xinjiang," in Starr, *Xinjiang*, 245–249; Igor Rotar, "The Growing Problem of Uighur Separatism," *China Brief* 4, no. 8 (April 15, 2004), The Jamestown Foundation, http://www.jamestown.org/single/?no_cache=1 &tx_ttnews[tt_news]=3644 (accessed April 24, 2009); Preeti Bhattacharji, "Uighurs and China's Xinjiang Region," Council on Foreign Relations Backgrounder, September 29,

2008, http://www.cfr.org/publication/16870/chinas_xinjiang_dilemma.html?breadcrumb
=%2F (accessed March 29, 2009).

2. Calla Weimer, "The Economy of Xinjiang," in Starr, *Xinjiang*, 169.

3. Statistics Bureau, *Xinjiang Statistical Yearbook*.

4. Toops, "The Demography of Xinjiang," 246–249.

5. Peter Ford, "Uighurs Struggle in a World Reshaped by Chinese Influx," *The Christian Science Monitor*, April 28, 2008, http://www.csmonitor.com/2008/0428/ p01s01-woap.htm (accessed March 31, 2009).

6. Justin Rudelson and William Jankowiak, "Acculturation and Resistance: Xinjiang Identities in Flux," in Starr, *Xinjiang*, 319.

7. Fuller and Starr, *The Xinjiang Problem*, 16.

8. Fuller and Starr, *The Xinjiang Problem*, 16; Justin Rudelson, "Xinjiang's Uyghurs in the Ensuing US-China Partnership," Uyghur Panel, Congressional-Executive Committee on China, Washington, DC, June 10, 2002, http://www.cecc.gov/pages/roundtables/ 061002/rudelsonStatement.php (accessed March 31, 2009).

9. People's Republic of China, "History and Development of Xinjiang."

10. Congressional-Executive Commission on China, "Civil Servant Recruitment in Xinjiang Favors Han Chinese," July 13, 2006, http://www.cecc.gov/pages/virtualAcad/ index.phpd?showsingle=61191 (accessed April 27, 2009).

11. Toops, "The Demography of Xinjiang," 256.

12. Ibid., 246.

13. Ibid., 257.

14. People's Republic of China, "History and Development of Xinjiang."

15. Fuller and Lipman, "Islam in Xinjiang," 323.

16. Fuller and Starr, *The Xinjiang Problem*, 17.

17. Rupert Wingfield-Hayes, "Language Blow for China's Muslims," BBC News, June 1, 2002, http://news.bbc.co.uk/2/hi/asia-pacific/2020009.stm (accessed September 13, 2009).

18. Linda Benson, "Education and Social Mobility among Minority Populations in Xinjiang," in Starr, *Xinjiang*, 205–206.

19. Fuller and Starr, *The Xinjiang Problem*, 6.

20. Benson, "Education and Social Mobility," 198.

21. Ibid., 194–197.

22. Ibid., 190.

23. Fuller and Lipman, "Islam in Xinjiang," 331.

24. Colin Mackerras, "Xinjiang at the Turn of the Century: The Causes of Separatism," *Central Asian Survey* 20, no. 3 (2001): 299, http://www.ingentaconnect.com/.

25. Benson, "Education and Social Mobility," 198.

26. Ibid., 191.

27. Fuller and Lipman, "Islam in Xinjiang," 335.

28. Human Rights Watch and Human Rights in China, "Devastating Blows," 3.

29. Agence France-Presse, "China Cracks Down on Its Muslims; Anti-Terrorist Drive Turned Against Uighurs," *The Washington Times*, November 23, 2001, http://www .infoweb.newsbank.com/.

30. Human Rights Watch and Human Rights in China, "Devastating Blows," 62.

31. Fuller and Starr, *The Xinjiang Problem*, 20.

32. Fuller and Lipman, "Islam in Xinjiang," 345.

33. Jackie Armijo, "Islamic Education in China," *Harvard Asia Quarterly* 10, no. 1 (2006), http://www.asiaquarterly.com/content/view/166/ (accessed March 29, 2009).

34. Human Rights Watch and Human Rights in China, "Devastating Blows," 3.

35. James Millward and Nabijan Tursun, "Political History and Strategies of Control, 1884–1978," in Starr, *Xinjiang*, 88–89.

36. Armijo, "Islamic Education in China."

37. Fuller and Starr, *The Xinjiang Problem*, 19.

38. Human Rights Watch and Human Rights in China, "Devastating Blows," 32.

39. Ibid., 48.

40. Dillon, "Uyghur Separatism," 101.

41. Fuller and Lipman, "Islam in Xinjiang," 338.

42. Jay Dautcher, "Public Health and Social Pathologies in Xinjiang," in Starr, *Xinjiang*, 286.

43. Michael Dillon, *Xinjiang: China's Muslim Far Northwest* (New York: Routledge-Curzon, 2004), 90.

44. Fuller and Lipman, "Islam in Xinjiang," 335.

45. Quoted in Human Rights Watch and Human Rights in China, "Devastating Blows," 46.

46. Fuller and Lipman, "Islam in Xinjiang," 325.

47. Human Rights Watch and Human Rights in China, "Devastating Blows," 32.

48. Fuller and Lipman, "Islam in Xinjiang," 333.

49. Millward, "Violent Separatism in Xinjiang," 15.

50. Ibid.

51. Human Rights Watch and Human Rights in China, "Devastating Blows," 50–52.

52. Fuller and Lipman, "Islam in Xinjiang," 324.

53. Ibid.

54. Toops, "Demography in Xinjiang," 261–262.

55. Ibid.

56. Dillon, "Uighur Separatism," 100.

57. Rudelson, *Oasis Identities*, 69.

58. Fuller and Lipman, "Islam in Xinjiang," 325.

59. Fuller and Starr, *The Xinjiang Problem*, 17.

60. Ibid., 18.

61. Ibid.

62. Weimer, "The Economy of Xinjiang," 180; Fuller and Starr, *The Xinjiang Problem*, 18.

63. Weimer, "The Economy of Xinjiang," 164, 188.

64. Fuller and Starr, *The Xinjiang Problem*, 18.

65. Rudelson, *Oasis Identities*, 75.

66. Richard Stone, "Fears Over Western Water Crisis," *Science* 321 (August 1, 2008): 630.

67. Toops, "The Ecology of Xinjiang: A Focus on Water," in Starr, *Xinjiang*, 273.

68. Ibid.

69. Ibid., 272.

70. Stone, "Fears Over Western Water Crisis," 630.

71. Toops, "The Ecology of Xinjiang," 274.

72. Yitzhak Shichor, "The Great Wall of Steel: Military and Strategy in Xinjiang," in Starr, *Xinjiang*, 146–147.

73. Andrew Buncombe, "China's Secret Nuclear Tests Leave Legacy of Cancer and Deformity," *The Independent* [London], October 5, 1998, http://www.lexisnexis.com/.

74. William J. Holstein, "China's Nuclear Tests May Be Causing Cancer," *United Press International*, August 24, 1981, http://www.lexisnexis.com/.

75. William D. Shingleton, "In Xinjiang, China's Consolidation Isn't Solid," *The Christian Science Monitor*, August 27, 1997, http://www.lexisnexis.com/; Cord Meyer, "Plight of the Uighur People," *The Washington Times*, September 5, 1997, http://www.lexisnexis.com/.

76. Anwar Yusuf Turani, "Declaration of the Formation of the E. T. Government in Exile," World Uighur Network News 2004, *SPARK* Uighur Press on Eastern Turkestan, news release, September 14, 2004, http://www.uygur.org/wunn04/09_14.htm (accessed April 5, 2009).

77. Buncombe, "China's Secret Nuclear Tests."

78. Holstein, "China's Nuclear Tests"; Bryan Johnson, "Cancer Increase in Chinese Province; Blight Rumored in Nuclear Test Area," *The Globe and Mail* [Canada], September 1, 1981, http://www.lexisnexis.com/.

79. Craig S. Smith, "China, in Harsh Crackdown, Executes Muslim Separatists," *The New York Times*, December 16, 2001, http://www.lexisnexis.com/.

80. June Teufel Dreyer, "China's Vulnerability to Minority Separatism," *Asian Affairs* 32, no. 2 (2005): 77, http://www.smhric.org/China's%20Vulnerability%20to%20Minority%20Separatism.pdf (accessed September 6, 2009).

81. Amnesty International, "People's Republic of China—Uighurs Fleeing Persecution as China Wages Its 'War on Terror,'" ASA 17/021/2004, July 7, 2004, 6, http://www.unhcr.org/refworld/docid/4129cc5d4.html (accessed April 6, 2009).

82. Fuller and Starr, *The Xinjiang Problem*, 21.

83. Dillon, "Uyghur Separatism," 105.

84. Amnesty International, "People's Republic of China—Uighurs Fleeing," 21.

85. Human Rights Watch and Human Rights in China, "Devastating Blows," 70–71.

86. Smith, "China, in Harsh Crackdown."

87. Human Rights Watch and Human Rights in China, "Devastating Blows," 71.

88. Dillon, *Xinjiang*, 89.

89. Ibid., 85, 102.

90. Ibid., 105.

91. Human Rights Watch and Human Rights in China, "Devastating Blows," 70.

92. Edward Wong, "Arrests Increased in Chinese Region," *The New York Times*, January 5, 2009, http://www.nytimes.com/2009/01/06/world/asia/06china.html (accessed April 24, 2009).

93. Human Rights Watch and Human Rights in China, "Devastating Blows," 67.

94. Dautcher, "Public Health," 277.

95. Ibid., 276.

96. Ibid., 279.

97. Rudelson and Jankowiak, "Acculturation and Resistance," 318.

98. Fuller and Lipman, "Islam in Xinjiang," 323.

99. Millward, "Violent Separatism," 6.

100. Gladney, "The Chinese Program," 101.

101. This breakdown is adapted from the work of Fuller and Lipman in "Islam in Xinjiang" and Fuller and Starr in *The Xinjiang Problem*.

102. Fuller and Lipman, "Islam in Xinjiang," 345.

103. Testimony of Dru C. Gladney, "Exploring the Nature."

104. Turkistan Islamic Party [Islam Awazi], "Jihad Lands."

105. Ibid.

106. For an example of this complaint, see Erkin Dolat, "Washington Betrays China's Uighurs," Uyghur Information Agency, September 5, 2002, http://www.atimes.com/atimes/China/DI05Ad03.html (accessed August 30, 2009).

107. Testimony of Dru C. Gladney, "Exploring the Nature"; Agence France-Presse, "Anti-American Sentiment Among China's Muslims Growing: Expert," March 31, 2003, http://www.lexisnexis.com/.

108. Shichor, "Fact and Fiction," 103.

109. Yitzhak Shichor, "Limping on Two Legs: Uyghur Diaspora Organizations and the Prospects for Eastern Turkestan Independence," *Central Asia and the Caucasus* 48, no. 6 (December 2007), http://www.ca-c.org/online/2007/journal_eng/cac-06/12.shtml (accessed April 26, 2009).

110. Ibid.

111. Uyghur activist Tursun Islam told Kyrgyz radio in 1999 that the East Turkistan National Congress considered gathering in Almaty or Bishkek instead of Munich but ultimately selected Munich because of Germany's democratic government and Munich's central location ("Uighur Community Sets Up Supreme Body, Resolves to Fight for Independence," Kyrgyz radio, translated from Kyrgyz by BBC Summary of World Broadcasts, November 3, 1999, http://www.lexisnexis.com/).

112. Yitzhak Shichor, "Changing the Guard at the World Uyghur Congress," *China Brief* 6, no. 25 (December 19, 2006), http://www.jamestown.org/single/?no_cache=1&tx_ttnews[tt_news]=32346 (accessed October 5, 2009); Lilith Volkert, "Public Enemy No. 1: The World Uighur Congress Champions the Rights of China's Muslim Minority," *The Atlantic Times*, August 2009, http://www.atlantic-times.com/archive_detail.php?recordID=1856 (accessed October 5, 2009).

113. Shichor, "Virtual Transnationalism," 294.

114. Shichor, "Fact and Fiction," 96–97.

115. Eastern Turkestan Union in Europe, "World National Congress Held," *Eastern Turkestan Information Bulletin* 2, no. 6 (December 1992), http://caccp.freedomsherald.org/et/etib/etib2_6.html (accessed September 4, 2009).

116. Shichor, "Virtual Transnationalism," 294.

117. Gladney, "Responses to Chinese Rule," 386.

118. World Uyghur Congress, "Introducing the World Uyghur Congress," http://www.uyghurcongress.org/En/AboutWUC.asp?mid=1095738888 (accessed September 3, 2009).

119. Turani, "Declaration of the Formation."

120. Shichor, "Fact and Fiction," 104.

121. National Endowment for Democracy (NED), "National Endowment for Democracy Support for Uyghur Human Rights and Prodemocracy Groups in Exile," last updated July 16, 2009, http://www.ned.org/grants/uyghur_factsheet.html (accessed September 4, 2009). The NED is a private, nonprofit organization funded by a U.S. congressional appropriation. In 2008, the NED's grants to the WUC, UAA, and IUHRDF totaled just under $550,000.

122. Li Hongmei, "Unveiled Rebiya Kadeer: A Uighur Dalai Lama," *Renmin Ribao*, July 7, 2009, http://www.lexisnexis.com/.

123. People's Republic of China, Information Office of the State Council, " 'East Turkistan' Terrorist Forces."

124. Ibid.

125. Xinhua General News Service, "First Batch of 'Eastern Turkistan' Terrorist Groups, Individuals Identified," December 15, 2003, http://www.lexisnexis.com/.

126. Ibid.

127. People's Republic of China, Information Office of the State Council, " 'East Turkistan' Terrorist Forces."

128. Xinhua General News Service, "First Batch."

129. Ibid.

130. Ibid.

131. Ibid.

132. Xinhua News Agency, "Official Says East Turkestan 'Great Terrorist Threat' to China," supplied by BBC Worldwide Monitoring, September 6, 2005, http://www.lexisnexis.com/.

133. Xinhua General News Service, "First Batch."

134. Ibid.

135. Ibid.

136. Ibid.

137. Ibid.

138. Radio Free Asia, "Separatist Leader Vows to Target Chinese Government; Uyghur Leader Denies Terror Charges," January 29, 2003, http://www.tibet.ca/en/newsroom/wtn/archive/old?y=2003&m=1&p=29-2_7 (accessed September 6, 2009).

139. Ibid.

140. Yu Song, "BBC Allegedly Has Received a Videotape Showing Masked Men from the East Turkestan Liberation Organization Declaring War on China," Zhongguo Tongxun She News Agency [Hong Kong], supplied by BBC Worldwide Monitoring, October 1, 2005, http://www.lexisnexis.com/.

141. Martin Wayne, *China's War on Terrorism: Counter-Insurgency, Politics, and Internal Security* (New York: Routledge, 2008), 46.

142. Millward, "Violent Separatism," 26.

143. Natsuko Oka, "The 'Triadic Nexus' in Kazakhstan: A Comparative Study of Russians, Uighurs, and Koreans," in *Beyond Sovereignty: From Status Law to Transnational Citizenship?*, ed. Osamu Ieda (Sapporo, Japan: Slavic Research Center, Hokkaido University, 2006), 371.

144. Millward, "Violent Separatism," 26.

145. Ibid., 24.

146. Ibid., 26.

147. Ibid., 25.

148. Ibid., 26.

149. Ibid.

150. Ibid.

151. Ibid.

152. People's Republic of China, "Terrorist Activities Perpetrated"; People's Republic of China, " 'East Turkistan' Terrorist Forces."

153. People's Republic of China, " 'East Turkistan' Terrorist Forces."

154. Cao Chang-Qing, "Fighting to Free Another Chinese 'Province,' " *Taipei Times*, October 11, 1999, http://www.taipeitimes.com/News/insight/archives/1999/10/11/6035 (accessed September 5, 2009).

155. Agence France-Presse, "China Executes Two Out of 18 Muslim Uighurs Convicted of Separatism," August 13, 2004, http://www.lexisnexis.com.

156. Zhang Yumo, "The Anti-Separatism Struggle and Its Historical Lessons Since the Liberation of Xinjiang," trans. Turdi Ghoja for the Uyghur American Association, in *Pan-Turkism & Pan-Islamism*, ed. Yang Faren, Li Ze, and Dong Sheng, August 1993, http://www.uyghurnews.com/ReadNews.asp?UighurNews=the-anti-separtism-struggle -and-its-historical-lessons-since-the-liberation-of-xinjiang&ItemID=ZH-217200857311 5318274840 (accessed September 5, 2009).

157. People's Republic of China, Information Office of the State Council, " 'East Turkistan' Terrorist Forces."

158. People's Republic of China, "Terrorist Activities Perpetrated."

159. "Law and Order: 'Islamic' 'Counter-Revolutionaries' Executed for Bomb Explosions," *Xinjiang Ribao*, BBC Summary of World Broadcasts, May 31, 1995, http://www .lexisnexis.com/.

160. World Uyghur Congress, "List of Political Prisoners," http://www.uyghurcongress .org/En/humanrights.asp?mid=2125209830&mid2=979265169 (accessed September 6, 2009).

161. Shichor, "Fact and Fiction," 102.

162. Andre Grabot, "The Uighurs—Sacrificed on Central Asia's Chess Board," Agence France-Presse, April 25, 1996, http://www.lexisnexis.com/.

163. Millward, "Violent Separatism," 27.

164. "Kazakh Paper Suggests USA Is Backing China's Uighur Separatists," *Komsomolskaya Pravda Kazakhstan*, trans. supplied by BBC Worldwide Monitoring, July 20, 2002, http://www.lexisnexis.com/.

165. Millward, "Violent Separatism," 27.

166. McNeal, "China's Relations," 8–9.

167. People's Republic of China, "Terrorist Activities Perpetrated"; He Huifeng, "Independence Bid in Xinjiang Unlikely to Succeed: Expert," *South China Morning Post* [Hong Kong], July 27, 2008, http://www.lexisnexis.com/; Rémi Castets, "The Uyghurs in Xinjiang—The Malaise Grows," trans. Philip Liddell, *China Perspectives*, September–October 2003, http://chinaperspectives.revues.org/document648.html (accessed September 5, 2009); Agence France-Presse, "China Breaks Silence on Bombings," *The Australian*, March 6, 1997, http://www.lexisnexis.com/.

168. People's Republic of China, "Terrorist Activities Perpetrated"; He, "Independence Bid."

169. People's Republic of China, Information Office of the State Council, " 'East Turkistan' Terrorist Forces."

170. Chow Chung-Yan, "Muslim Put to Death for Seeking Separate State," *South China Morning Post* [Hong Kong], October 24, 2003, http://www.lexisnexis.com/.

171. People's Republic of China, Information Office of the State Council, " 'East Turkistan' Terrorist Forces."

172. Chien-peng Chung, "China's 'War on Terror,' " *Foreign Affairs* 81, no. 4 (July–August 2002): 8–12, http://www.ebscohost.com/.

173. John C. K. Daly and Martin Sieff, "UPI Intelligence Watch," *United Press International*, November 4, 2004, http://www.lexisnexis.com/; Aditya Bhagat, "China Tries to Quell the Xinjiang Uprising," *The Pioneer*, February 27, 1997, http://www.hvk.org/ articles/0397/0020.html (accessed September 5, 2009). Bhagat's article states that the Baren Rebellion occurred on April 5, 1992, but the correct date is April 5, 1990.

174. K. Imatov, "The Question of the Uighur Question," *Slovo Kyrgyzstana*, in Russian, trans. supplied by BBC Worldwide Monitoring under the title "Kyrgyz Newspaper Analyses Threat from Uighur 'Extremists,'" November 1, 2001, http://www.lexisnexis.com/.

175. Andre Grabot, "Uighur Radical Says His Creed Is to 'Kill the Chinese,'" Agence France-Presse, March 4, 1997, http://www.lexisnexis.com/.

176. Inside China Mainland, "Xinjiang Separatist Movement Intensifies," June 1, 1999, http://www.lexisnexis.com.

177. James Meek, "Ancient Warriors Feel China's Cosh," *The Observer*, October 12, 1997, http://www.lexisnexis.com/.

178. Millward, "Violent Separatism," 8–9.

179. See http://www.uygur.org/spark/archiv/14/index.html.

180. People's Republic of China, "Terrorist Activities Perpetrated"; He, "Independence Bid."

181. Amnesty International, "People's Republic of China—Gross Violations of Human Rights in the Xinjiang Uighur Autonomous Region," ASA 17/018/1999, April 1, 1999, http://asiapacific.amnesty.org/library/Index/ENGASA170181999?open&of=ENG-CHN (accessed September 5, 2009).

182. People's Republic of China, "Terrorist Activities Perpetrated."

183. Unrepresented Nations and Peoples Organization, "Nonviolence and Conflict: Conditions for Effective Peaceful Change," July 1997, http://www.unpo.org/downloads/nonviolencereport97.pdf (accessed September 5, 2009).

184. Agence France-Presse, "Uygur Terror Group."

185. People's Republic of China, Information Office of the State Council, "'East Turkistan' Terrorist Forces."

186. Jasper Becker, "China's 'Home-Grown' Terror," *South China Morning Post* [Hong Kong], November 16, 2001, http://www.lexisnexis.com/.

187. Agence France-Presse, "Uygur Terror Group"; Becker, "China's 'Home-Grown' Terror." Such an exact count of a militant group's members (113) is unusual. The precision suggests the number may be arbitrary or based on a single source.

188. People's Republic of China, Information Office of the State Council, "'East Turkistan' Terrorist Forces."

189. Nadira Artykova, "Xinjiang: Uighur People Seek Independence from Chinese Influence," Inter Press Service, August 28, 1993, http://www.lexisnexis.com/.

190. Shichor, "Blow Up," 135.

191. David Filipov, "Islamic Separatists Claim China Bombings," *Boston Globe*, March 9, 1997, http://www.lexisnexis.com/; Agence France-Presse, "China Breaks Silence"; Grabot, "Uighur Radical Says."

192. People's Republic of China, "Terrorist Activities Perpetrated"; He, "Independence Bid"; Castets, "The Uyghurs in Xinjiang."

193. Agence France-Presse, "China Breaks Silence."

194. Ibid.; Grabot, "Uighur Radical Says."

195. Eastern Turkestan Union in Europe, "Organizations Unite Their Efforts," *Eastern Turkestan Information Bulletin* 4, no. 4 (October 1994), http://caccp.freedomsherald.org/et/etib/etib4_4.html (accessed September 5, 2009).

196. Ibid.

197. Cao, "Fighting to Free."

198. Shichor, "Fact and Fiction," 94.

199. Ibid., 102.

200. People's Republic of China, "Terrorist Activities Perpetrated."

201. Ibid.

202. Ibid.

203. Ibid.

204. *Times of India*, "Laden Had Links with Xinjiang Terrorist Groups," November 18, 2001, http://timesofindia.indiatimes.com/articleshow/1528111876.cms (accessed September 5, 2009).

205. People's Republic of China, "Terrorist Activities Perpetrated."

206. Fuller and Lipman, "Islam in Xinjiang," 327.

207. Chung, "China's 'War on Terror.'"

208. Gladney, "The Chinese Program," 104.

209. Yasushi Shinmen, "The Eastern Turkistan Republic (1933–34) in Historical Perspective," in *Islam in Politics in Russia and Central Asia: Early Eighteenth to Late Twentieth Centuries*, ed. Stephane A. Dudoignon and Komatsu Hisao, 151.

210. Fuller and Lipman, "Islam in Xinjiang," 329.

211. Ibid.

212. Ibid.

213. Ibid.

214. Ibid.

215. Ibid.

216. Fuller and Starr, *The Xinjiang Problem*, 20–21.

217. Shichor, "Virtual Transnationalism," 302.

218. Ibid., 297, 309.

219. Dru Gladney, "Cyber-Separatism and Uyghur Ethnic Nationalism in China," Center for Strategic and International Studies, June 5, 2003, 19, http://www.csis.org/china/030605gladney.pdf (accessed April 10, 2009).

220. Shichor, "Virtual Transnationalism," 290.

CHAPTER 3

1. Turkistan Islamic Party [Islam Awazi], "Steadfastness and Preparations."

2. The first PRC news release calling attention to the ETIM was "Terrorist Activity Perpetrated by 'Eastern Turkistan' Organizations and Their Links with Osama bin Laden and the Taliban," dated November 2001.

3. The ETIM's website was http://www.tipislamawazi.com/. To our knowledge, it had not been revitalized or replaced as of this writing (September 2009).

4. The first public mentions of the ETIM that we can identify date from 1990, when news accounts of the Baren Rebellion referred to the Islamic Party of East Turkistan. See Andrew Higgins, "'Holy War' Rages in Western China," *The Independent*, April 24, 1990, 15, http://www.lexisnexis.com/; United Press International, "Authorities in Western China Blame Fanatics for 'Holy War,'" April 23, 1990, http://www.lexisnexis.com/; James L. Tyson, "Foreign Muslims Blamed for Unrest," *Christian Science Monitor*, May 31, 1990, 4, http://www.lexisnexis.com/; and "Further Report on 5th–6th April Rebellion in Xinjiang," Xinjiang Television, Urumqi, April 22, 1990, transcript in BBC Summary of World Broadcasts, http://www.lexisnexis.com/.

5. Gao Chaoming, "National Splittism Is the Main Danger in Xinjiang," *Xinjiang Ribao* [Urumqi], reprinted in BBC Summary of World Broadcasts, October 19, 1990, http://www.lexisnexis.com/.

6. Catherine Field, "Dateline: Happy, Smiling Workers—China's Latest Fakes," *The Observer*, May 21, 1994, http://www.lexisnexis.com/.

7. All three articles appeared in the Russian publication *Nezavisimaya Gazeta* and identify the ETIM as one of the primary Islamic militant groups coming from Xinjiang. See Michael Falco, "Islamic Movement of Uzbekistan (IMU): History, Financial Base and Military Structure," [in Russian], *Nezavisimaya Gazeta*, August 24, 2000, http://www.ng.ru/net/2000-08-24/0_idu.html (accessed August 16, 2009); Igor Rotar, "Explode Whether Central Asia?" [in Russian], *Nezavisimaya Gazeta*, November 29, 2000, http://www.ng.ru/cis/2000-11-29/5_central.html (accessed August 16, 2009); and Stanislav Alexeyev, "A Tough International," [in Russian], *Nezavisimaya Gazeta*, October 6, 2000, http://nvo.ng.ru/wars/2000-10-06/2_international.html (accessed August 16, 2009).

8. Boaz Ganor, "Xinjiang: Profile of a Restless Province," September 10, 2000, International Institute for Counter-Terrorism, http://212.150.54.123/spotlight/comment .cfm?id=482 (accessed August 20, 2009). Ganor's article refers to a meeting the ETIM attended in 1994.

9. Turkistan Islamic Party [Islam Awazi], "Jihad Lands"; STRATFOR, "China: The Evolution of ETIM."

10. STRATFOR, "China."

11. Turkistan Islamic Party [Islam Awazi], "Jihad Lands."

12. STRATFOR, "China."

13. U.S. Department of Defense, Administrative Review Board, Unclassified Summary of Evidence for Administrative Review Board in the Case of Noori, Adel, July 1, 2005, http://projects.nytimes.com/guantanamo/detainees/584-adel-noori#3 (accessed August 2, 2009).

14. STRATFOR, "China"; "Further Report."

15. STRATFOR, "China."

16. Field, "Dateline."

17. STRATFOR, "China"; People's Republic of China, "First Batch."

18. STRATFOR, "China."

19. People's Republic of China, "First Batch"; STRATFOR, "China"; Turkistan Islamic Party [Islam Awazi], "Jihad Lands."

20. STRATFOR, "China."

21. Ibid.; Turkistan Islamic Party [Islam Awazi], "Jihad Lands."

22. Turkistan Islamic Party [Islam Awazi], "Jihad Lands."

23. People's Republic of China, "First Batch"; STRATFOR, "China."

24. Turkistan Islamic Party [Islam Awazi], "Jihad Lands."

25. The group's website notes, "The understanding of Hasan Makhdoom underwent a radical transformation in that he decided alongside other group members, that peaceful, non-resistant . . . efforts were only producing limited success." See Turkistan Islamic Party [Islam Awazi], "Jihad Lands."

26. "Profiles of 11 Terrorists Identified," *China Daily*, December 16, 2003, http://www.chinadaily.com.cn/en/doc/2003-12/16/content_290652.htm (accessed August 17, 2008); Murad Batal Al-Shishani, "Journal of the Turkistan Islamic Party Urges Jihad in China," *Terrorism Monitor* 7, no. 9 (April 10, 2009): 3–4, The Jamestown Foundation, http://www.jamestown.org/single/?no_cache=1&tx_ttnews[tt_news]=34838 (accessed August 18, 2009); STRATFOR, "China"; Turkistan Islamic Party [Islam Awazi], "Jihad

Lands"; People's Republic of China, "First Batch"; People's Republic of China, "Terrorist Activities Perpetrated"; People's Republic of China, Ministry of Public Security, "China Identifies Alleged 'Eastern Turkistan' Terrorists," news release, October 21, 2008, http://www.gov.cn/english/2008-10/21/content_1126738.htm (accessed April 20, 2009); People's Republic of China, Information Office of the State Council, " 'East Turkistan' Terrorist Forces."

27. STRATFOR, "China."

28. Some of the videos were found on the now-defunct website http://www.tipislamawazi.com/. Other videos and additional copies of some of the original videos can also be found at YouTube and other file-sharing sites. For example, see Turkistan Islamic Party [Islam Awazi], "Shaheed Hasan Mahsum Rahimallah," video in four parts, May 21, 2004, http://www.youtube.com/watch?v=3lx5lwRm9UA (accessed August 22, 2009); Turkistan Islamic Party [Islam Awazi], "Birlik wa Tayyarlik Togrisida," video, September 11, 2003, http://www.tipislamyultuzi.com/mazmun/8/video/05.wmv (accessed April 22, 2008); and Turkistan Islamic Party [Islam Awazi], "TIP Islam Awazi," video in two parts, n.d., http://www.youtube.com/watch?v=s3A-BbBixWI (accessed August 22, 2009).

29. Turkistan Islamic Party [Islam Awazi], "Steadfastness and Preparations."

30. Al-Shishani, "Journal of the Turkistan Islamic Party."

31. Islamic Party of Turkistan, "Jihad Lands."

32. U.S. Department of Defense, Combatant Status Review Board, Summarized Detainee Sworn Statement [Ahmed Mohamed, ISN 328], n.d., http://www.dod.gov/pubs/foi/detainees/csrt_arb/index.html (accessed August 2, 2009).

33. U.S. Department of Defense, Combatant Status Review Board, Summarized Detainee Unsworn Statement [Yusef Abbas, ISN 275], n.d., http://www.dod.gov/pubs/foi/detainees/csrt_arb/index.html (accessed August 2, 2009); U.S. Department of Defense, Combatant Status Review Board, Summarized Detainee Unsworn Statement [Abdulla Abdulqadir, ISN 285], n.d., http://www.dod.gov/pubs/foi/detainees/csrt_arb/index.html (accessed August 2, 2009); U.S. Department of Defense, Combatant Status Review Board, Detainee Unsworn Statement—ISN 289 [Dawut Abdurehim], n.d., http://www.dod.gov/pubs/foi/detainees/csrt_arb/index.html (accessed August 2, 2009); U.S. Department of Defense, Combatant Status Review Board, Summarized Detainee Sworn Statement [Ahmed Mohamed, ISN 328].

34. U.S. Department of Defense, Administrative Review Board, Unclassified Summary of Evidence for Combatant Status Review Tribunal—Abdul Rahman, Abdul Ghappar, October 29, 2004, http://www.dod.gov/pubs/foi/detainees/csrt_arb/index.html (accessed August 2, 2009).

35. STRATFOR, "China"; People's Republic of China, "First Batch."

36. At least eight of the Uyghur GTMO detainees referred to Abdul Haq. For an example, see U.S. Department of Defense, Combatant Status Review Board, Summarized Detainee Unsworn Statement [Abdul Ghappar Abdul Rahman, ISN 281], n.d., http://www.dod.gov/pubs/foi/detainees/csrt_arb/index.html (accessed August 2, 2009).

37. Alexeyev, "A Tough International"; IntelCenter, "Turkistan Islamic Party (TIP): Threat Awareness Wall Chart," August 12, 2008, v. 1.1; Turkistan Islamic Party, "Regarding the Death of Hesen Mexsum," May 30, 2004, trans. Open Source Center, January 12, 2006, CPP20060112075001.

38. Turkistan Islamic Party [Islam Awazi], "Why Are We Fighting China?" translated by ceifiT LTD on behalf of the Nine Eleven/Finding Answers (NEFA) TerrorWatch subscription service, July 2008, http://www.nefafoundation.org/miscellaneous/FeaturedDocs/nefatip0409-3.pdf (accessed August 19, 2009).

39. Turkistan Islamic Party, "Apparent Full Text."

40. Ibid. The Congressional Research Service analyst Shirley Kan has noted that Uyghurs traditionally practiced sharia law until the Communist takeover, so on its own, a call for the reinstatement of sharia is not necessarily radical. See U.S. House of Representatives, Foreign Affairs Committee, "Exploring the Nature of Uighur Nationalism: Freedom Fighters or Terrorists?"

41. Turkistan Islamic Party [Islam Awazi], "Jihad Lands."

42. Ibid.

43. Turkistan Islamic Party [Islam Awazi], "Steadfastness and Preparations."

44. Turkistan Islamic Party, "Apparent Full Text."

45. Turkistan Islamic Party [Islam Awazi], "Steadfastness and Preparations."

46. Mansur [Islam Awazi], "The Enemy Is Terrified."

47. Al-Shishani, "Journal of the Turkistan Islamic Party"; Turkistan Islamic Party [Islam Awazi], "Steadfastness and Preparations."

48. Al-Shishani, "Journal of the Turkistan Islamic Party."

49. Turkistan Islamic Party [Islam Awazi], "Apparent Full Text."

50. Turkistan Islamic Party [Islam Awazi], "Why Are We Fighting China?"

51. Turkistan Islamic Party [Islam Awazi], "Jihad Lands."

52. Ibid.

53. For an example of this rhetoric, see Turkistan Islamic Party [Islam Awazi], "Steadfastness and Preparations."

54. Turkistan Islamic Party [Islam Awazi], "Steadfastness and Preparations."

55. Turkistan Islamic Party, "Apparent Full Text."

56. Turkestan Islamic Party, "Commander Abdelhaqq al-Turkestani: Response from the Turkestan Islamic Party to the Olympic Games to Be Held in China in 2008," trans. ceifiT LTD on behalf of the Nine Eleven/Finding Answers (NEFA) TerrorWatch subscription service, March 1, 2008, http://www.nefafoundation.org/miscellaneous/FeaturedDocs/nefatip0409.pdf (accessed August 23, 2009).

57. Turkestan Islamic Party, "On the Occasion of Our Blessed Jihad in the Chinese City of Yunnan," trans. ceifiT LTD on behalf of the Nine Eleven/Finding Answers (NEFA) TerrorWatch subscription service, July 23, 2008, http://www.nefafoundation.org/miscellaneous/FeaturedDocs/nefatip0409-2.pdf (accessed August 23, 2009).

58. Ibid.

59. The Aviation Safety Network website, last updated May 4, 2009, http://aviation-safety.net/database/record.php?id=20080307-0&lang=fr (accessed May 4, 2009); Xinhua, "Suspect Confesses to Terrorist Attempt on China Flight," China Daily, March 27, 2008, http://www.chinadaily.com.cn/china/2008-03/27/content_6570512.htm (accessed May 4, 2009); Tak-ho Fong, " 'Terror' Attack a Warning Shot for Beijing," March 14, 2008, Asia Times, http://www.atimes.com/atimes/China/JC14Ad01.html (accessed May 4, 2009).

60. Parry, "Female Suicide Bombers"; Xinhua, "Serial Explosions"; Geoff Dyer and Jamil Anderlini, "Distant Thunder: Separatism Stirs on China's Forgotten Frontier," Financial Times, August 17, 2008, http://www.ft.com/cms/s/0/26082e82-6c7b-11dd-96dc-0000779fd18c,dwp_uuid=723ba534-41c2-11dc-8328-0000779fd2ac.html?nclick_check=1

(accessed April 10, 2009); Parry, "Renewed Bomb Attacks"; Yardley, "Police in Western China Kill 5 Suspected Militants After Bombing Attack"; Yardley, "New Spasm."

61. Asian News International, "3 Suicide Bombers Enter Islamabad, Lahore, May Target Key Installations," June 19, 2009, http://www.lexisnexis.com/.

62. Rohan Gunaratna and Kenneth George Pereire, "An Al-Qaeda Associate Group Operating in China?" *China and Eurasian Forum Quarterly* 4, no. 2 (2006): 56, http://www.silkroadstudies.org/new/docs/CEF/Quarterly/May_2006/GunaratnaPereire.pdf (accessed August 23, 2009).

63. Millward, "Violent Separatism," 13.

64. STRATFOR, "China."

65. Millward, "Violent Separatism," 14.

66. Higgins, " 'Holy War' Rages"; United Press International, "Authorities in Western China"; Tyson, "Foreign Muslims"; "Further Report."

67. Many organizations in China, including government ones, are organized as compounds. Depending on the size of the organization, the compound may include dormitories, apartments, schools, medical offices, or administrative buildings, as well as the actual organization itself.

68. "Further Report."

69. Ibid.

70. Ibid.

71. Ibid.

72. Dreyer, "China's Vulnerability," 72.

73. "Further Report."

74. Ibid.

75. Millward, "Violent Separatism," 14; STRATFOR, "China."

76. "Further Report"; United Press International, "Authorities in Western China."

77. People's Republic of China, Information Office of the State Council, " 'East Turkistan' Terrorist Forces."

78. Ibid.

79. Ibid.

80. Ibid.

81. Ibid.

82. Ibid.

83. Ibid.

84. Ibid.

85. Ibid.

86. Agence France-Presse, "Chronology of China Bombs and Mystery Blasts," January 29, 1999, http://www.lexisnexis.com/ (accessed August 16, 2009).

87. Charles Hutzler, "Despite Crackdown, Ethnic Tensions Persist in China's Northwest," Associated Press, March 12, 1998, http://www.uygur.org/enorg/wunn98/wunn031198.htm (accessed August 16, 2009).

88. People's Republic of China, Information Office of the State Council, " 'East Turkistan' Terrorist Forces"; Teresa Poole, "Peking Rocked by Bomb Blast," *The Independent*, May 14, 1997, http://www.independent.co.uk/news/world/peking-rocked-by-bomb-blast-1261381.html (accessed March 15, 2009).

89. Agence France-Presse, "China Rocked as Bombs on Xinjiang Buses Kill Seven," February 26, 1997, http://www.uygur.org/enorg/wunn97/wunn022697.htm (accessed August 16, 2009).

90. People's Republic of China, Information Office of the State Council, " 'East Turkistan' Terrorist Forces."

91. Ibid.

92. The original reporting said damage totaled more than 1 million Chinese yuan.

93. People's Republic of China, Information Office of the State Council, " 'East Turkistan' Terrorist Forces."

94. Ibid.

95. "Profiles of 11 Terrorists Identified."

96. STRATFOR, "China."

97. People's Republic of China, Ministry of Public Security, "First Batch."

98. "Profiles of 11 Terrorists Identified."

99. Radio Free Europe/Radio Liberty Kyrgyz News, "Kyrgyzstan Deports Two Uyghurs to China," May 23, 2002, http://www.eurasianet.org/resource/kyrgyzstan/hypermail/200205/0062.shtml (accessed August 29, 2009); NCA, "Kyrgyzstan Deports Two Uyghurs Back to China," May 23, 2002, http://www.uygur.org/wunn02/2002_05_23a.htm (accessed August 16, 2009). The assassination in 2000 was reported in Alexeyev, "A Tough International."

100. *People's Daily*, "U.S. Has Evidence ETIM Plans Attack," *People's Daily Online*, August 30, 2002, http://english.peopledaily.com.cn/200208/30/eng20020830_102348.shtml (accessed August 16, 2009); Philip Pan, "U.S. Warns of Plot by Group in W. China," *The Washington Post*, August 29, 2002, A27.

101. Ibid.

102. BBC News, "Bomb Explodes on S China Bus," August 8, 2005, http://newsvote.bbc.co.uk/mpapps/pagetools/print/news.bbc.co.uk/2/hi/asia-pacific/4131916.stm (accessed August 17, 2009).

103. Turkistan Islamic Party [Islam Awazi], "Our Blessed Jihad in Yunnan," video, July 23, 2008, http://www.youtube.com/watch?v=E6DLGShOnEg&feature=related (accessed August 17, 2009).

104. "Xinjiang Foils Air Crash Attempt with an Emergency Landing," *People's Daily Online*, March 10, 2008, http://english.peopledaily.com.cn/90001/90776/90882/6370043.html (accessed February 1, 2009); Fong, " 'Terror' Attack."

105. Aviation Safety Network website; Xinhua, "Suspect Confesses"; Fong, " 'Terror' Attack."

106. Xinhua, "Seven Killed, 36 Injured in China Truck Explosion," March 13, 2008, http://news.smashits.com/NewsPrint.asp?nid=234790 (accessed August 19, 2009).

107. Jill Drew, "China Group Asserts That It Bombed Buses," *The Washington Post*, July 27, 2008, http://www.washingtonpost.com/wp-dyn/content/article/2008/07/26/AR2008072601370.html (accessed August 17, 2008).

108. Xinhua, "Three Firefighters Die, Nine Injured in Factory Fire," *China Daily*, July 18, 2008, http://www.chinadaily.com.cn/china/2008-07/18/content_6858653.htm (accessed August 18, 2009).

109. The website that hosted this video, www.alhesbah.bz, is no longer operational. The ETIM logo was reportedly superimposed over one of the first frames. However, this video did not display the Islam Awazi logo or contact information for the ETIM, as other ETIM videos have.

The execution video was first reported by MEMRI ("Islamic Party of Turkestan Releases Video Showing Execution of Three Chinese Hostages"). The MEMRI report sparked discussion about the video's authenticity at the New Dominion website. See New Dominion,

"Follow-Up: Video of Attack on Chinese Men in Pakistan," April 26, 2008, http://www
.thenewdominion.net/149/follow-up-video-of-attack-on-chinese-men-in-pakistan/
(accessed September 13, 2009); and "Report of Chinese Hostage Execution Video, Possible
Central Asia Link," April 15, 2008, http://www.thenewdominion.net/137/report-of-chinese
-hostage-execution-video-possible-central-asia-link/ (accessed September 13, 2009).
New Dominion reported the video appeared to be related to the shooting of three Chinese
citizens in Peshawar, Pakistan, on July 9, 2007. Police said the shooting in Peshawar was a
robbery, but one witness said the attackers had covered faces and shouted religious slogans.
See Xinhua, "Three Chinese Killed in NW Pakistan," July 9, 2007, http://news.xinhuanet
.com/english/2007-07/09/content_6346549.htm (accessed September 13, 2009).

110. Xinhua News Agency, "Chinese Police Deny 'Terrorist Attacks' Behind Recent
Explosions," July 26, 2008, http://news.xinhuanet.com/english/2008-07/26/content
_8775123.htm (accessed August 23, 2009); Drew, "China Group Asserts"; Tania Branigan,
"Olympics Threatened by Islamic Separatists," *The Guardian*, July 27, 2008, http://
www.guardian.co.uk/sport/2008/jul/27/olympicgames2008.terrorism/print (accessed
August 18, 2009).

111. Xinhua, "Fatal Explosion Linked to Gambling Dispute in East China," May 19,
2008, Embassy of Switzerland in Beijing, http://www.sinoptic.ch/embassy/presseschau/
2008/20080519-0523.htm#21 (accessed August 18, 2009); Associated Press, "Bus Crash
in China Kills 14," *USA Today*, May 17, 2008, http://www.usatoday.com/news/world/
2008-05-17-4025066727_x.htm (accessed August 18, 2009).

112. Agence France-Presse, "Chinese Authorities Deny Uighur Group Behind Attacks:
State Media," July 25, 2008, http://afp.google.com/article/ALeqM5hn-RS89mZLpCR
_CyIATJLUlG8YDQ (accessed August 19, 2009); Xinhua News Agency, "Chinese Police
Deny"; Drew, "China Group Asserts."

113. Drew, "China Group Asserts."

114. Reuters, "Bizarre Text Message Precedes China Bus Bomb Blasts," *TheStar*,
July 22, 2008, http://thestar.com.my/news/story.asp?file=/2008/7/22/worldupdates/
2008-07-22T134257Z_01_NOOTR_RTRMDNC_0_-346179-2&sec=Worldupdates
(accessed August 18, 2009).

115. Ibid.

116. Xinhua, "Bus Explosions Leave Two Dead in SW China, Police Say Deliberately Set,"
July 21, 2008, Xinhua News Agency, http://news.xinhuanet.com/english/2008-07/21/content
_8739304.htm (accessed August 19, 2009); Xinhua News Agency, "Chinese Police Deny."

117. Commander Abdelhaq Al-Turkestani, "Response from the Turkestan Islamic Party
to the Olympic Games to Be Held in China in 2008," March 1, 2008, trans. Nine Eleven/
Finding Answers (NEFA) TerrorWatch subscription service, http://www.nefafoundation
.org/miscellaneous/FeaturedDocs/nefatip0409.pdf (accessed August 23, 2009).

118. Turkestan Islamic Party, "On the Occasion."

119. Turkistan Islamic Party [Islam Awazi], "General Call to Muslims of the World,"
August 1, 2008, http://www.youtube.com/watch?v=pwO_wX5olNQ (accessed August 22,
2009), trans. Open Source Center, CPP200808074800001.

120. *China Daily*, "Xinjiang Official Vows to Crack Down on Terrorists," August 2,
2008, http://www.china.org.cn/china/local/2008-08/02/content_16120593.htm (accessed
August 22, 2008).

121. Mansur [Islam Awazi], "The Enemy Is Terrified."

122. Xinhua, "16 Police Officer Die in Kashgar Terror Strike," [sic], *China Daily*,
August 5, 2008, http://www.chinadaily.com.cn/china/2008-08/05/content_6903132.htm

(accessed March 8, 2009); Xinhua, "Serial Explosions"; DPA, "Blasts, Gunfire Kill at Least Eight in China," *Thaindian News*, August 10, 2008, http://www.thaindian.com/newsportal/uncategorized/blasts-gunfire-kill-at-least-eight-in-china-lead_10082196.html (accessed August 20, 2009); B. Raman, "Chinese Delink Xinjiang Incident from Olympics," Chennai Centre for China Studies, August 6, 2008, http://www.c3sindia.org/terrorismandsecurity/297 (accessed August 20, 2009).

123. Ibid.

124. Mansur [Islam Awazi], "The Enemy Is Terrified."

125. Ibid.

126. Reporting on this incident is confusing and sometimes contradictory. This account synthesizes information presented in the following news articles: Parry, "Renewed Bomb Attacks"; Parry, "Female Suicide Bombers"; Xinhua, "Serial Explosions"; Yardley, "Police in Western China"; Yardley, "New Spasm of Violence"; *China Daily*, "Blasts Rock Xinjiang"; Foreman, "Bombing Spree"; Foreman, "City in China's West"; Agence France-Presse, "Police Attacked"; Moore, "China Beefs Up Security in Kuqa After New Terror Attack"; Elegant, "A China Threat"; Xinhua News Agency, "Civilian Dies from Injuries"; and Ho, "Muslim Separatists." This account also includes information from the ETIM statement Mansur [Islam Awazi], "The Enemy Is Terrified."

127. Edward Wong, "Attack in West China Kills 3 Security Officers," *The New York Times*, August 13, 2008, http://www.nytimes.com/2008/08/13/sports/olympics/13china.html?ref=world (accessed August 17, 2008); Mansur [Islam Awazi], "The Enemy Is Terrified"; Xinhua News Agency, "Police Arrest Three Over Xinjiang Killings," August 29, 2008, http://news.xinhuanet.com/english/2008-08/29/content_9737543.htm (accessed August 23, 2009); Jonathan Watts, "Chinese Police Officers Stabbed to Death at Checkpoint," *The Guardian*, August 12, 2008, http://www.guardian.co.uk/sport/2008/aug/12/olympics2008.china?gusrc=rss&feed=networkfront (accessed August 23, 2009).

128. Mansur [Islam Awazi], "The Enemy Is Terrified"; Agence France-Presse, "Chinese Police Kill Six in Xinjiang Clash: Reports," August 29, 2008, http://afp.google.com/article/ALeqM5g9DGAcpJC22ojD44TodVyRFQJ4WA (accessed August 23, 2009); Xinhua News Agency, "Police Arrest Three."

129. Xinhua, "Police Destroy Terrorist Camp, Killing 18," January 8, 2007, *China Daily*, http://www.chinadaily.com.cn/china/2007-01/08/content_777852.htm (accessed March 13, 2009).

130. Gulnoza Saidazimova, "China: Officials Say Uyghur Group Involved in Olympic Terror Plot," GlobalSecurity.org, http://www.globalsecurity.org/security/library/news/2008/04/sec-080411-rferl01.htm (accessed August 29, 2009); Zhu Zhe, "Police Foil Terrorist Attempts to Derail Games," April 11, 2008, *China Daily*, http://www.chinadaily.com.cn/olympics/2008-04/11/content_6607933.htm (accessed August 23, 2009).

131. "Xinjiang Foils Air Crash Attempt."

132. Edward Wong and Keith Bradshier, "China Orders Highest Alert for Olympics," *The New York Times*, August 4, 2008, http://www.nytimes.com/2008/08/04/sports/olympics/04china.html (accessed August 22, 2009).

CHAPTER 4

1. Rohan Gunaratna, "China Under Threat: Uighur Group Poses Biggest Terror Threat to Olympics," *The Straits Times*, August 3, 2008, http://www.straitstimes.com/Free/Story/STIStory_264004.html (accessed April 10, 2009).

2. Falco, "Islamic Movement of Uzbekistan (IMU)."

3. People's Republic of China, "Terrorist Activities Perpetrated."

4. People's Republic of China, "China Identifies"; People's Republic of China, Information Office of the State Council, " 'East Turkistan' Terrorist Forces"; People's Republic of China, Ministry of Public Security, "First Batch."

5. UN Security Council, "The Consolidated List Established and Maintained by the 1267 Committee with Respect to Al-Qaida, Usama bin Laden, and the Taliban and Other Individuals, Groups, Undertakings and Entities Associated with Them," last updated August 10, 2009, http://www.un.org/sc/committees/1267/consolist.shtml (accessed August 23, 2009).

6. U.S. Department of the Treasury, Office of Public Affairs, "Press Statement."

7. U.S. Department of State, "Patterns of Global Terrorism 2002," April 2003, http://www.state.gov/documents/organization/20177.pdf (accessed August 27, 2009), p. 132.

8. U.S. Department of State, "Patterns of Global Terrorism 2003," April 2004, http://www.state.gov/documents/organization/31912.pdf (accessed August 27, 2009), p. 144.

9. Radio Free Asia, "Uyghur Separatist Denies Links to Taliban, Al-Qaeda," January 27, 2002, http://www.rfa.org/english/news/politics/2002/01/27/85871/ (accessed April 20, 2008).

10. David S. Cloud and Ian Johnson, "Friend or Foe: In Post-9/11 World, Chinese Dissidents Pose U.S. Dilemma," *The Wall Street Journal*, August 3, 2004, http://www.proquest.umi.com.

11. Turkestan Islamic Party, "Why Are We Fighting China?"

12. Al-Shishani, "Journal of the Turkistan Islamic Party."

13. Murad Batal Al-Shishani of the Jamestown Foundation characterizes this as a standard jihadi argument. See "Journal of the Turkistan Islamic Party"; Turkistan Islamic Party, "Apparent Full Text"; Turkistan Islamic Party [Islam Awazi], "Steadfastness and Preparations"; Turkistan Islamic Party [Islam Awazi], "Why Are We Fighting China?"; and Turkistan Islamic Party [Islam Awazi], "Statement on the Events, Chinese Aggression v. Uyghurs," video, July 8, 2009, http://www.youtube.com/watch?v=e-K6gkbRqNw (accessed August 22, 2009).

14. People's Republic of China, Ministry of Public Security, "China Identifies."

15. U.S. Department of the Treasury, Office of Public Affairs, "Press Statement."

16. United Nations, "The Consolidated List."

17. Cloud and Johnson, "In Post-9/11 World."

18. Ibid.

19. Turkestan Islamic Party, "Steadfastness and Preparations."

20. Clifford J. Levy, "Central Asia Sounds Alarm on Islamic Radicalism," *The New York Times*, August 17, 2009, http://www.nytimes.com/2009/08/18/world/asia/18kyrgyz.html?hpw (accessed September 12, 2009).

21. Deirdre Tynan, "Uzbekistan: Authorities Link Tashkent Shootout in August to Islamic Movement of Uzbekistan," EurasiaNet.org, September 9, 2009, http://www.eurasianet.org/departments/insightb/articles/eav090909.shtml (accessed September 12, 2009).

22. Bruno De Cordier, "The Islamic Movement of Uzbekistan and the Islamic Jihad Union: A Jihadi Nebulous in Central Asia and the EU," Caucaz.com, February 7, 2008, http://www.caucaz.com/home_eng/breve_contenu.php?id=344 (accessed September 12, 2009).

23. People's Republic of China, Ministry of Public Security, "First Batch."

24. Alexeyev, "A Tough International"; Falco, "Islamic Movement of Uzbekistan."

25. Al-Shishani, "Journal of the Turkistan Islamic Party."

26. Alexeyev, "A Tough International."

27. BBC World Service, "Tajik Opposition Blames Uzbekistan for Bombings," October 6, 1999, http://usproxy.bbc.com/2/low/asia-pacific/466820.stm (accessed September 12, 2009); GlobalSecurity.org, "Tajikistan Civil War," last modified April 27, 2005, http://www.globalsecurity.org/military/world/war/tajikistan.htm (accessed September 12, 2009).

28. Gunaratna and Pereire, "An Al-Qaeda Associate Group"; Gunaratna, "China Under Threat."

29. Gunaratna, "China Under Threat."

30. Ibid.

31. Hassan Abbas, "A Profile of Tehrik-i-Taliban Pakistan," CTC Sentinel 1 (January 2008): 2, 1–4, http://belfercenter.ksg.harvard.edu/publication/17868/profile_of_tehrikitaliban_pakistan.html (accessed September 12, 2009).

32. Gunaratna and Pereire, "An Al-Qaeda Associate Group."

33. Imatov, "The Question of the Uighur Question."

34. People's Republic of China, Ministry of Public Security, "First Batch."

35. Falco, "Islamic Movement of Uzbekistan"; Hashim Ibragimov, "Frightening Image of Extremism" [in Russian], Nezavisimaya Gazeta, February 3, 2000, http://www.ng.ru/net/2000-02-03/5_lik.html (accessed August 16, 2009).

36. Alexeyev, "A Tough International"; Falco, "Islamic Movement of Uzbekistan"; Rotar, "Explode Whether Central Asia?"

37. People's Republic of China, Information Office of the State Council, " 'East Turkistan' Terrorist Forces Cannot Get Away with Impunity."

38. Alexeyev, "A Tough International."

39. Developing a precise figure for the Uyghur diaspora is practically impossible. In 2003, Shichor estimated the Uyghur diaspora at just under 486,000 ("Virtual Transnationalism"); by 2009, he estimated that up to 600,000 Uyghurs live outside China ("The Uyghurs and China"). The WUC estimates on its website that 500,000 Uyghurs live in "West Turkistan," with another 75,000 Uyghurs living in Pakistan, Afghanistan, Saudi Arabia, Europe, and the United States.

40. World Uyghur Congress, "Brief History of the Uyghurs," http://www.uyghurcongress.org/En/Uyghurs.asp?mid=1195916276&mid2=-1500528155 (accessed August 30, 2009).

41. Turkistan Islamic Party [Islam Awazi], "Jihad Lands."

42. Falco, "Islamic Movement of Uzbekistan."

43. Yu Zheng, "Woman Behind Xinjiang Riot Caught Self-Contradictory," Xinhua News Agency, July 11, 2009, http://news.xinhuanet.com/english/2009-07/11/content_11689948.htm (accessed August 29, 2009); Associated Press, "China Against Muslim Activist for Nobel Prize," The Jerusalem Post, September 12, 2006, http://www.jpost.com/servlet/Satellite?cid=1157913614559&pagename=JPost%2FJPArticle%2FShowFull (accessed August 29, 2009); Peter Ford, "Spiritual Mother of Uighurs or Terrorist?" The Christian Science Monitor, July 9, 2009, http://www.csmonitor.com/2009/0709/p06s15-woap.html (accessed August 29, 2009).

44. The Uyghurs at the ETIM training camp were Abdu Helil Mamut, Abdul Ghappar Abdul Rahman, Abdul Razak, Abdul Semet, Abu Bakr Qasim, Adel Abdulhehim, Ahmed Adil, Ahmed Mohamed, Akhdar Qasem, Bahtiyar Mahnut, Dawut Abdurehim,

Haji Mohammed Ayub, Hasan Anvar, Huzaifa Parhat, Jalal Jalaldin, Sabir Osman, Saidullah Khalik, and Yusef Abbas.

Unless otherwise specified, information here comes from Combatant Status Review Tribunal and Administrative Review Board documents. See http://www.dod.gov/pubs/foi/detainees/csrt_arb/index.html for a complete archive of these documents. Many of the GTMO Uyghurs used aliases at different points during their detention, so their names may differ across documents. The unique Internment Serial Number (ISN) is the best way to identify a specific detainee.

45. U.S. Department of Defense, Administrative Review Board, Unclassified Summary of Evidence.

46. U.S. Department of Defense, Combatant Status Review Board, Summarized Detainee Sworn Statement [Ahmed Mohamed, ISN 328].

47. At least eight of the GTMO Uyghurs followed this route. Sources include U.S. Department of Defense, Combatant Status Review Board, Summarized Detainee Unsworn Statement [Akhdar Qasem, ISN 276], n.d., http://www.dod.gov/pubs/foi/detainees/csrt_arb/index.html (accessed August 2, 2009); U.S. Department of Defense, Combatant Status Review Board, Summarized Detainee Unsworn Statement [Abu Bakr Qasim, ISN 283], n.d., http://www.dod.gov/pubs/foi/detainees/csrt_arb/index.html (accessed August 2, 2009); and U.S. Department of Defense, Combatant Status Review Board, Summarized Detainee Sworn Statement [Adel Abdulhehim, ISN 293], n.d., http://www.dod.gov/pubs/foi/detainees/csrt_arb/index.html (accessed August 2, 2009).

48. U.S. Department of Defense, Combatant Status Review Board, Summarized Detainee Unsworn Statement [Sabir Osman, ISN 282], November 5, 2004, http://www.dod.gov/pubs/foi/detainees/csrt_arb/index.html (accessed August 2, 2009).

49. U.S. Department of Defense, Administrative Review Board, Unclassified Summary of Evidence.

50. U.S. Department of Defense, Combatant Status Review Board, Summarized Detainee Unsworn Statement [Abu Bakr Qasim, ISN 283].

51. U.S. Department of Defense, Combatant Status Review Board, Summarized Detainee Sworn Statement [Bahtiyar Mahnut, ISN 277], n.d., http://www.dod.gov/pubs/foi/detainees/csrt_arb/index.html (accessed August 2, 2009).

52. U.S. Department of Defense, Combatant Status Review Board, Summarized Detainee Unsworn Statement [Abu Bakr Qasim, ISN 283]; U.S. Department of Defense, Combatant Status Review Board, Summarized Detainee Sworn Statement [Bahtiyar Mahnut, ISN 277].

53. Ibid.

54. U.S. Department of Defense, Combatant Status Review Board, Summarized Detainee Sworn Statement [Huzaifa Parhat, ISN 320], n.d., http://www.dod.gov/pubs/foi/detainees/csrt_arb/index.html (accessed August 2, 2009); U.S. Department of Defense, Combatant Status Review Board, Summarized Detainee Sworn Statement [Ahmed Mohamed, ISN 328].

55. U.S. Department of Defense, Administrative Review Board, Summary of Administrative Review Board Proceedings for ISN 277, n.d., http://projects.nytimes.com/guantanamo/detainees/277-bahtiyar-mahnut/documents/2/pages/2884#23 (accessed August 15, 2009).

56. U.S. Department of Defense, Combatant Status Review Board, Summarized Detainee Unsworn Statement [Yusef Abbas, ISN 275]; U.S. Department of Defense, Combatant Status Review Board, Summarized Detainee Unsworn Statement [Abu Bakr Qasim, ISN 283].

57. Abu Bakker Qasim, "The View from Guantanamo," *The New York Times*, September 16, 2006, http://query.nytimes.com/gst/fullpage.html?res=9D0CEFDB1331 F934A2575AC0A9609C8B63 (accessed August 15, 2009).

58. Richard J. Leon, *"Lakhdar Boumediene et al. v. George W. Bush et al.*—Civil Action No. 04-1166 (RJL): Memorandum Order," U.S. District Court for the District of Columbia, October 27, 2008, http://www.scotusblog.com/wp/wp-content/uploads/ 2008/10/boumediene-order-10-27-08.pdf (accessed August 15, 2009). The exact definition of an "enemy combatant" is "an individual who was part of or supporting Taliban or al Qaeda forces that are engaged in hostilities against the United States or its coalition partners. This includes any person who has committed a belligerent act or has directly supported hostilities in aid of enemy armed forces."

59. BBC News, "Albania Takes Guantanamo Uighurs," May 6, 2006, http://news.bbc .co.uk/go/pr/fr/-/2/hi/americas/4979466.stm (accessed August 9, 2009).

60. U.S. District Court for the District of Columbia, "Memorandum Opinion: Granting the Petitioners' Motions for Judgment on Their Pending Habeas Petitions and Denying as Moot the Petitioners' Motions for Immediate Release of Parole into the United States," October 9, 2008, https://ecf.dcd.uscourts.gov/cgi-bin/show_public_doc?2008cv1310-45 (accessed August 9, 2009).

61. BBC News, "Bermuda Takes Guantanamo Uighurs," June 11, 2009, http://news .bbc.co.uk/go/pr/fr/-/2/hi/americas/8095582.stm (accessed August 9, 2009).

62. U.S. Department of Defense, Combatant Status Review Board, Summarized Detainee Sworn Statement [Huzaifa Parhat, ISN 320].

63. Adel Abdulhehim, ISN 293, was called as a witness at the Combatant Status Review Board for GTMO detainee Abdul Ghappar Abdul Rahman.

64. U.S. Department of Defense, Combatant Status Review Board, Summarized Detainee Unsworn Statement [Abdul Ghappar Abdul Rahman, ISN 281].

65. U.S. District Court for the District of Columbia, *Nag Mohammed v. George W. Bush: Civil Action No. 05-1602 (ESH)*, September 19, 2005, http://www.dod.mil/pubs/foi/ detainees/csrt_arb/publicly_filed_CSRT_records_698-814.pdf (accessed September 12, 2009).

66. Turkestan Islamic Party, "Steadfastness and Preparations."

67. Falco, "Islamic Movement of Uzbekistan."

68. Al-Shishani, "Journal of the Turkistan Islamic Party."

69. Gunaratna, "China Under Threat."

70. Turkistan Islamic Party [Islam Awazi], "Jihad Lands."

71. Alexeyev, "A Tough International."

72. "Separatist Leader Handed Over to China," *Dawn*, May 28, 2002, http://www. hartford-hwp.com/archives/55/456.html (accessed April 12, 2009); Al-Jazeera, "China 'Executes' Uighur Activist," February 9, 2007, http://english.aljazeera.net/news/ asia-pacific/2007/02/2008525143353859811.html (accessed March 7, 2009).

73. Turkistan Islamic Party [Islam Awazi], "Jihad Lands"; Turkestan Islamic Party, "Steadfastness and Preparations."

74. Amir Mir, "10 Terror Suspects Extradited to China," *The News*, June 6, 2009, http:// www.thenews.com.pk/top_story_detail.asp?Id=22569 (accessed September 12, 2009).

75. Turkistan Islamic Party, "The Chinese and Pakistani Media Are Full of Lies and Accusations," trans. on behalf of the Nine Eleven/Finding Answers (NEFA) TerrorWatch subscription service, May 1, 2009, http://www.nefafoundation.org/miscellaneous/ FeaturedDocs/nefatip0509.pdf (accessed August 23, 2009).

76. Alexeyev, "A Tough International"; Seva Gunitskiy, "In the Spotlight: East Turkistan Islamic Movement (ETIM)," Center for Defense Information, December 9, 2002, http://www.cdi.org/terrorism/etim.cfm (accessed August 29, 2009); Gunaratna and Pereire, "An Al-Qaeda Associate Group."

77. Pan, "U.S. Warns."

78. Evan Kohlmann, "Prominent Jihad Media Organizations in Central Asia," the Nine Eleven/Finding Answers (NEFA) Foundation, 2009, http://www.nefafoundation.org/miscellaneous/FeaturedDocs/nefajihadmedia0309.pdf (accessed August 29, 2009); Evan Kohlmann, "Al-Qaida's Online Couriers: The Al-Fajr Media Center and the Global Islamic Media Front (GIMF)," the Nine Eleven/Finding Answers (NEFA) Foundation, May 2009, http://nefafoundation.org/fajrchart.html (accessed August 29, 2009).

79. Ibid.

80. We last accessed the site on April 21, 2008. On August 7, 2008, the blog of Internet Haganah (a research and activism group focused on combating global jihad) reported the site was "currently suspended."

81. These URLs appeared on the ETIM's website, in ETIM videos, and in the ETIM magazine.

82. Society for Internet Research (SOFIR), "kanzhassan.com: Site of Cleric Abdel Hakim Hassan (Abu Amrw)," n.d., http://www.sofir.org/reports/2006-06-10-kanzhassan.html (accessed August 29, 2009). Tipawazi.com was registered to "naeem Khan (info@kanzhassan.com), 5pl ranchor line Saddar, Karachi, sindh, pk 74200, P: +021.090078601 F: +201.090078601."

83. Society for Internet Research, "kanzhassan.com."

84. Will McCants, "Important Al-Qaeda Scholar Identified," *Jihadica*, June 4, 2008, http://www.jihadica.com/important-al-qaeda-scholar-identified/ (accessed August 29, 2009); Will McCants, "Al-Qaeda Cleric Linked to Chinese Terrorist Group," *Jihadica*, August 11, 2008, http://www.jihadica.com/al-qaeda-cleric-linked-to-chinese-terrorist-group/ (accessed September 12, 2009).

85. These e-mail addresses appeared on the ETIM's website, in ETIM videos, and in the ETIM magazine.

86. Al-Shishani, "Journal of the Turkistan Islamic Party," 3.

87. Thomas Hegghammer, "Infighting over Distribution of New Uighur Magazine," *Jihadica*, February 20, 2009, http://www.jihadica.com/infighting-over-distribution-of-new-uighur-magazine/ (accessed August 29, 2009).

88. Al-Shishani, "Journal of the Turkistan Islamic Party"; Turkestan Islamic Party, "Steadfastness and Preparations"; Associated Press, "Islamic Group Threatens Olympic Transport," August 7, 2008, http://www.msnbc.msn.com/id/26074595/ (accessed August 31, 2009).

CHAPTER 5

1. Dyer and Anderlini, "Distant Thunder."

2. Edward Cody, "China Cracks Down on Corruption," *The Washington Post*, February 15, 2006, A18.

3. Luo Bing, "Chinese Leader States Corruption Will Destroy the Chinese Communist Party," *The Epoch Times*, February 29, 2008, http://en.epochtimes.com/tools/printer.asp?id=66784 (accessed March 28, 2009).

4. Jamie P. Horsley, "Village Elections: Training Ground for Democratization," *The China Business Review*, March–April 2001, http://www.chinabusinessreview.com/public/0103/horsley.html (accessed February 3, 2009).

5. Girish Sawlani, "Hong Kong's Democracy Advocate Bows Out of Elections," Australian Broadcasting Corporation, July 9, 2009, http://www.abc.net.au/ra/program guide/stories/200807/s2298623.htm (accessed March 28, 2009).

6. These observations are based on the experience of author J. Todd Reed, who spent time in China from 1994 through 2004.

7. Pitman B. Potter, "Belief in Control: Regulation of Religion in China," *The China Quarterly* 174 (June 2003), http://www.jstor.org/, p. 320.

8. Dreyer, "China's Vulnerability."

9. Katie Xiao, "China Continues to Persecute Religious Groups, State's Birkle Says," July 21, 2005, U.S. Department of State: United States Diplomatic Mission to Italy, http://www.usembassy.it/viewer/article.asp?article=/file2005_07/alia/a5072204.htm (accessed March 28, 2009).

10. Falun Dafa Information Center, "Falun Gong: The Practice," May 17, 2008, http://www.faluninfo.net/print/210/ (accessed April 11, 2009).

11. Potter, "Belief in Control."

12. Richard C. Morais, "China's Fight with Falun Gong," *Forbes*, February 9, 2006, http://www.forbes.com/2006/02/09/falun-gong-china_cz_rm_0209falungong.html (accessed February 22, 2009).

13. Joseph Kahn, "Notoriety Now for Movement's Leader," *The New York Times*, April 27, 1999, http://www.nytimes.com/1999/04/27/world/notoriety-now-for-movement-s-leader.html (accessed March 28, 2009).

14. Xinhua, "Xinhua Commentary Calls for Long-Term Fight Against Falun Gong Cult," Permanent Mission of the People's Republic of China to the UN, September 7, 2003, http://www.china-un.org/eng/zt/flgwt/t29534.htm (accessed February 28, 2009).

15. Francesco Sisci, "Falungong, Part 1: From Sport to Suicide," *Asia Times Online*, January 21, 2001, http://atimes.com/china/CA27Ad01.html (accessed February 22, 2009).

16. Francesco Sisci, "Falungong, Part 2: A Rude Awakening," *Asia Times Online*, January 30, 2001, http://atimes.com/china/CA30Ad01.html (accessed February 22, 2009).

17. Thomas Lum, "China and Falun Gong," Congressional Research Service, Report for Congress, May 25, 2006, http://fpc.state.gov/documents/organization/67820.pdf (accessed March 28, 2009).

18. Evan Osnos, "Jesus in China: Christianity's Rapid Rise," *Chicago Tribune*, June 22, 2008, http://www.chicagotribune.com/news/local/chi-jesus-1-1-webjun22,0,2458211.story (accessed March 28, 2009); "Christianity in China: Sons of Heaven," *The Economist*, October 2, 2008, http://www.economist.com/world/asia/PrinterFriendly.cfm?story_id=12342509 (accessed March 28, 2009).

19. Jane Macartney, "One Billion Souls to Save," *The Times*, March 28, 2009, http://www.timesonline.co.uk/tol/news/article5960010.ece (accessed March 28, 2009).

20. Kate McGeown, "China's Christians Suffer for Their Faith," BBC News, November 9, 2004, http://news.bbc.co.uk/2/hi/asia-pacific/3993857.stm (accessed March 28, 2009).

21. Macartney, "One Billion Souls to Save."

22. Armijo, "Islamic Education in China."

23. Igor Rotar, "Xinjiang: Strict Control of China's Uighur Muslims Continues," Forum 18 News Service via WorldWide Religious News, August 15, 2006, http://www.wwrn.org/article.php?idd=22434&sec=33&con=17 (accessed August 15, 2009).

24. People's Republic of China, Information Office of the State Council, "China's National Defense in 2008," January 2009, http://english.gov.cn/official/2009-01/20/content_1210227.htm (accessed April 5, 2009).

25. Agence France-Presse, "China Vows 'Severe Crackdown' on Tibet Separatists," March 28, 2009, http://www.google.com/hostednews/afp/article/ALeqM5iR_h4oql XBVVpm8RCEGOcW15jQcg (accessed March 29, 2009).

26. Ibid.

27. BBC News, "Tibetan Riots Continue in China," March 24, 2008, http://news.bbc.co.uk/2/hi/asia-pacific/7311289.stm (accessed September 13, 2009); BBC News, "Timeline: Tibet," May 13, 2009, http://news.bbc.co.uk/2/hi/asia-pacific/country_profiles/6299565.stm (accessed September 13, 2009).

28. BBC News, "Regions and Territories: Tibet," May 13, 2009, http://news.bbc.co.uk/2/hi/asia-pacific/country_profiles/4152353.stm (accessed September 13, 2009).

29. Agence France-Presse, "Tibet's Panchen Lama, Beijing's Propaganda Tool," March 27, 2009, http://www.google.com/hostednews/afp/article/ALeqM5g4z56PSsE15a H9AaSUAtI4-M_AaQ (accessed March 29, 2009).

30. Hongjiang Wang, "Tibetan Separatists Attack Chinese Embassy in Washington," Xinhua, April 2, 2008, http://www.china-embassy.org/eng/gyzg/t420556.htm (accessed March 28, 2009).

31. "Not Much of a Celebration," *The Economist*, February 26, 2009, http://www.economist.com/opinion/displaysotry.cfm?story_id=13184929 (accessed February 28, 2009).

32. Tseten Samdup, "Chinese Population—Threat to Tibetan Identity," the Government of Tibet in Exile, 1993, http://www.tibet.com/Humanrights/poptrans.html (accessed March 28, 2009).

33. Yang Fang, "Backgrounder: Basic Facts about Tibet," Xinhua, March 9, 2009, http://news.xinhuanet.com/english/2009-03/09/content_10976310.htm (accessed March 28, 2009).

34. Xinhua, "Report: Tibetan Population Grows Fast, Language Education Stressed," April 1, 2009, http://news.xinhuanet.com/english/2009-04/01/content_11112488.htm (accessed September 13, 2009).

35. People's Republic of China, National Bureau of Statistics of China, "2-25 Population in Minority National Autonomous Areas," *China Statistical Yearbook* 1996, http://www.stats.gov.cn/english/statisticaldata/yearlydata/YB1996e/B2-25e.htm (accessed September 13, 2009).

36. Sim Chi Yin, "Potential in Qinghai," *The Straits Times*, August 21, 2009, http://www.straitstimes.com/Breaking%2BNews/Singapore/Story/STIStory_419561.html (accessed September 13, 2009).

37. Erik Eckholm, "China Army Renews Threat Against Taiwan Separatism," *The New York Times*, March 7, 2008, http://www.nytimes.com/2000/03/07/world/china-army-renews-threat-against-taiwan-separatism.html?n=Top/News/World/Countries%20and%20Territories/China (accessed April 5, 2009).

38. Kent Ewing, "Trying Times for Journalists in China," *Asia Times*, August 29, 2006, http://www.atimes.com/atimes/China/HH29Ad01.html (accessed March 28, 2009).

39. Carin Zissis, "Media Censorship in China," Council on Foreign Relations, March 18, 2008, http://www.cfr.org/publication/11515 (accessed March 8, 2009).

40. Lucie Morillon, "China Blocks Blogs, Search Results on Tainted Milk Scandal," PBS, October 22, 2008, http://www.pbs.org/mediashift/2008/10/china-blocks-blogs -search-results-on-tainted-milk-scandal.html (accessed February 28, 2009).

41. Ewing, "Trying Times."

42. Ibid.

43. Richard Taylor, "The Great Firewall of China," BBC News, January 6, 2006, http:// newsvote.bbc.co.uk/1/hi/programmes/click_online/4587622.stm (accessed February 28, 2009).

44. Stephen Sackur, "Red Alert: As the Tibet Protests Erupted, Television and Online Reports from Foreign Broadcasters Were Being Monitored and Shut Down, Proving That Old Habits Die Hard in 'New China,'" *The Guardian*, March 24, 2008, http:// www.guardian.co.uk/media/2008/mar/24/chinathemedia.china (accessed March 7, 2009).

45. Author J. Todd Reed experienced this event on a trip to Xi'an in 2004.

46. Benjamin Kang Lim, "Thousands Protest Against S. China Chemical Plant," Reuters, June 1, 2007, http://www.alertnet.org/thenews/newsdesk/PEK112258.htm# (accessed March 28, 2009).

47. Mark Magnier, "Beijing Olympics Visitors to Come Under Widespread Surveil-lance," *LA Times*, August 7, 2008, http://articles.latimes.com/2008/aug/07/world/ fg-snoop7 (accessed April 9, 2009).

48. Ibid.

49. Andrew F. Nathan, "The Tiananmen Papers," *Foreign Affairs*, January–February 2001.

50. Michael Bristow, "China 'Yet to Approve Protests,'" BBC News, August 18, 2008, http://news.bbc.co.uk/2/hi/asia-pacific/7567703.stm (accessed February 28, 2009).

51. Luis Ramirez, "China Hands Stiff Sentences to 27 Farmers Over Land Seizure Protest," *VOA News*, January 24, 2005, http://www.voanews.com/english/2005-01-24 -voa22.cfm (accessed March 1, 2009).

52. "Sharp Rise in Group Protests in China," *The Epoch Times*, October 16, 2006, http://theepochtimes.com/tools/printer.asp?id=47044 (accessed February 28, 2009).

53. Alex Watts, "Beijing: A Protest-Free Zone?" Sky News, August 20, 2008, http://news .sky.com/skynews/Home/World-News/Beijing-Olympics-Protest-Free-Despite-Protest -Zones/Article/200808315082849 (accessed September 13, 2009).

54. Reuters, "China Says Headed Off Olympic Protest Permits," September 17, 2008, http://www.reuters.com/article/worldNews/idUSPEK9159120080918 (accessed September 13, 2009).

55. Ibid.

56. Bristow, "China 'Yet to Approve Protests.'"

57. Gao, "National Splittism."

58. Xinhua News Agency, "Official: Dalai Lama 'Stubborn in Talks, Not True to His Word,'" March 26, 2009, http://news.xinhuanet.com/english/2009-03/26/content _11076912.htm (accessed March 28, 2009).

59. Human Rights Watch and Human Rights in China, "Devastating Blows."

60. Liu Zhenmin, "Statement by H. E. Ambassador LIU Zhenmin, Deputy Permanent Representative of China to the United Nations, at the Sixth Committee of the 63rd Session of the UN General Assembly on Item 99 'Measures to Eliminate International

Terrorism,'" October 8, 2008, http://www.china-un.org/eng/ldhy/63rd_unga/t517213
.htm (accessed August 23, 2009).

61. Zhu Zhe, "Experts: Anti-Terrorism Law on Cards," *China Daily*, May 31, 2007,
http://www.chinadaily.com.cn/china/2007-05/31/content_883861.htm (accessed
August 23, 2009).

62. Ibid.

63. Shichor, "Blow Up," 124.

64. Millward, "Violent Separatism," 11.

65. Ibid.

66. People's Republic of China, Ministry of Foreign Affairs, "Foreign Ministry Spokesman Qin Gang's Press Conference on 8 September 2005," transcript, September 9, 2005,
http://www.fmprc.gov.cn/eng/xwfw/s2510/2511/t211142.htm (accessed August 29, 2009).

67. Shichor, "Fact and Fiction," 100–101.

68. Xinhua News Agency, "Chinese Police Deny"; Drew, "China Group Asserts";
Branigan, "Olympics Threatened"; Xinhua, "Bus Explosions."

69. Shirley A. Kan, "U.S.-China Counter-Terrorism Cooperation: Issues for U.S. Policy," Congressional Research Service, CRS Report for Congress, version last updated
May 7, 2009, http://www.fas.org/sgp/crs/terror/RL33001.pdf (accessed August 29,
2009), 19.

70. Xinhua, "Fatal Explosion Linked"; Associated Press, "Bus Crash."

71. Xinhuanet, "Anti-Terrorism Law Urged After Urumqi Riot: Expert," last updated
July 22, 2009, http://en.ce.cn/subject/urumqiriot/urumqirioto/200907/22/t20090722
_19594550.shtml (accessed August 23, 2009).

72. Wayne, *China's War on Terrorism*, 45.

73. People's Republic of China, "Spokesperson's Remarks on the Death of Hasan
Mahsum, Head of the 'East Turkistan Islamic Movement,'" n.d., http://www.china-embassy
.org/eng/fyrth/t57039.htm (accessed March 15, 2009). The statement itself is undated, but
it refers to Mahsum's death on October 2 (which we know from other sources to be
October 2, 2003), and to Liu Jianchao's confirmation of that death on October 24 (presumably of the same year). It was almost certainly posted online in October 2003. We accessed
and printed this statement from the website of the Chinese embassy to the United States on
March 15, 2009, but it had been taken down as of April 24, 2009. As of April 24, 2009, the
same statement was still available on the website of the Chinese embassy to Bulgaria.

74. Xinhua News Agency, "Chinese Foreign Ministry Confirms Death of East Turkistan 'Terrorist' Leader," December 24, 2003, http://www.lexisnexis.com/.

75. BBC News, "Chinese Militant 'Shot Dead,'" December 23, 2003, http://news
.bbc.co.uk/2/hi/asia-pacific/3343241.stm (accessed April 21, 2009).

76. Stephen Sullivan, "China's bin Laden: The Terrorist Leader China Forgot," Media
Monitors Network, December 22, 2003, http://usa.mediamonitors.net/Headlines/China
-s-Bin-Laden-The-Terrorist-leader-China-forgot (accessed April 21, 2009).

77. Shichor, "Fact and Fiction," 107–108.

CHAPTER 6

1. Blacklists are commonly confused with watch lists, but they are two different tools of
counterterrorism policy. Placement on a blacklist confers a set of sanctions that restricts
access to funding, mobility, or both. The sole purpose of a watch list is to identify terrorists
as they try to enter a specific territory. Blacklists are published openly, but watch lists are

not. Blacklists can include individuals, organizations, or even whole countries, as in the U.S. list of State Sponsors of Terrorism; by contrast, watch lists include only individuals.

2. See 22 U.S. Code § 2656f(d), 18 U.S. Code § 2331, 28 Code of Federal Regulations Section 0.85, Executive Order 13224, the *2002 National Security Strategy of the United States*, and the *U.S. Department of Defense Dictionary of Military and Associated Terms* for definitions of terrorism. Also see the Immigration and Nationality Act, 8 U.S. Code § 1182(a)(3)(b), for a description of terrorist activity.

3. Turkestan Islamic Party, "Steadfastness and Preparations."

4. Alex Schmid and Albert J. Jongman, *Political Terrorism: A New Guide to Actors, Authors, Concepts, Data Bases, Theories, & Literature* (New Brunswick, NJ: Transaction Books, 1988), 1–2.

5. Michael Scharf, "Defining Terrorism as the Peacetime Equivalent of War Crimes," *Case Western Reserve Journal of International Law* 36, no. 2/3 (2004): 369.

6. Xinhua, "16 Police Officer Die in Kashgar Terror Strike" [*sic*]; Xinhua, "Serial Explosions"; DPA, "Blasts, Gunfire"; Raman, "Chinese Delink."

7. Mansur [Islam Awazi], "The Enemy Is Terrified."

8. Turkestan Islamic Party, "On the Occasion."

9. Edward Wong, "Group Says Video Warns of Olympic Attack," *The New York Times*, August 8, 2008, http://www.nytimes.com/2008/08/08/sports/08iht-08china.15100553.html (accessed August 23, 2009).

10. Turkestan Islamic Party, "Steadfastness and Preparations."

11. Ibid.

12. Cloud and Johnson, "Friend or Foe."

13. U.S. Department of the Treasury, Office of Public Affairs, "Treasury Targets Leader of Group Tied to Al Qaida," news release, April 20, 2009, http://www.treas.gov/press/releases/tg92.htm (accessed August 20, 2009).

14. UN Security Council, "The Consolidated List."

15. HM Treasury, "Financial Sanctions Notification, Al-Qaida and Taliban," October 6, 2008, http://www.hm-treasury.gov.uk/d/fin_sanc_notification_al_qaida_061008.pdf (accessed August 20, 2009). The Arabic term *djamaat* essentially means "group," "collective," or "assembly." It can refer specifically to a group of related villages. In some contexts it assumes a religious connotation, much like "congregation" in English. In the northern Caucasus, it may refer to fundamentalist Muslim groups. Some Westerners have defined the term to mean "militant group," but the word *djamaat* itself does not imply militancy.

Few English-language or translated media sources refer to "Djamaat Turkistan." For examples, see Interfax-Kazakhstan, "Kazakh Special Services Report on Fighting Terror, Illegal Migration in 2007," trans. supplied by BBC Worldwide Monitoring, February 27, 2008, http://www.lexisnexis.com/; and "Kazakh Court Declares Islamic Group as 'Terrorist' Organization," trans. supplied by BBC Worldwide Monitoring, March 5, 2008, http://www.lexisnexis.com/.

16. Audrey Kurth Cronin, "The 'FTO List' and Congress: Sanctioning Designated Foreign Terrorist Organizations," Congressional Research Service, CRS Report for Congress, p. 5, October 21, 2003, https://www.policyarchive.org/handle/10207/1865 (accessed August 22, 2009).

17. The State Department's annual published report on terrorism was called "Patterns of Global Terrorism" through the 2003 edition. The 2004 edition and subsequent editions have been called "Country Reports on Terrorism."

18. Cronin, "The 'FTO List' and Congress," 5.

19. U.S. Department of State, Office of the Coordinator for Counterterrorism, "Fact Sheet: Foreign Terrorist Organizations," July 7, 2009, http://www.state.gov/s/ct/rls/other/des/123085.htm (accessed August 23, 2009).

20. Testimony of Randall G. Schriver, "Exploring the Nature of Uighur Nationalism: Freedom Fighters or Terrorists?" Hearing before the International Organizations, Human Rights, and Oversight Subcommittee.

21. Dru C. Gladney, *Dislocating China: Muslims, Minorities, and Other Subaltern Subjects* (Chicago: University of Chicago Press, 2004), 251.

22. Tamora Vidaillet, "U.S. Seeks Nod for FBI Post in Beijing—Says Muslims in Xinjiang Are Not Necessarily Terrorists," Reuters News Agency, published in the *Washington Times*, December 7, 2001, http://www.infoweb.newsbank.com/. Fuller and Lipman ("Islam in Xinjiang," 343) also note the contrast between Gen. Francis X. Taylor's statements in December 2001 and the eventual U.S. blacklisting.

23. For further information on U.S. political controversy associated with the blacklisting, see the transcripts of congressional hearings on Uyghur issues chaired by Rep. Bill Delahunt (D–Mass.). Transcripts are available through the Federal News Service database at http://www.fnsg.com/.

24. Gunaratna and Pereire, "An Al-Qaeda Associate Group," 56.

25. Shirley Kan, "U.S.-China Counter-Terrorism Cooperation: Issues for U.S. Policy," Congressional Research Service, CRS Report for Congress, p. 5, updated May 12, 2005, http://www.fas.org/sgp/crs/row/RS21995.pdf (accessed August 23, 2009).

26. Holly Fletcher and Jayshree Bajoria, "Backgrounder: The East Turkestan Islamic Movement," Council on Foreign Relations, updated July 31, 2008, http://www.cfr.org/publication/9179/ (accessed August 23, 2009).

27. Shaun Tandon, "US Lawmakers Seek Review of Uighur 'Terror' Label," Agence France-Presse, June 16, 2009, http://www.google.com/hostednews/afp/article/ALeqM5izqnr8jZRqX1Taz8MSCFzUlS_Zjg (accessed August 29, 2009).

28. Testimony of Dru C. Gladney, "Exploring the Nature of Uighur Nationalism: Freedom Fighters or Terrorists?" Hearing before the International Organizations, Human Rights, and Oversight Subcommittee.

29. Millward, "Violent Separatism," 29, 31.

30. U.S. Department of the Treasury, Office of Public Affairs, "Press Statement"; People's Republic of China, Information Office of the State Council, " 'East Turkistan' Terrorist Forces."

31. In a congressional hearing on June 16, 2009, Rep. Dana Rohrabacher (R–Calif.) charged, "We used weasel words to make sure that we could use information that obviously was spoon-fed us by the intelligence arm of the world's worst human rights abuser." Rep. Bill Delahunt (D–Mass.) made a similar statement: "It appears to me that we took substantial intelligence information from the Chinese communist regime and then used that questionable evidence as our own." See "Exploring the Nature of Uighur Nationalism: Freedom Fighters or Terrorists?" Hearing before the International Organizations, Human Rights, and Oversight Subcommittee.

32. Testimony of Randall G. Schriver, "Exploring the Nature of Uighur Nationalism: Freedom Fighters or Terrorists?" Hearing before the International Organizations, Human Rights, and Oversight Subcommittee. Schriver actually referred to "a group that went by the acronym SHAT," another acronym for ETLO.

33. Radio Free Europe/Radio Liberty Kyrgyz News, "Kyrgyzstan Deports Two Uyghurs to China."

34. *People's Daily*, "U.S. Has Evidence"; Pan, "U.S. Warns of Plot."

35. Pan, "U.S. Warns of Plot."

36. U.S. Department of State, Office of International Information Programs, "Kelly Stresses U.S. Cooperation, Consultation with East Asia; Assistant Secretary of State Remarks on Terrorism, Other Threats," December 11, 2002, http://www.america.gov/st/washfile-english/2002/December/20021211155813nsiak@pd.state.gov0.1011011.html (accessed August 29, 2009).

37. Turkestan Islamic Party, "The Chinese and Pakistani Media."

38. Dolat, "Washington Betrays China's Uighurs." Note that the United States had added the ETIM to the OFAC list and the TEL but did not actually designate the ETIM an FTO as Dolat asserts. He likely did not recognize the FTO as a specific blacklist and assumed that all groups blacklisted by the United States are FTOs.

39. Cloud and Johnson, "Friend or Foe."

40. For a transcript of Craner's speech, see U.S. Department of State, Office of International Information Programs, "Text: Craner Says Government Can't Ignore Human Rights in War on Terrorism (Security and Human Rights Support Each Other)," includes transcript, December 26, 2002, http://usinfo.org/wf-archive/2002/021226/epf402.htm (accessed August 29, 2009).

41. Cronin, "The 'FTO List' and Congress," 9.

42. Ibid.

43. Cloud and Johnson, "Friend or Foe."

APPENDIX B

1. People's Republic of China, "Terrorist Activities Perpetrated."

2. People's Republic of China, Information Office of the State Council, " 'East Turkistan' Forces."

3. Xinhua General News Service, "First Batch."

4. People's Republic of China, "China Identifies."

APPENDIX C

1. Xinhua News Agency, "China Announces List of ETIM Terrorists," October 21, 2008, http://www.china.org.cn/international/photos/2008-10/21/content_16642708.htm (accessed April 21, 2009); People's Republic of China, "China Identifies"; Turkestan Islamic Party [Islam Awazi], "Steadfastness and Preparations"; U.S. Department of the Treasury, Office of Foreign Assets Control, "What You Need to Know about U.S. Sanctions," July 2, 2009, http://www.treas.gov/offices/enforcement/ofac/programs/terror/terror.pdf (accessed August 27, 2009); Turkestan Islamic Party [Islam Awazi], "Jihad Lands."

2. Turkestan Islamic Party, "Regarding the Death." Both the PRC and the ETIM itself (on its website, in its videos, and in the pages of its magazine) have identified Abdul Haq al-Turkistani as the leader of the ETIM.

3. At least eight of the Uyghur GTMO detainees referred to Abdul Haq. For an example, see U.S. Department of Defense, Combatant Status Review Board, Summarized Detainee Unsworn Statement [Abdul Ghappar Abdul Rahman, ISN 281].

4. Al-Shishani, "Journal of the Turkistan Islamic Party"; Turkestan Islamic Party [Islam Awazi], "Steadfastness and Preparations"; Xinhua News Agency, "China Announces List of ETIM Terrorists"; People's Republic of China, "China Identifies."

5. People's Republic of China, "China Identifies."

6. Ibid.

7. Turkistan Islamic Party [Islam Awazi], "Steadfastness and Preparations."

8. Al-Shishani, "Journal of the Turkistan Islamic Party."

9. "Profiles of 11 Terrorists Identified"; Cloud and Johnson, "Friend or Foe"; Jin Yan and Wu Qi, " 'East Turkistan' Gang Leader Hasan and His Organization," *Beijing Sanlian Shenghuo Zhoukan*, January 5, 2004, trans. FBIS, CPP20040114000198; People's Republic of China, Ministry of Public Security, "First Batch."

10. "Profiles of 11 Terrorists Identified."

11. Cloud and Johnson, "Friend or Foe."

12. "Profiles of 11 Terrorists Identified."

13. Al-Shishani, "Journal of the Turkistan Islamic Party"; Turkistan Islamic Party [Islam Awazi], "Steadfastness and Preparations"; Associated Press, "Islamic Group Threatens."

14. We assess that Abdullah Mansour and Abu Ja'afar al-Mansour are the same individual based on the similarity of their names and the similar messages they deliver in ETIM statements.

15. Associated Press, "Islamic Group Threatens."

16. Turkistan Islamic Party [Islam Awazi], "Steadfastness and Preparations."

17. Al-Shishani, "Journal of the Turkistan Islamic Party."

18. Ibid.

19. Turkestan Islamic Party, "Why Are We Fighting China?"

20. Xinhua News Agency, "China Announces List of ETIM Terrorists"; People's Republic of China, "China Identifies."

21. Ibid.

22. Ibid.

23. Ibid.

24. Ibid.

25. Ibid.

26. "Profiles of 11 Terrorists Identified"; Jin and Wu, " 'East Turkistan' Gang Leader"; People's Republic of China, Ministry of Public Security, "First Batch."

27. STRATFOR, "China."

28. "Profiles of 11 Terrorists Identified"; People's Republic of China, Ministry of Public Security, "First Batch."

29. "Profiles of 11 Terrorists Identified"; Jin and Wu, " 'East Turkistan' Gang Leader"; People's Republic of China, Ministry of Public Security, "First Batch."

30. INTERPOL, "INTERPOL Notices," http://www.interpol.int/Public/Notices/default.asp (accessed on September 12, 2009); People's Republic of China, Ministry of Public Security, "First Batch."

31. People's Republic of China, "China Identifies."

32. People's Republic of China, Information Office of the State Council, " 'East Turkistan' Terrorist Forces."

33. People's Republic of China, Ministry of Public Security, "First Batch."

34. Ibid.

35. U.S. Department of Defense, Combatant Status Review Board, Summarized Detainee Sworn Statement [Adel Abdulhehim, ISN 293]; U.S. Department of Defense, Combatant Status Review Board, Summarized Detainee Unsworn Statement [Abu Bakr Qasim, ISN 283].

36. STRATFOR, "China"; Islamic Party of Turkistan [Islam Awazi], "Jihad Lands."

37. STRATFOR, "China."

38. Islamic Party of Turkistan [Islam Awazi], "Jihad Lands."

39. STRATFOR, "China."

40. Wong, "Attack in West China."

41. People's Republic of China, Embassy of the People's Republic of China in the State of Israel, "Xinjiang Public Security Authorities Unearthed Two Terrorist Rings," April 16, 2008, http://www.chinaembassy.org.il/eng/xwdt/t425814.htm (accessed April 20, 2008).

42. Xinhua, "Townspeople in Xinjiang Mourn 16 Slain Police," *People's Daily Online*, August 7, 2008, http://english.peopledaily.com.cn/90001/90776/90882/6468861.html (accessed February 1, 2009).

43. Ibid.

44. B. Raman, "Explosions in Xinjiang," South Asia Analysis Group, January 25, 2005, http://www.southasiaanalysis.org/papers13/paper1232.html (accessed March 8, 2009).

45. Shichor, "Fact and Fiction."

46. Shichor, "Fact and Fiction"; Jin and Wu, " 'East Turkistan' Gang Leader."

47. Xinhua, "Chinese Court Rejects Appeal of Convicted Xinjiang Terrorist," supplied by BBC Worldwide Monitoring, July 10, 2007, http://www.lexisnexis.com/.

48. People's Republic of China, Ministry of Public Security, "First Batch."

49. Turkistan Islamic Party [Islam Awazi], "Steadfastness and Preparations"; Turkistan Islamic Party [Islam Awazi], "Jihad Lands."

50. "Profiles of 11 Terrorists Identified"; Al-Shishani, "Journal of the Turkistan Islamic Party"; STRATFOR, "China"; Turkistan Islamic Party [Islam Awazi], "Jihad Lands"; People's Republic of China, Ministry of Public Security, "First Batch."

51. "Profiles of 11 Terrorists Identified"; People's Republic of China, Ministry of Public Security, "First Batch."

52. Turkistan Islamic Party [Islam Awazi], "Jihad Lands."

53. STRATFOR, "China."

54. STRATFOR, "China"; Falco, "Islamic Movement of Uzbekistan (IMU)"; Alexeyev, "A Tough International."

55. Turkistan Islamic Party [Islam Awazi], "Jihad Lands."

56. Al-Jazeera, "China 'Executes' Uighur Activist."

57. "Further Report on 5th–6th April Rebellion in Xinjiang."

58. Turkistan Islamic Party [Islam Awazi], "Pidayi Usama" [video in eight parts], http://www.youtube.com/watch?v=Ucpq6IqJgw8 (accessed August 22, 2009).

59. Turkistan Islamic Party [Islam Awazi], "Jihad Lands."

60. U.S. Department of Defense, Combatant Status Review Board, Summarized Detainee Unsworn Statement [Abdul Helil Mamut, ISN 278].

61. U.S. Department of Defense, Combatant Status Review Board, Summary of Evidence for Combatant Status Review Tribunal—Abdul Rahman, Abdul Ghappar; U.S. Department of Defense, Combatant Status Review Board, Summarized Detainee Unsworn Statement [Abdul Ghappar Abdul Rahman, ISN 281].

62. U.S. Department of Defense, Combatant Status Review Board, Summarized Detainee Sworn Statement [Abdul Razak, ISN 219].

63. U.S. Department of Defense, Combatant Status Review Board, Summarized Detainee Unsworn Statement [Salahidin Abdulahat, ISN 295], n.d., http://www.dod.gov/pubs/foi/detainees/csrt_arb/index.html (accessed August 2, 2009).

64. U.S. Department of Defense, Combatant Status Review Board, Summarized Detainee Unsworn Statement [Abu Bakr Qasim, ISN 283].

65. U.S. Department of Defense, Combatant Status Review Board, Summarized Detainee Sworn Statement [Adel Abdulhehim, ISN 293].

66. U.S. Department of Defense, Administrative Review Board, Unclassified Summary of Evidence for Administrative Review Board in the Case of Noori, Adel.

67. U.S. Department of Defense, Combatant Status Review Board, Summarized Detainee Statement [Ahmad Tourson, ISN 201], n.d., http://www.dod.gov/pubs/foi/detainees/csrt_arb/index.html (accessed August 2, 2009).

68. U.S. Department of Defense, Combatant Status Review Board, Detainee Unsworn Statement—ISN 260 [Ahmed Adil], n.d., http://www.dod.gov/pubs/foi/detainees/csrt_arb/index.html (accessed August 2, 2009).

69. U.S. Department of Defense, Combatant Status Review Board, Summarized Detainee Sworn Statement [Ahmed Mohamed, ISN 328].

70. U.S. Department of Defense, Combatant Status Review Board, Summary of Evidence for Combatant Status Review Tribunal—Basit, Akhdar, November 12, 2004, http://www.dod.gov/pubs/foi/detainees/csrt_arb/index.html (accessed August 2, 2009); U.S. Department of Defense, Combatant Status Review Board, Summarized Detainee Unsworn Statement [Akhdar Qasem, ISN 276].

71. U.S. Department of Defense, Combatant Status Review Board, Summarized Detainee Unsworn Statement [Arkin Mahmud, ISN 103], n.d., http://www.dod.gov/pubs/foi/detainees/csrt_arb/index.html (accessed August 2, 2009).

72. U.S. Department of Defense, Administrative Review Board, Summary of Administrative Review Board Proceedings for ISN 277; U.S. Department of Defense, Combatant Status Review Board, Summarized Detainee Sworn Statement [Bahtiyar Mahnut, ISN 277].

73. U.S. Department of Defense, Combatant Status Review Board, Detainee Unsworn Statement—ISN 289 [Dawut Abdurehim].

74. U.S. Department of Defense, Combatant Status Review Board, Summarized Detainee Sworn Statement [Haji Mohammed Ayub, ISN 279], n.d., http://www.dod.gov/pubs/foi/detainees/csrt_arb/index.html (accessed August 2, 2009).

75. U.S. Department of Defense, Combatant Status Review Board, Unclassified Summary of Basis for Tribunal Decision [Hasan Anvar, ISN 250], n.d., http://www.dod.gov/pubs/foi/detainees/csrt_arb/index.html (accessed August 2, 2009).

76. U.S. Department of Defense, Combatant Status Review Board, Summarized Detainee Sworn Statement [Huzaifa Parhat, ISN 320].

77. U.S. Department of Defense, Combatant Status Review Board, Summarized Detainee Unsworn Statement [Abdulla Abdulqadir, ISN 285]; U.S. Department of Defense, Office for the Administrative Review of the Detention of Enemy Combatants, "Summarized Detainee Unsworn Statement" [Abdullah Abdulqadirakhum], n.d., http://www.dod.gov/pubs/foi/detainees/csrt_arb/Set_20_1606-1644.pdf (accessed April 11, 2009).

78. U.S. District Court for the District of Columbia, Declaration of Joseph S. Imburiga, September 19, 2005, http://www.dod.gov/pubs/foi/detainees/csrt_arb/index.html (accessed August 2, 2009).

79. U.S. Department of Defense, Combatant Status Review Board, Summarized Detainee Unsworn Statement [Sabir Osman, ISN 282].

80. U.S. Department of Defense, Combatant Status Review Board, Summary of Evidence for Combatant Status Review Tribunal—Khalik, Saidullah, October 29, 2004, http://www.dod.gov/pubs/foi/detainees/csrt_arb/index.html (accessed August 2, 2009).

81. U.S. Department of Defense, Combatant Status Review Board, Summarized Detainee Unsworn Statement [Yusef Abbas, ISN 275].

Bibliography

Abbas, Hassan. "A Profile of Tehrik-i-Taliban Pakistan." *CTC Sentinel* 1 (January 2008): 2, 1–4. http://belfercenter.ksg.harvard.edu/publication/17868/profile_of _tehrikitaliban_pakistan.html (accessed September 12, 2009).

Agence France-Presse. "Anti-American Sentiment Among China's Muslims Growing: Expert." March 31, 2003. http://www.lexisnexis.com/.

———. "China Breaks Silence on Bombings." *The Australian.* March 6, 1997. http:// www.lexisnexis.com/.

———. "China Cracks Down on Its Muslims; Anti-Terrorist Drive Turned Against Uighurs." *The Washington Times.* November 23, 2001. http://www.infoweb .newsbank.com/.

———. "China Executes Two Out of 18 Muslim Uighurs Convicted of Separatism." August 13, 2004. http://www.lexisnexis.com/.

———. "China Rocked as Bombs on Xinjiang Buses Kill Seven." February 26, 1997. http:// www.uygur.org/enorg/wunn97/wunn022697.htm (accessed August 16, 2009).

———. "China Vows 'Severe Crackdown' on Tibet Separatists." March 28, 2009. http:// www.google.com/hostednews/afp/article/ALeqM5iR_h4oqlXBVVpm8RCEGOcW 15jQcg (accessed March 29, 2009).

———. "Chinese Authorities Deny Uighur Group Behind Attacks: State Media." July 25, 2008. http://afp.google.com/article/ALeqM5hn-RS89mZLpCR_CyIATJLUlG8YDQ (accessed August 19, 2009).

———. "Chinese Police Kill Six in Xinjiang Clash: Reports." August 29, 2008. http:// afp.google.com/article/ALeqM5g9DGAcpJC22ojD44TodVyRFQJ4WA (accessed August 23, 2009).

———. "Chronology of China Bombs and Mystery Blasts." January 29, 1999. http:// www.lexisnexis.com/ (accessed August 16, 2009).

———. "Police Attacked in China's Muslim Northwest." *Straits Times.* Undated. http:// www.straitstimes.com/Breaking%2BNews/World/Story/STIStory_266584.html (accessed October 24, 2009).

————. "Tibet's Panchen Lama, Beijing's Propaganda Tool." March 27, 2009. http://www.google.com/hostednews/afp/article/ALeqM5g4z56PSsE15aH9AaSUAtI4-M_AaQ (accessed March 29, 2009).

————. "Uygur Terror Group Smashed in Raids." *Hong Kong iMail.* January 23, 2001. http://www.hartford-hwp.com/archives/55/459.html (accessed August 19, 2009).

Alexeyev, Stanislav. "A Tough International" [in Russian]. *Nezavisimaya Gazeta.* October 6, 2000. http://nvo.ng.ru/wars/2000-10-06/2_international.html (accessed August 16, 2009).

Al-Jazeera. "China 'Executes' Uighur Activist." February 9, 2007. http://english.aljazeera.net/news/asia-pacific/2007/02/2008525143353859811.html (accessed March 7, 2009).

Al-Shishani, Murad Batal. "Journal of the Turkistan Islamic Party Urges Jihad in China." *Terrorism Monitor* 7, vol. 9 (April 10, 2009): 3–4. The Jamestown Foundation. http://www.jamestown.org/single/?no_cache=1&tx_ttnews[tt_news]=34838 (accessed August 18, 2009).

Al-Turkestani, Commander Abdelhaq [Islam Awazi]. "Response from the Turkestan Islamic Party to the Olympic Games to Be Held in China in 2008." March 1, 2008. Translated by the Nine Eleven/Finding Answers (NEFA) TerrorWatch subscription service. http://www.nefafoundation.org/miscellaneous/FeaturedDocs/nefatip0409.pdf (accessed August 23, 2009).

Amnesty International. "People's Republic of China—Gross Violations of Human Rights in the Xinjiang Uighur Autonomous Region." ASA 17/018/1999. April 1, 1999. http://asiapacific.amnesty.org/library/Index/ENGASA170181999?open&of=ENG-CHN (accessed September 5, 2009).

————. "People's Republic of China—Uighurs Fleeing Persecution as China Wages Its 'War on Terror.'" ASA 17/021/2004. July 7, 2004. http://www.unhcr.org/refworld/docid/4129cc5d4.html (accessed April 6, 2009).

Armijo, Jackie. "Islamic Education in China." *Harvard Asia Quarterly* 10, no. 1 (2006). http://www.asiaquarterly.com/content/view/166/ (accessed March 29, 2009).

Artykova, Nadira. "Xinjiang: Uighur People Seek Independence from Chinese Influence." Inter Press Service. August 28, 1993. http://www.lexisnexis.com/.

Asian News International (ANI). "China Warns Against Pak Based 'Terror Movement' Threatening Strikes Inside Mainland." *Thaindian News.* April 9, 2009. http://www.thaindian.com/newsportal/south-asia/china-warns-against-pak-based-terror-movement-threatening-strikes-inside-mainland_100177391.html (accessed August 20, 2009).

————. "3 Suicide Bombers Enter Islamabad, Lahore, May Target Key Installations." June 19, 2009. http://www.lexisnexis.com/.

AsiaPulse News. "China 2009 Cotton Planting Area Down 12 Pct in 2009: Assoc." May 20, 2009. http://www.highbeam.com/doc/1G1-200160264.html (accessed August 2, 2009).

————. "Gold Reserves in China's Xinjiang Region Estimated to Be 9 Mln Tons." March 8, 2001. http://www.highbeam.com/doc/1G1-71353999.html (accessed August 2, 2009).

Associated Press. "Bus Crash in China Kills 14." *USA Today.* May 17, 2008. http://www.usatoday.com/news/world/2008-05-17-4025066727_x.htm (accessed August 18, 2009).

————. "China Against Muslim Activist for Nobel Prize." *The Jerusalem Post.* September 12, 2006. http://www.jpost.com/servlet/Satellite?cid=1157913614559 &pagename=JPost%2FJPArticle%2FShowFull (accessed August 29, 2009).

————. "Islamic Group Threatens Olympic Transport." August 7, 2008. http://www .msnbc.msn.com/id/26074595/ (accessed August 31, 2009).

Aviation Safety Network website. Last updated May 4, 2009. http://aviation-safety.net/ database/record.php?id=20080307-0&lang=fr (accessed May 4, 2009).

BBC. "Islam in China (650–Present)." October 2, 2002. http://www.bbc.co.uk/religion/ religions/islam/history/china_print.html (accessed March 28, 2009).

BBC News. "Albania Takes Guantanamo Uighurs." May 6, 2006. http://news.bbc.co.uk/ go/pr/fr/-/2/hi/americas/4979466.stm (accessed August 9, 2009).

————. "Bermuda Takes Guantanamo Uighurs." June 11, 2009. http://news.bbc.co.uk/ go/pr/fr/-/2/hi/americas/8095582.stm (accessed August 9, 2009).

————. "Bomb Explodes on S China Bus." August 8, 2005. http://newsvote.bbc.co.uk/ mpapps/pagetools/print/news.bbc.co.uk/2/hi/asia-pacific/4131916.stm (accessed August 17, 2009).

————. "Chinese Border Assault Kills 16." August 4, 2008. http://news.bbc.co.uk/2/hi/ asia-pacific/7540138.stm (accessed March 7, 2009).

————. "Chinese Militant 'Shot Dead.'" December 23, 2003. http://news.bbc.co.uk/2/hi/ asia-pacific/3343241.stm (accessed April 21, 2009).

————. "Language Blow for China's Muslims." June 1, 2002. http://news.bbc.co.uk/1/hi/ world/asia-pacific/2020009.stm (accessed March 28, 2009).

————. "Regions and Territories: Tibet." May 13, 2009. http://news.bbc.co.uk/2/hi/ asia-pacific/country_profiles/4152353.stm (accessed September 13, 2009).

————. "Tibetan Riots Continue in China." March 24, 2008. http://news.bbc.co.uk/2/hi/ asia-pacific/7311289.stm (accessed September 13, 2009).

————. "Timeline: Tibet." May 13, 2009. http://news.bbc.co.uk/2/hi/asia-pacific/country _profiles/6299565.stm (accessed September 13, 2009).

————. "Yahoo 'Helped Jail China Writer.'" September 7, 2005. http://news.bbc.co.uk/ go/pr/fr/-/2/hi/asia-pacific/4221538.stm (accessed September 5, 2009).

BBC World Service. "Tajik Opposition Blames Uzbekistan for Bombings." October 6, 1999. http://usproxy.bbc.com/2/low/asia-pacific/466820.stm (accessed September 12, 2009).

Becker, Jasper. "China's 'Home-Grown' Terror." *South China Morning Post* [Hong Kong]. November 16, 2001. http://www.lexisnexis.com/.

Becquelin, Nicolas. "Xinjiang in the Nineties." *The China Journal* 44 (July 2000): 65–90. http://www.jstor.org/.

Benson, Linda. "Education and Social Mobility among Minority Populations in Xinjiang." In *Xinjiang: China's Muslim Borderland*, edited by S. Frederick Starr, 190–215. Armonk, NY: M.E. Sharpe, 2004.

Bhagat, Aditya. "China Tries to Quell the Xinjiang Uprising." *The Pioneer.* February 27, 1997. http://www.hvk.org/articles/0397/0020.html (accessed September 5, 2009).

Bhattacharji, Preeti. "Uighurs and China's Xinjiang Region." Council on Foreign Relations Backgrounder. September 29, 2008. http://www.cfr.org/publication/16870/ chinas_xinjiang_dilemma.html?breadcrumb=%2F (accessed March 29, 2009).

Bhattacharya, Abanti. "Conceptualising Uyghur Separatism in Chinese Nationalism." *Strategic Analysis* 27, no. 3 (July–September 2003): 357–381.

Bing, Luo. "Chinese Leader States Corruption Will Destroy the Chinese Communist Party." *The Epoch Times*. February 29, 2008. http://en.epochtimes.com/tools/printer.asp?id=66784 (accessed March 28, 2009).

Bovingdon, Gardner. "Autonomy in Xinjiang: Han Nationalist Imperatives and Uyghur Discontent." *Policy Studies* 11. http://www.eastwestcenter.org/fileadmin/stored/pdfs/PS011.pdf (accessed April 10, 2009).

Branigan, Tania. "Muslim 'Separatists' Protest as Unrest Spreads in China." *The Guardian*. April 2, 2008. http://www.guardian.co.uk/world/2008/apr/02/china/print (accessed April 9, 2009).

———. "Olympics Threatened by Islamic Separatists." *The Guardian*. July 27, 2008. http://www.guardian.co.uk/sport/2008/jul/27/olympicgames2008.terrorism/print (accessed August 18, 2009).

Bristow, Michael. "China 'Yet to Approve Protests.'" BBC News. August 18, 2008. http://news.bbc.co.uk/2/hi/asia-pacific/7567703.stm (accessed February 28, 2009).

Buncombe, Andrew. "China's Secret Nuclear Tests Leave Legacy of Cancer and Deformity." *The Independent* [London]. October 5, 1998. http://www.lexisnexis.com/.

Cao Chang-Qing. "Fighting to Free Another Chinese 'Province.'" *Taipei Times*. October 11, 1999. http://www.taipeitimes.com/News/insight/archives/1999/10/11/6035 (accessed September 5, 2009).

Castets, Rémi. "The Uyghurs in Xinjiang—The Malaise Grows." Translated by Philip Liddell. *China Perspectives*. September–October 2003. http://chinaperspectives.revues.org/document648.html (accessed September 5, 2009).

Center for Nonproliferation Studies. "Draft Convention on International Terrorism." Inventory of International Nonproliferation Organizations and Regimes. Last updated May 27, 2009. http://www.cns.miis.edu/inventory/pdfs/intlterr.pdf (accessed August 22, 2009).

China Daily. "Blasts Rock Xinjiang, Guard Killed." August 11, 2008. http://www.chinadaily.com.cn/china/2008-08/11/content_6923306.htm (accessed October 24, 2009).

———. "Xinjiang Official Vows to Crack Down on Terrorists." August 2, 2008. http://www.china.org.cn/china/local/2008-08/02/content_16120593.htm (accessed August 22, 2008).

China Internet Information Center. "Xinjiang: The Call of the West." 2004. http://www.china.org.cn/english/en-xj/5.htm (accessed August 2, 2009).

China Mining Association. "China's Xinjiang Coal Reserves Adds 18.98 Billion Tons." May 8, 2008. http://www.chinamining.org/News/2008-05-08/1210233199d13585.html (accessed August 2, 2009).

Chow Chung-Yan. "Muslim Put to Death for Seeking Separate State." *South China Morning Post* [Hong Kong]. October 24, 2003. http://www.lexisnexis.com/.

"Christianity in China: Sons of Heaven." *The Economist*. October 2, 2008. http://www.economist.com/world/asia/PrinterFriendly.cfm?story_id=12342509 (accessed March 28, 2009).

Christofferson, Gaye. "Constituting the Uyghur in U.S.-China Relations: The Geopolitics of Identity Formation in the War on Terrorism." *Strategic Insights* 1, no. 7 (September 2002). http://www.ccc.nps.navy.mil/si/sept02/eastAsia.asp (accessed August 15, 2009).

————. "Islam and Ethnic Minorities in Central Asia: The Uyghurs." In *Islam, Oil, and Geopolitics: Central Asia After September 11*, edited by Elizabeth Van Wie Davis and Rouben Azizan, 45–60. Lanham, MD: Rowman & Littlefield, 2006.

Chung, Chien-peng. "China's 'War on Terror.'" *Foreign Affairs* 81, no. 4 (July–August 2002): 8–12. http://www.ebscohost.com/.

Chung, Grace. "U.S. Military Helped Chinese Interrogate Uighur Prisoners at Guantanamo." McClatchy Newspapers. July 16, 2009. http://www.cleveland.com/world/index.ssf/2009/07/us_military_helped_chinese_int.html (accessed August 30, 2009).

Cloud, David S., and Ian Johnson. "Friend or Foe: In Post-9/11 World, Chinese Dissidents Pose U.S. Dilemma; Uighur Nationalists Have Peaceful, Violent Wings; Deciding Who Is a Threat; 'Omar Is Not a Bomb Thrower.'" *The Wall Street Journal*. August 3, 2004. http://www.proquest.umi.com.

CNN. "U.S.: China Separatists 'Plotted Embassy Attacks.'" *CNN*. August 30, 2002. http://edition.cnn.com/2002/WORLD/asiapcf/east/08/30/kyrgyz.china.terror/index.html (accessed March 8, 2009).

Cody, Edward. "China Cracks Down on Corruption." *The Washington Post*. February 15, 2006, A18.

"Combating Terrorism, We Have No Choice." *People's Daily*. December 16, 2003. http://english1.peopledaily.com.cn/200312/18/eng20031218_130652.shtml (accessed September 13, 2009).

Congressional-Executive Commission on China. "Civil Servant Recruitment in Xinjiang Favors Han Chinese." July 13, 2006. http://www.cecc.gov/pages/virtualAcad/index.phpd?showsingle=61191 (accessed April 27, 2009).

Cronin, Audrey Kurth. "The 'FTO List' and Congress: Sanctioning Designated Foreign Terrorist Organizations." Congressional Research Service, CRS Report for Congress. October 21, 2003. https://www.policyarchive.org/handle/10207/1865 (accessed August 22, 2009).

Cui Xiaohuo. "Chinese Police Seek Extradition of Terrorists." *China Daily*. October 22, 2008. http://www.chinadaily.com.cn/china/2008-10/22/content_7126884.htm (accessed August 23, 2009).

Daly, John C. K., and Martin Sieff. "UPI Intelligence Watch." *United Press International*. November 4, 2004. http://www.lexisnexis.com/.

Dautcher, Jay. "Public Health and Social Pathologies in Xinjiang." In *Xinjiang: China's Muslim Borderland*, edited by S. Frederick Starr, 276–295. Armonk, NY: M.E. Sharpe, 2004.

De Cordier, Bruno. "The Islamic Movement of Uzbekistan and the Islamic Jihad Union: A Jihadi Nebulous in Central Asia and the EU." Caucaz.com. February 7, 2008. http://www.caucaz.com/home_eng/breve_contenu.php?id=344 (accessed September 12, 2009).

Dillon, Michael. "Uyghur Separatism and Nationalism in Xinjiang." In *Conflict, Terrorism and the Media in Asia*, edited by Benjamin Cole, 98–116. New York: Routledge, 2006.

————. *Xinjiang: China's Muslim Far Northwest*. New York: RoutledgeCurzon, 2004.

Dolat, Erkin. "Washington Betrays China's Uighurs." Uyghur Information Agency. September 5, 2002. http://www.atimes.com/atimes/China/DI05Ad03.html (accessed August 30, 2009).

DPA. "Blasts, Gunfire Kill at Least Eight in China." *Thaindian News.* August 10, 2008. http://www.thaindian.com/newsportal/uncategorized/blasts-gunfire-kill-at-least -eight-in-china-lead_10082196.html (accessed August 20, 2009).

Drew, Jill. "China Group Asserts That It Bombed Buses." *The Washington Post.* July 27, 2008. http://www.washingtonpost.com/wp-dyn/content/article/2008/07/26/ AR2008072601370.html (accessed August 17, 2008).

Dreyer, June Teufel. "China's Vulnerability to Minority Separatism." *Asian Affairs* 32, no. 2 (2005): 69–85. 'http://www.smhric.org/China's%20Vulnerability%20to %20Minority%20Separatism.pdf (accessed September 6, 2009).

Dyer, Geoff, and Jamil Anderlini. "Distant Thunder: Separatism Stirs on China's Forgot- ten Frontier." *Financial Times.* August 17, 2008. http://www.ft.com/cms/s/0/ 26082e82-6c7b-11dd-96dc-0000779fd18c,dwp_uuid=723ba534-41c2-11dc-8328 -0000779fd2ac.html?nclick_check=1 (accessed April 10, 2009).

Eastern Turkestan Union in Europe. "Organizations Unite Their Efforts." *Eastern Turke- stan Information Bulletin* 4, no. 4. October 1994. http://caccp.freedomsherald.org/ et/etib/etib4_4.html (accessed September 5, 2009).

———. "World National Congress Held." *Eastern Turkestan Information Bulletin* 2, no. 6. December 1992. http://caccp.freedomsherald.org/et/etib/etib2_6.html (accessed September 4, 2009).

Eckholm, Erik. "China Army Renews Threat Against Taiwan Separatism." *The New York Times.* March 7, 2008. http://www.nytimes.com/2000/03/07/world/china-army -renews-threat-against-taiwan-separatism.html?n=Top/News/World/Countries %20and%20Territories/China (accessed April 5, 2009).

Elegant, Simon. "A China Threat from Pakistan?" *Time.* August 10, 2008. http:// www.time.com/time/world/article/0,8599,1831216,00.html (accessed October 24, 2009).

———. "A Video Threat to the Olympics." *Time.* July 27, 2008. http://www.time.com/ time/world/article/0,8599,1826953,00.html?iid=sphere-inline-bottom (accessed February 1, 2009).

Eranosian, Nancy. "Chinese National Unity vs. Uyghur Separatism." MA thesis, Tufts University. July 21, 2005.

Ewing, Kent. "Trying Times for Journalists in China." *Asia Times.* August 29, 2006. http://www.atimes.com/atimes/China/HH29Ad01.html (accessed March 28, 2009).

Eye on the U.N. "There Is No UN Definition of Terrorism." No date. http://www .eyeontheun.org/facts.asp?1=1&p=61 (accessed August 23, 2009).

Falco, Michael. "Islamic Movement of Uzbekistan (IMU): History, Financial Base and Military Structure" [in Russian]. *Nezavisimaya Gazeta.* August 24, 2000. http:// www.ng.ru/net/2000-08-24/0_idu.html (accessed August 16, 2009).

Falun Dafa Information Center. "Falun Gong: The Practice." May 17, 2008. http://www .faluninfo.net/print/210/ (accessed April 11, 2009).

Fang, Yang. "Backgrounder: Basic Facts about Tibet." Xinhua. March 9, 2009. http://news .xinhuanet.com/english/2009-03/09/content_10976310.htm (accessed March 28, 2009).

Field, Catherine. "Dateline: Happy, Smiling Workers—China's Latest Fakes." *The Observer.* May 21, 1994. http://www.lexisnexis.com/.

Filipov, David. "Islamic Separatists Claim China Bombings." *Boston Globe.* March 9, 1997. http://www.lexisnexis.com/.

Fischer, Sebastian. "Uighur Exiles in Munich: 'The Reality Is Far Worse than Television Pictures Suggest.'" *Spiegel Online International.* July 9, 2009. http://www.spiegel.de/international/world/0,1518,635249,00.html (accessed August 16, 2009).

Fletcher, Holly, and Jayshree Bajoria. "Backgrounder: The East Turkestan Islamic Movement." Council on Foreign Relations. Updated July 31, 2008. http://www.cfr.org/publication/9179/ (accessed August 23, 2009).

Fletcher, Joseph F. *Studies on Chinese and Islamic Inner Asia.* Brookfield, VT: Ashgate Publishing Company, 1995.

Fong, Tak-ho. "'Terror' Attack a Warning Shot for Beijing." March 14, 2008. *Asia Times.* http://www.atimes.com/atimes/China/JC14Ad01.html (accessed May 4, 2009).

Ford, Peter. "Spiritual Mother of Uighurs or Terrorist?" *The Christian Science Monitor.* July 9, 2009. http://www.csmonitor.com/2009/0709/p06s15-woap.html (accessed August 29, 2009).

———. "Uighurs Struggle in a World Reshaped by Chinese Influx." *The Christian Science Monitor.* April 28, 2008. http://www.csmonitor.com/2008/0428/p01s01-woap.htm (accessed March 31, 2009).

Foreman, William. "Bombing Spree Exposes Ethnic Divisions in China." *USA Today.* August 12, 2008. http://www.usatoday.com/news/world/2008-08-11-2286247682_x.htm (accessed October 24, 2009).

———. "City in China's West Locks Down After Bombings." Associated Press, published in the *Washington Post.* August 10, 2008. http://www.washingtonpost.com/wp-dyn/content/article/2008/08/10/AR2008081000455.html (accessed October 24, 2009).

French, Howard W. "Ethnic Unrest Continues in China." *The New York Times.* http://www.nytimes.com/2008/04/05/world/asia/05china.html?_r=1&ref=asia&pagewanted=print (accessed April 9, 2009).

Fuller, Graham E., and Jonathan N. Lipman. "Islam in Xinjiang." In *Xinjiang: China's Muslim Borderland,* edited by S. Frederick Starr, 320–352. Armonk, NY: M.E. Sharpe, 2004.

Fuller, Graham E., and S. Frederick Starr. *The Xinjiang Problem.* Washington, DC: Central Asia–Caucasus Institute, 2003.

"Further Report on 5th–6th April Rebellion in Xinjiang." Xinjiang Television, Urumqi. April 22, 1990. Transcript in BBC Summary of World Broadcasts. April 24, 1990. http://www.lexisnexis.com/.

Ganor, Boaz. "Xinjiang: Profile of a Restless Province." September 10, 2000. International Institute for Counter-Terrorism. http://212.150.54.123/spotlight/comment.cfm?id=482 (accessed August 20, 2009).

Gao Chaoming. "National Splittism Is the Main Danger in Xinjiang." *Xinjiang Ribao* [Urumqi], reprinted in BBC Summary of World Broadcasts. October 19, 1990. http://www.lexisnexis.com/.

Gittings, John. "China Prepares for New Offensive Against 'Dangerous' Sect." *The Guardian.* January 29, 2001. http://www.guardian.co.uk/world/2001/jan/29/china.johngittings (accessed March 28, 2009).

Gladney, Dru C. "The Chinese Program of Development and Control, 1978–2001." In *Xinjiang: China's Muslim Borderland,* edited by S. Frederick Starr, 101–119. Armonk, NY: M.E. Sharpe, 2004.

———. "Cyber-Separatism and Uyghur Ethnic Nationalism in China." Center for Strategic and International Studies. June 5, 2003. http://www.csis.org/china/030605 gladney.pdf (accessed April 10, 2009).

———. *Dislocating China: Muslims, Minorities, and Other Subaltern Subjects.* Chicago: University of Chicago Press, 2004.

———. "Islam in China: Accommodation or Separatism?" *The China Quarterly* 174 (June 2003): 451–467. http://www.jstor.org/.

———. "Responses to Chinese Rule: Patterns of Cooperation and Opposition." In *Xinjiang: China's Muslim Borderland,* edited by S. Frederick Starr, 375–396. Armonk, NY: M.E. Sharpe, 2004.

GlobalSecurity.org. "Tajikistan Civil War." Last modified April 27, 2005. http://www .globalsecurity.org/military/world/war/tajikistan.htm (accessed September 12, 2009).

Global Times. "Armed Police Protect Uygur Community Against Revenge." July 8, 2009. http://china.globaltimes.cn/top-photo/2009-07/443843_3.html (accessed August 16, 2009).

Grabot, Andre. "Uighur Radical Says His Creed Is to 'Kill the Chinese.'" Agence France-Presse. March 4, 1997. http://www.lexisnexis.com/.

———. "The Uighurs—Sacrificed on Central Asia's Chess Board." Agence France-Presse. April 25, 1996. http://www.lexisnexis.com/.

Gunaratna, Rohan. "China Under Threat: Uighur Group Poses Biggest Terror Threat to Olympics." *The Straits Times.* August 3, 2008. http://www.straitstimes.com/Free/ Story/STIStory_264004.html (accessed April 10, 2009).

Gunaratna, Rohan, and Kenneth George Pereire. "An Al-Qaeda Associate Group Operating in China?" *China and Eurasian Forum Quarterly,* 4(2), 2006: 56. http:// www.silkroadstudies.org/new/docs/CEF/Quarterly/May_2006/ GunaratnaPereire.pdf (accessed August 23, 2009).

Gunitskiy, Seva. "In the Spotlight: East Turkistan Islamic Movement (ETIM)." Center for Defense Information. December 9, 2002. http://www.cdi.org/terrorism/etim.cfm (accessed August 29, 2009).

He Huifeng. "Independence Bid in Xinjiang Unlikely to Succeed: Expert." *South China Morning Post* [Hong Kong]. July 27, 2008. http://www.lexisnexis.com/.

Hegghammer, Thomas. "Infighting over Distribution of New Uighur Magazine." *Jihadica.* February 20, 2009. http://www.jihadica.com/infighting-over-distribution-of-new -uighur-magazine/ (accessed August 29, 2009).

Higgins, Andrew. "'Holy War' Rages in Western China." *The Independent.* April 24, 1990, 15. http://www.lexisnexis.com/.

HM Treasury. "Financial Sanctions Notification, Al-Qaida and Taliban." October 6, 2008. http://www.hm-treasury.gov.uk/d/fin_sanc_notification_al_qaida_061008 .pdf (accessed August 20, 2009).

Ho, Stephanie. "Muslim Separatists Blamed for Blasts in China's Far Western Xinjian Region." August 10, 2008. http://www.globalsecurity.org/security/library/news/ 2008/08/sec-080810-voa01.htm (accessed October 24, 2009).

Holstein, William J. "China's Nuclear Tests May Be Causing Cancer." *United Press International.* August 24, 1981. http://www.lexisnexis.com/.

Hornby, Lucy, and Benjamin Kang Lim. "China Fire Protesters Were Uighurs." *Reuters.* February 26, 2009. http://uk.reuters.com/article/worldNews/idUKTRE51P241 20090226 (accessed February 28, 2009).

Horsley, Jamie P. "Village Elections: Training Ground for Democratization." *The China Business Review*. March–April 2001. http://www.chinabusinessreview.com/public/0103/horsley.html (accessed February 3, 2009).

"Hu Orders 'Great Wall' to Fight Tibet Separatism." *The Standard*. March 10, 2009. http://www.thestandard.com.hk/news_print.asp?art_id=79334&sid=23036576 (accessed March 28, 2009).

Human Rights Watch and Human Rights in China. "Devastating Blows: Religious Repression of Uighurs in Xinjiang" (a Human Rights in China special report). *Human Rights Watch* 17, no. 2(c). April 2005. http://www.hrw.org/en/reports/2005/04/11/devastating-blows (accessed April 24, 2009).

Hutzler, Charles. "Despite Crackdown, Ethnic Tensions Persist in China's Northwest." Associated Press. March 12, 1998. http://www.uygur.org/enorg/wunn98/wunn 031198.htm (accessed August 16, 2009).

Ibragimov, Hashim. "Frightening Image of Extremism" [in Russian]. *Nezavisimaya Gazeta*. February 3, 2000. http://www.ng.ru/net/2000-02-03/5_lik.html (accessed August 16, 2009).

Imatov, K. "The Question of the Uighur Question." *Slovo Kyrgyzstana*. In Russian. Translation supplied by BBC Worldwide Monitoring under the title "Kyrgyz Newspaper Analyses Threat from Uighur 'Extremists.' " November 1, 2001. http://www.lexisnexis.com/.

Inside China Mainland. "Xinjiang Separatist Movement Intensifies." June 1, 1999. http://www.lexisnexis.com/.

IntelCenter. "Turkistan Islamic Party (TIP): Threat Awareness Wall Chart." August 12, 2008. v. 1.1.

Interfax-Kazakhstan. "Kazakh Court Declares Islamic Group as 'Terrorist' Organization." Translation supplied by BBC Worldwide Monitoring. March 5, 2008. http://www.lexisnexis.com/.

———. "Kazakh Special Services Report on Fighting Terror, Illegal Migration in 2007." Translation supplied by BBC Worldwide Monitoring. February 27, 2008. http://www.lexisnexis.com/.

Internet Haganah. "Of Turkistanis and Their Videos." August 7, 2008. http://internet -haganah.com/harchives/006366.html#006366 (accessed on October 4, 2009).

INTERPOL. "INTERPOL Notices." http://www.interpol.int/Public/Notices/default.asp (accessed on September 12, 2009).

ITAR-TASS News Agency [Moscow]. "Kyrgyzstan Hands Chinese Diplomat's Suspected Killers Over to China." Supplied by BBC Worldwide Monitoring. August 9, 2002. http://www.lexisnexis.com/.

Jin Yan and Wu Qi. " 'East Turkistan' Gang Leader Hasan and His Organization." *Beijing Sanlian Shenghuo Zhoukan*. January 5, 2004. Translated by FBIS. CPP200401140 00198.

Johnson, Bryan. "Cancer Increase in Chinese Province; Blight Rumored in Nuclear Test Area." *The Globe and Mail* [Canada]. September 1, 1981. http://www.lexisnexis.com/.

Johnson, Tim. "Throngs of Migrants Flooding China's Ancient Silk Road Cities." Knight Ridder Newspapers. September 22, 2004. http://www.lexisnexis.com/.

Kahn, Joseph. "Notoriety Now for Movement's Leader." *The New York Times*. April 27, 1999. http://www.nytimes.com/1999/04/27/world/notoriety-now-for-movement-s -leader.html (accessed March 28, 2009).

Kan, Shirley. "U.S.-China Counter-Terrorism Cooperation: Issues for U.S. Policy." Congressional Research Service, CRS Report for Congress. Updated May 12, 2005. http://www.fas.org/sgp/crs/row/RS21995.pdf (accessed August 23, 2009).
———. "U.S.-China Counter-Terrorism Cooperation: Issues for U.S. Policy." Congressional Research Service, CRS Report for Congress. Updated May 7, 2009. http://www.fas.org/sgp/crs/terror/RL33001.pdf (accessed August 29, 2009).
"Kazakh Paper Suggests USA Is Backing China's Uighur Separatists." *Komsomolskaya Pravda Kazakhstan*, translation supplied by BBC Worldwide Monitoring. July 20, 2002. http://www.lexisnexis.com/.
Knickmeyer, Ellen, and Jonathan Fine. "Insurgent Leader Al-Zarqawi Killed in Iraq." *The Washington Post*. June 8, 2006. http://www.washingtonpost.com/wp-dyn/content/article/2006/06/08/AR2006060800114.html (accessed September 12, 2009).
Kohlmann, Evan. "Al-Qaida's Online Couriers: The Al-Fajr Media Center and the Global Islamic Media Front (GIMF)." The Nine Eleven/Finding Answers (NEFA) Foundation. May 2009. http://nefafoundation.org/fajrchart.html (accessed August 29, 2009).
———. "Prominent Jihad Media Organizations in Central Asia." The Nine Eleven/Finding Answers (NEFA) Foundation. 2009. http://www.nefafoundation.org/miscellaneous/FeaturedDocs/nefajihadmedia0309.pdf (accessed August 29, 2009).
Lattimore, Owen. *Pivot of Asia: Sinkiang and the Inner Asian Frontiers of China and Russia.* Boston: Little, Brown and Company, 1950.
"Law and Order: 'Islamic' 'Counter-Revolutionaries' Executed for Bomb Explosions." *Xinjiang Ribao.* BBC Summary of World Broadcasts. May 31, 1995. http://www.lexisnexis.com/.
Leon, Richard J. *"Lakhdar Boumediene et al. v. George W. Bush et al.*—Civil Action No. 04-1166 (RJL): Memorandum Order." U.S. District Court for the District of Columbia. October 27, 2008. http://www.scotusblog.com/wp/wp-content/uploads/2008/10/boumediene-order-10-27-08.pdf (accessed August 15, 2009).
Levy, Clifford J. "Central Asia Sounds Alarm on Islamic Radicalism." *The New York Times.* August 17, 2009. http://www.nytimes.com/2009/08/18/world/asia/18kyrgyz.html?hpw (accessed September 12, 2009).
Li Hongmei. "Unveiled Rebiya Kadeer: A Uighur Dalai Lama." *Renmin Ribao.* July 7, 2009. http://www.lexisnexis.com/.
Lim, Benjamin Kang. "Thousands Protest Against S. China Chemical Plant." Reuters. June 1, 2007. http://www.alertnet.org/thenews/newsdesk/PEK112258.htm# (accessed March 28, 2009).
Liu Zhenmin. "Statement by H.E. Ambassador LIU Zhenmin, Deputy Permanent Representative of China to the United Nations, at the Sixth Committee of the 63rd Session of the UN General Assembly on Item 99 'Measures to Eliminate International Terrorism.'" October 8, 2008. http://www.china-un.org/eng/ldhy/63rd_unga/t517213.htm (accessed August 23, 2009).
Lu Yanan, Ed. "Two Hospitalized After Car Fire in Downtown Beijing." Xinhua. February 25, 2009. http://news.xinhuanet.com/english/2009-02/25/content_10893344.htm (accessed February 28, 2009).
Lum, Thomas. "China and Falun Gong." Congressional Research Service Report for Congress. May 25, 2006. http://fpc.state.gov/documents/organization/67820.pdf (accessed March 28, 2009).

Macartney, Jane. "One Billion Souls to Save." *The Times*. March 28, 2009. http://www.timesonline.co.uk/tol/news/article5960010.ece (accessed March 28, 2009).

Mackerras, Colin. "Xinjiang at the Turn of the Century: The Causes of Separatism." *Central Asian Survey* 20, no. 3 (2001): 289–303. http://www.ingentaconnect.com/.

Magnier, Mark. "Beijing Olympics Visitors to Come Under Widespread Surveillance." *LA Times*. August 7, 2008. http://articles.latimes.com/2008/aug/07/world/fg-snoop7 (accessed April 9, 2009).

Mansur, Abdullah [Islam Awazi]. "The Enemy Is Terrified by Our Operations." November 2008. Islamic Turkistan [Turkistan al-Muslimah]. Translated by the Nine Eleven/Finding Answers (NEFA) TerrorWatch subscription service. http://www.nefafoundation.org/miscellaneous/nefa_tipenemyterrified0809.pdf (accessed August 23, 2009).

McCants, Will. "Al-Qaeda Cleric Linked to Chinese Terrorist Group." *Jihadica*. August 11, 2008. http://www.jihadica.com/al-qaeda-cleric-linked-to-chinese-terrorist-group/ (accessed September 12, 2009).

———. "Important Al-Qaeda Scholar Identified." *Jihadica*. June 4, 2008. http://www.jihadica.com/important-al-qaeda-scholar-identified/ (accessed August 29, 2009).

McDermott, Josephine. "The Battle to Scale the Great Firewall of China." *Telegraph* [United Kingdom]. August 5, 2009. http://www.telegraph.co.uk/expat/5976173/The-battle-to-scale-the-Great-Firewall-of-China.html (accessed August 15, 2009).

McGeown, Kate. "China's Christians Suffer for Their Faith." BBC News. November 9, 2004. http://news.bbc.co.uk/2/hi/asia-pacific/3993857.stm (accessed March 28, 2009).

McNeal, Dewardric L. "China's Relations with Central Asian States and Problems with Terrorism." Congressional Research Service, CRS Report for Congress. December 17, 2001. https://www.policyarchive.org/handle/10207/1315 (accessed April 26, 2009).

Meek, James. "Ancient Warriors Feel China's Cosh." *The Observer*. October 12, 1997. http://www.lexisnexis.com/.

MEMRI. "Islamic Party of Turkestan Releases Video Showing Execution of Three Chinese Hostages." *Jihad and Terrorism Threat Monitor*. April 9, 2008. http://www.memrijttm.org/content/en/blog_personal.htm?id=373&param=GJN (accessed September 13, 2009).

Meyer, Cord. "Plight of the Uighur People." *The Washington Times*. September 5, 1997. http://www.lexisnexis.com/.

Millward, James A. "Violent Separatism in Xinjiang: A Critical Assessment." *Policy Studies* 6. Washington, DC: East-West Center, 2004. http://www.eastwestcenter.org/fileadmin/stored/pdfs/PS006.pdf (accessed April 24, 2009).

Millward, James A., and Nabijan Tursun. "Political History and Strategies of Control, 1884–1978." In *Xinjiang: China's Muslim Borderland*, edited by S. Frederick Starr, 63–98. Armonk, NY: M.E. Sharpe, 2004.

Millward, James A., and Peter C. Perdue. "Political and Cultural History of the Xinjiang Region through the Late Nineteenth Century." In *Xinjiang: China's Muslim Borderland*, edited by S. Frederick Starr, 27–62. Armonk, NY: M.E. Sharpe, 2004.

Mir, Amir. "10 Terror Suspects Extradited to China." *The News*. June 6, 2009. http://www.thenews.com.pk/top_story_detail.asp?Id=22569 (accessed September 12, 2009).

Moore, Malcolm. "China Beefs Up Security in Kuqa After New Terror Attack." *Telegraph*. August 10, 2008. http://www.telegraph.co.uk/news/worldnews/asia/china/

2533765/China-beefs-up-security-in-Kuqa-after-new-terror-attack.html (accessed October 24, 2009).

Morais, Richard C. "China's Fight with Falun Gong." *Forbes.* February 9, 2006. http://www.forbes.com/2006/02/09/falun-gong-china_cz_rm_0209falungong.html (accessed February 22, 2009).

Morillon, Lucie. "China Blocks Blogs, Search Results on Tainted Milk Scandal." PBS. October 22, 2008. http://www.pbs.org/mediashift/2008/10/china-blocks -blogs-search-results-on-tainted-milk-scandal.html (accessed February 28, 2009).

Nathan, Andrew F. "The Tiananmen Papers." *Foreign Affairs.* January–February 2001.

National Endowment for Democracy. "National Endowment for Democracy Support for Uyghur Human Rights and Prodemocracy Groups in Exile." Last updated July 16, 2009. http://www.ned.org/grants/uyghur_factsheet.html (accessed September 4, 2009).

NCA. "Kyrgyzstan Deports Two Uyghurs Back to China." May 23, 2002. http://www .uygur.org/wunn02/2002_05_23a.htm (accessed August 16, 2009).

New Dominion. "Follow-Up: Video of Attack on Chinese Men in Pakistan." April 26, 2008. http://www.thenewdominion.net/149/follow-up-video-of-attack-on -chinese-men-in-pakistan/ (accessed September 13, 2009).

———. "Report of Chinese Hostage Execution Video, Possible Central Asia Link." April 15, 2008. http://www.thenewdominion.net/137/report-of-chinese-hostage -execution-video-possible-central-asia-link/ (accessed September 13, 2009).

"Not Much of a Celebration." *The Economist.* February 26, 2009. http://www.economist .com/opinion/displaysotry.cfm?story_id=13184929 (accessed February 28, 2009).

Oka, Natsuko. "The 'Triadic Nexus' in Kazakhstan: A Comparative Study of Russians, Uighurs, and Koreans." In *Beyond Sovereignty: From Status Law to Transnational Citizenship?*, edited by Osamu Ieda, 359–380. Sapporo, Japan: Slavic Research Center, Hokkaido University, 2006.

Osnos, Evan. "Jesus in China: Christianity's Rapid Rise." *Chicago Tribune.* June 22, 2008. http://www.chicagotribune.com/news/local/chi-jesus-1-1-webjun22,0,2458211.story (accessed March 28, 2009).

Pan, Philip. "China May Charge Foreign Reporters over Tiananmen Burning." *The Washington Post.* February 9, 2001, A23.

———. "U.S. Warns of Plot by Group in W. China." *The Washington Post.* August 29, 2002, A27.

Panda, Jagannath. "China's Anti-Terror Raid in Xinjiang." Institute for Defence Studies & Analysis. May 11, 2007. http://www.idsa.in/publications/stratcomments/Jagannath Panda110507.htm (accessed February 1, 2009).

Pannier, Bruce. "Central Asia: IMU Leader Says Group's Goal Is 'Return of Islam.'" Radio Free Europe/Radio Liberty. June 6, 2001. http://www.rferl.org/content/ article/1096618.html (accessed August 19, 2001).

Parry, Richard Lloyd. "Chinese Separatists 'Planning Year-Long' Terror Campaign." *Times Online.* August 5, 2008. http://www.timesonline.co.uk/tol/news/world/ asia/article4464246.ece (accessed August 23, 2009).

———. "Female Suicide Bombers in Uighur Separatist War in Xinjiang Province." *Times Online.* August 11, 2008. http://www.timesonline.co.uk/tol/news/world/asia/ article4507446.ece (accessed September 12, 2009).

——. "Renewed Bomb Attacks Kill Five in China." *Times Online*. August 10, 2009. http://www.timesonline.co.uk/tol/news/world/asia/article4495365.ece (accessed August 20, 2009).

Pasquet, Yannick. "Munich Fights to Welcome the Uighurs of Guantanamo." Agence France-Presse. March 17, 2009. http://www.infoweb.newsbank.com/.

People's Daily. "U.S. Has Evidence ETIM Plans Attack." *People's Daily Online*. August 30, 2002. http://english.peopledaily.com.cn/200208/30/eng20020830_102348.shtml (accessed August 16, 2009).

People's Republic of China. "Amendment of the Criminal Law of the People's Republic of China (III)." December 29, 2001. http://www.fdi.gov.cn/pub/FDI_EN/Laws/law_en_info.jsp?docid=50898 (accessed August 23, 2009).

——. "China Identifies Alleged 'Eastern Turkistan' Terrorists." October 21, 2008. News release. http://www.gov.cn/english/2008-10/21/content_1126738.htm (accessed April 20, 2009).

——. "Measures for the Administration of Financial Institutions' Report of Transactions Suspicious of Financing for Terrorist Purposes." June 11, 2007. http://www.fdi.gov .cn/pub/FDI_EN/Laws/law_en_info.jsp?docid=79879 (accessed August 23, 2009).

——. "Spokesperson's Remarks on the Death of Hasan Mahsum, Head of the 'East Turkistan Islamic Movement.'" No date. http://www.china-embassy.org/eng/fyrth/t57039.htm (accessed March 15, 2009).

People's Republic of China, Embassy of the People's Republic of China in the State of Israel. "Xinjiang Public Security Authorities Unearthed Two Terrorist Rings." April 16, 2008. http://www.chinaembassy.org.il/eng/xwdt/t425814.htm (accessed April 20, 2008).

People's Republic of China, Information Office of the State Council. "China's National Defense in 2008." January 2009. http://english.gov.cn/official/2009-01/20/content_1210227.htm (accessed April 5, 2009).

——. "'East Turkistan' Terrorist Forces Cannot Get Away with Impunity." January 21, 2002. News release. http://www.china-un.ch/eng/rqrd/jzzdh/t85075.htm (accessed April 20, 2009).

——. "History and Development of Xinjiang." White paper. May 26, 2003. http://www.china.org.cn/e-white/20030526/index.htm (accessed March 31, 2009).

——. "Regional Autonomy for Ethnic Minorities in China." White paper. February 2005. http://www.bjreview.com.cn/nation/txt/2009-05/27/content_197768.htm (accessed August 3, 2009).

People's Republic of China, Ministry of Foreign Affairs. "Foreign Ministry Spokesman Qin Gang's Press Conference on 8 September 2005." Transcript. September 9, 2005. http://www.fmprc.gov.cn/eng/xwfw/s2510/2511/t211142.htm (accessed August 29, 2009).

People's Republic of China, Ministry of Public Security. "First Batch of 'Eastern Turkistan' Terrorist Groups, Individuals Identified." *Xinhua*. December 15, 2003. http://groups.yahoo.com/group/RMSMC/message/3011 (accessed April 9, 2009).

People's Republic of China, National Bureau of Statistics of China. "2-25 Population in Minority National Autonomous Areas." *China Statistical Yearbook* 1996. http://www.stats.gov.cn/english/statisticaldata/yearlydata/YB1996e/B2-25e.htm (accessed September 13, 2009).

People's Republic of China, Permanent Mission of the People's Republic of China to the UN. "Terrorist Activities Perpetrated by 'Eastern Turkistan' Organizations and

Their Links with Osama bin Laden and the Taliban." November 29, 2001. http://www.china-un.org/eng/zt/fk/t28937.htm (accessed August 23, 2009).

Poole, Teresa. "Peking Rocked by Bomb Blast." *The Independent*. May 14, 1997. http://www.independent.co.uk/news/world/peking-rocked-by-bomb-blast-1261381.html (accessed March 15, 2009).

"Population of Major Nationalities by Prefecture, Autonomous Prefecture, City and County." *Xinjiang Statistical Yearbook* 2008. Table: 307.

Potter, Pitman B. "Belief in Control: Regulation of Religion in China." *The China Quarterly* 174 (June 2003): 317–337. http://www.jstor.org/.

"Profiles of 11 Terrorists Identified." *China Daily*. December 16, 2003. http://www.chinadaily.com.cn/en/doc/2003-12/16/content_290652.htm (accessed August 17, 2008).

Qasim, Abu Bakker. "The View from Guantanamo." *The New York Times*. September 16, 2006. http://query.nytimes.com/gst/fullpage.html?res=9D0CEFDB1331F934A2575AC0A9609C8B63 (accessed August 15, 2009).

Radio Free Asia. "Separatist Leader Vows to Target Chinese Government; Uyghur Leader Denies Terror Charges." January 29, 2003. http://www.tibet.ca/en/newsroom/wtn/archive/old?y=2003&m=1&p=29-2_7 (accessed September 6, 2009).

———. "Uyghur Separatist Denies Links to Taliban, Al-Qaeda." January 27, 2002. http://www.rfa.org/english/news/politics/2002/01/27/85871/ (accessed April 20, 2008).

Radio Free Europe/Radio Liberty Kyrgyz News. "Kyrgyzstan Deports Two Uyghurs to China." May 23, 2002. http://www.eurasianet.org/resource/kyrgyzstan/hypermail/200205/0062.shtml (accessed August 29, 2009).

Raman, B. "Chinese Delink Xinjiang Incident from Olympics." Chennai Centre for China Studies. August 6, 2008. http://www.c3sindia.org/terrorismandsecurity/297 (accessed August 20, 2009).

———. "Explosions in Xinjiang." South Asia Analysis Group. January 25, 2005. http://www.southasiaanalysis.org/papers13/paper1232.html (accessed March 8, 2009).

———. "Jihadi Terrorism in Central Asia: An Update." *International Terrorism Monitor*, Paper No. 1691 (February 1, 2006). http://www.saag.org/common/uploaded_files/paper1691.html (accessed August 18, 2009).

Ramirez, Luis. "China Hands Stiff Sentences to 27 Farmers over Land Seizure Protest." *VOA News*. January 24, 2005. http://www.voanews.com/english/2005-01-24-voa22.cfm (accessed March 1, 2009).

Reuters. "Bizarre Text Message Precedes China Bus Bomb Blasts." *TheStar*. July 22, 2008. http://thestar.com.my/news/story.asp?file=/2008/7/22/worldupdates/2008-07-22T134257Z_01_NOOTR_RTRMDNC_0_-346179-2&sec=Worldupdates (accessed August 18, 2009).

———. "China Says Headed Off Olympic Protest Permits." September 17, 2008. http://www.reuters.com/article/worldNews/idUSPEK9159120080918 (accessed September 13, 2009).

Roggio, Bill. "Senior Al Qaeda Leaders Reported Killed in North Waziristan Strike." *The Long War Journal*. September 8, 2009. http://www.longwarjournal.org/archives/2009/09/senior_al_qaeda_lead_6.php (accessed September 12, 2009).

Rotar, Igor. "Explode Whether Central Asia?" [in Russian]. *Nezavisimaya Gazeta*. November 29, 2000. http://www.ng.ru/cis/2000-11-29/5_central.html (accessed August 16, 2009).

———. "The Growing Problem of Uighur Separatism." *China Brief* 4, no. 8 (April 15, 2004). The Jamestown Foundation. http://www.jamestown.org/single/?no_cache =1&tx_ttnews[tt_news]=3644 (accessed April 24, 2009).

———. "Xinjiang: Strict Control of China's Uighur Muslims Continues." Forum 18 News Service via WorldWide Religious News. August 15, 2006. http://www.wwrn .org/article.php?idd=22434&sec=33&con=17 (accessed August 15, 2009).

Rudelson, Justin. *Oasis Identities: Uyghur Nationalism Along China's Silk Road.* New York: Columbia University Press, 1997.

———. "Xinjiang's Uyghurs in the Ensuing US-China Partnership." Uyghur Panel, Congressional-Executive Committee on China, Washington, DC. June 10, 2002. http://www.cecc.gov/pages/roundtables/061002/rudelsonStatement.php (accessed March 31, 2009).

Rudelson, Justin, and William Jankowiak. "Acculturation and Resistance: Xinjiang Identities in Flux." In *Xinjiang: China's Muslim Borderland*, edited by S. Frederick Starr, 299–319. Armonk, NY: M.E. Sharpe, 2004.

Sackur, Stephen. "Red Alert: As the Tibet Protests Erupted, Television and Online Reports from Foreign Broadcasters Were Being Monitored and Shut Down, Proving That Old Habits Die Hard in 'New China.'" *The Guardian*. March 24, 2008. http://www.guardian.co.uk/media/2008/mar/24/chinathemedia.china (accessed March 7, 2009).

Saidazimova, Gulnoza. "China: Officials Say Uyghur Group Involved in Olympic Terror Plot." GlobalSecurity.org. http://www.globalsecurity.org/security/library/news/ 2008/04/sec-080411-rferl01.htm (accessed August 29, 2009).

Samdup, Tseten. "Chinese Population—Threat to Tibetan Identity." The Government of Tibet in Exile. 1993. http://www.tibet.com/Humanrights/poptrans.html (accessed March 28, 2009).

Sawlani, Girish. "Hong Kong's Democracy Advocate Bows Out of Elections." Australian Broadcasting Corporation. July 9, 2009. http://www.abc.net.au/ra/programguide/ stories/200807/s2298623.htm (accessed March 28, 2009).

Scharf, Michael. "Defining Terrorism as the Peacetime Equivalent of War Crimes." *Case Western Reserve Journal of International Law* 36, no. 2/3 (2004): 369.

Schmid, Alex, and Albert J. Jongman. *Political Terrorism: A New Guide to Actors, Authors, Concepts, Data Bases, Theories, & Literature.* New Brunswick, NJ: Transaction Books, 1988.

"Separatist Leader Handed Over to China." *Dawn.* May 28, 2002. http://www.hartford-hwp .com/archives/55/456.html (accessed April 12, 2009).

"Sharp Rise in Group Protests in China." *The Epoch Times.* October 16, 2006. http:// theepochtimes.com/tools/printer.asp?id=47044 (accessed February 28, 2009).

Shichor, Yitzhak. "Blow Up: Internal and External Challenges of Uyghur Separatism and Islamic Radicalism to Chinese Rule in Xinjiang." *Asian Affairs* 32, no. 2 (2005): 119–135. http://vnweb.hwwilsonweb.com/hww/Journals/index.jhtml.

———. "Changing the Guard at the World Uyghur Congress." *China Brief* 6, no. 25 (December 19, 2006). http://www.jamestown.org/single/?no_cache=1&tx_ttnews [tt_news]=32346 (accessed October 5, 2009).

———. "Fact and Fiction: A Chinese Documentary on Eastern Turkestan Terrorism." *China and Eurasia Forum Quarterly* 4, no. 2 (2006): 89–108. http://www.silkroad studies.org/new/docs/CEF/Quarterly/May_2006/Shichor.pdf (accessed April 24, 2009).

————. "The Great Wall of Steel: Military and Strategy in Xinjiang." In *Xinjiang: China's Muslim Borderland*, edited by S. Frederick Starr, 120–160. Armonk, NY: M.E. Sharpe, 2004.

————. "Limping on Two Legs: Uyghur Diaspora Organizations and the Prospects for Eastern Turkestan Independence." *Central Asia and the Caucasus* 48, no. 6 (December 2007). http://www.ca-c.org/online/2007/journal_eng/cac-06/12.shtml (accessed April 26, 2009).

————. "The Uyghurs and China: Lost and Found Nation." June 7, 2009. http://www.opendemocracy.net/article/the-uighurs-and-china-lost-and-found-nation (accessed August 16, 2009).

————. "Virtual Transnationalism: Uygur Communities in Europe and the Quest for Eastern Turkestan Independence." In *Muslim Networks and Transnational Communities in and Across Europe*, edited by Stefano Allievi and Jørgen S. Nielsen, 281–311. Leiden, Netherlands: Koninklijke, 2003.

Shingleton, William D. "In Xinjiang, China's Consolidation Isn't Solid." *The Christian Science Monitor*. August 27, 1997. http://www.lexisnexis.com/.

Shinmen, Yasushi. "The Eastern Turkistan Republic (1933–34) in Historical Perspective." In *Islam in Politics in Russia and Central Asia: Early Eighteenth to Late Twentieth Centuries*, edited by Stephane A. Dudoignon and Komatsu Hisao, 133–164 (New York: Kegan Paul, 2001).

Sisci, Francesco. "Falungong, Part 1: From Sport to Suicide." *Asia Times Online*. January 21, 2001. http://atimes.com/china/CA27Ad01.html (accessed February 22, 2009).

————. "Falungong, Part 2: A Rude Awakening." *Asia Times Online*. January 30, 2001. http://atimes.com/china/CA30Ad01.html (accessed February 22, 2009).

Smith, Craig S. "China, in Harsh Crackdown, Executes Muslim Separatists." *The New York Times*. December 16, 2001. http://www.lexisnexis.com/.

Society for Internet Research (SOFIR). "kanzhassan.com: Site of Cleric Abdel Hakim Hassan (Abu Amrw)." No date. http://www.sofir.org/reports/2006-06-10-kanzhassan.html (accessed August 29, 2009).

"Sons of Heaven: Inside China's Fastest-Growing Non-Governmental Organization." *The Economist*. October 2, 2008. http://www.economist.com/world/asia/displaystory.cfm?story_id=12342509 (accessed September 5, 2009).

Statistics Bureau of Xinjiang Uygur Autonomous Region. *Xinjiang Statistical Yearbook 2008*. Beijing: China Statistics Press, 2008.

Stone, Richard. "Fears Over Western Water Crisis." *Science* 321 (August 1, 2008): 630.

STRATFOR. "China: The Evolution of ETIM." May 13, 2008. http://www.stratfor.com/analysis/china_evolution_etim (accessed August 19, 2009).

Sullivan, Stephen. "China's bin Laden: The Terrorist Leader China Forgot." Media Monitors Network. December 22, 2003. http://usa.mediamonitors.net/Headlines/China-s-Bin-Laden-The-Terrorist-leader-China-forgot (accessed April 21, 2009).

Tandon, Shaun. "US Lawmakers Seek Review of Uighur 'Terror' Label." Agence France-Presse. June 16, 2009. http://www.google.com/hostednews/afp/article/ALeqM5izqnr8jZRqX1Taz8MSCFzUlS_Zjg (accessed August 29, 2009).

Taylor, Richard. "The Great Firewall of China." BBC News. January 6, 2006. http://newsvote.bbc.co.uk/1/hi/programmes/click_online/4587622.stm (accessed February 28, 2009).

Tibetan Centre for Human Rights and Democracy. " 'Strike Hard' Campaign: China's Crackdown on Political Dissidence." 2004. http://www.tchrd.org/publications/

topical_reports/strike_hard-2004/strike_hard-2004.pdf (accessed April 6, 2009).

Times of India. "Laden Had Links with Xinjiang Terrorist Groups." November 18, 2001. http://timesofindia.indiatimes.com/articleshow/1528111876.cms (accessed September 5, 2009).

Toops, Stanley W. "The Demography of Xinjiang." In *Xinjiang: China's Muslim Borderland*, edited by S. Frederick Starr, 241–263. Armonk, NY: M.E. Sharpe, 2004.

———. "The Ecology of Xinjiang: A Focus on Water." In *Xinjiang: China's Muslim Borderland*, edited by S. Frederick Starr, 264–275. Armonk, NY: M.E. Sharpe, 2004.

Turani, Anwar Yusuf. "Declaration of the Formation of the E. T. Government in Exile." World Uighur Network News 2004, *SPARK* Uighur Press on Eastern Turkestan. September 14, 2004. News release. http://www.uygur.org/wunn04/09_14.htm (accessed April 5, 2009).

Turkestan Islamic Party. "The Chinese and Pakistani Media Are Full of Lies and Accusations." Translated on behalf of the Nine Eleven/Finding Answers (NEFA) TerrorWatch subscription service. May 1, 2009. http://www.nefafoundation.org/miscellaneous/FeaturedDocs/nefatip0509.pdf (accessed August 23, 2009).

———. "Commander Abdelhaqq al-Turkestani: Response from the Turkestan Islamic Party to the Olympic Games to Be Held in China in 2008." Translated by ceifiT LTD on behalf of the Nine Eleven/Finding Answers (NEFA) TerrorWatch subscription service. March 1, 2008. http://www.nefafoundation.org/miscellaneous/FeaturedDocs/nefatip0409.pdf (accessed August 23, 2009).

———. "On the Occasion of Our Blessed Jihad in the Chinese City of Yunnan." Translated by ceifiT LTD on behalf of the Nine Eleven/Finding Answers (NEFA) TerrorWatch subscription service. July 23, 2008. http://www.nefafoundation.org/miscellaneous/FeaturedDocs/nefatip0409-2.pdf (accessed August 23, 2009).

———. "Steadfastness and Preparations for Jihad in the Cause of Allah." Translated by the Nine Eleven/Finding Answers (NEFA) TerrorWatch subscription service. January 20, 2009. http://www.nefafoundation.org/miscellaneous/FeaturedDocs/nefatip0409-4.pdf (accessed August 19, 2009).

———. "Why Are We Fighting China?" Translated by ceifiT LTD on behalf of the Nine Eleven/Finding Answers (NEFA) TerrorWatch subscription service. July 2008. http://www.nefafoundation.org/miscellaneous/FeaturedDocs/nefatip0409-3.pdf (accessed August 19, 2009).

"Turkistan." *Encyclopædia Britannica* Online. http://www.britannica.com/EBchecked/topic/610093/Turkistan (accessed August 12, 2009).

Turkistan Islamic Party. "Apparent Full Text of Turkistan Islamic Party 'Constitution.'" No date. Translated by the Open Source Center on January 29, 2008. CPP2008 0129480002.

———. "Regarding the Death of Hesen Mexsum." May 30, 2004. Translated by the Open Source Center. January 12, 2006. CPP20060112075001.

Turkistan Islamic Party [Islam Awazi]. "Birlik wa Tayyarlik Togrisida" [video]. September 11, 2003. http://www.tipislamyultuzi.com/mazmun/8/video/05.wmv (accessed April 22, 2008).

———. "General Call to Muslims of the World." August 1, 2008. http://www.youtube.com/watch?v=pwO_wX5olNQ (accessed August 22, 2009). Translated by Open Source Center. CPP200808074800001.

———. "Jihad Lands: Turkestan." No date. http://tipislamyultuzi.com/mazmun/
summary/summary.html (accessed April 21, 2008).

———. "Our Blessed Jihad in Yunnan" [video]. July 23, 2008. http://www.youtube.com/
watch?v=E6DLGShOnEg&feature=related (accessed August 17, 2009).

———. "Pidayi Usama" [video in eight parts]. No date. http://www.youtube.com/watch
?v=Ucpq6IqJgw8 (accessed August 22, 2009).

———. "Shaheed Hasan Mahsum Rahimallah" [video in four parts]. May 21, 2004.
http://www.youtube.com/watch?v=3lx5lwRm9UA (accessed August 22, 2009).

———. "Statement on the Events, Chinese Aggression v. Uyghurs" [video]. July 8, 2009.
http://www.youtube.com/watch?v=e-K6gkbRqNw (accessed August 22, 2009).

———. "Steadfastness and Preparations for Jihad in the Cause of Allah" [video in four
parts]. January 20, 2009. http://www.youtube.com/watch?v=6T2cmMVY9hE
(accessed August 22, 2009). Translated on behalf of the Nine Eleven/Finding
Answers (NEFA) TerrorWatch subscription service. http://www.nefafoundation.org.

———. "TIP Islam Awazi" [video in two parts]. No date. http://www.youtube.com/
watch?v=s3A-BbBixWI (accessed August 22, 2009).

Tyler, Christian. Wild West China: The Taming of Xinjiang. New Brunswick, NJ: Rutgers
University Press, 2004.

Tynan, Deirdre. "Uzbekistan: Authorities Link Tashkent Shootout in August to Islamic
Movement of Uzbekistan." EurasiaNet.org. September 9, 2009. http://www
.eurasianet.org/departments/insightb/articles/eav090909.shtml (accessed
September 12, 2009).

Tyson, James L. "Foreign Muslims Blamed for Unrest." The Christian Science Monitor.
May 31, 1990, 4. http://www.lexisnexis.com/.

"Uighur Community Sets Up Supreme Body, Resolves to Fight for Independence."
Kyrgyz radio, translated from Kyrgyz by BBC Summary of World Broadcasts.
November 3, 1999. http://www.lexisnexis.com/.

United Nations. "Measures to Eliminate International Terrorism: Ad Hoc Committee
Established by General Assembly Resolution 51/210 of 17 December 1996." Last
updated July 30, 2009. http://www.un.org/law/terrorism/index.html (accessed
August 23, 2009).

UN Security Council. "The Consolidated List Established and Maintained by the 1267
Committee with Respect to Al-Qaida, Usama bin Laden, and the Taliban and
Other Individuals, Groups, Undertakings and Entities Associated with Them."
Last updated August 10, 2009. http://www.un.org/sc/committees/1267/consolist
.shtml (accessed August 23, 2009).

UN Security Council, Department of Public Information, News and Media Division.
"Security Council Al-Qaida and Taliban Sanctions Committee Adds Name of
One Individual to Consolidated List." April 16, 2009. http://www.un.org/News/
Press/docs/2009/sc9636.doc.htm (accessed August 20, 2009).

United Press International. "Authorities in Western China Blame Fanatics for 'Holy
War.'" April 23, 1990. http://www.lexisnexis.com/.

———. "Insider Notes from United Press International for Nov. 19." November 19,
2001. http://www.lexisnexis.com/.

Unrepresented Nations and Peoples Organization. "Nonviolence and Conflict:
Conditions for Effective Peaceful Change." July 1997. http://www.unpo.org/
downloads/nonviolencereport97.pdf (accessed September 5, 2009).

U.S. Department of Defense. "U.S. Department of Defense Dictionary of Military and Associated Terms." April 12, 2001, as amended through March 17, 2009. Joint Publication 1-02. http://www.dtic.mil/doctrine/jel/new_pubs/jp1_02.pdf (accessed August 22, 2009).

U.S. Department of Defense, Administrative Review Board. Summary of Administrative Review Board Proceedings for ISN 277. No date. http://projects.nytimes.com/guantanamo/detainees/277-bahtiyar-mahnut/documents/2/pages/2884#23 (accessed August 15, 2009).

———. Unclassified Summary of Evidence for Administrative Review Board in the Case of Noori, Adel. July 1, 2005. http://projects.nytimes.com/guantanamo/detainees/584-adel-noori#3 (accessed August 2, 2009).

U.S. Department of Defense, Combatant Status Review Board. Summary of Evidence for Combatant Status Review Tribunal – Abdul Rahman, Abdul Ghappar. October 29, 2004. http://www.dod.gov/pubs/foi/detainees/csrt_arb/index.html (accessed August 2, 2009).

———. Summary of Evidence for Combatant Status Review Tribunal – Basit, Akhdar. November 12, 2004. http://www.dod.gov/pubs/foi/detainees/csrt_arb/index.html (accessed August 2, 2009).

———. Detainee Unsworn Statement – ISN 260 [Ahmed Adil]. No date. http://www.dod.gov/pubs/foi/detainees/csrt_arb/index.html (accessed August 2, 2009).

———. Detainee Unsworn Statement – ISN 289 [Dawut Abdurehim]. No date. http://www.dod.gov/pubs/foi/detainees/csrt_arb/index.html (accessed August 2, 2009).

———. Summarized Detainee Statement [Ahmad Tourson, ISN 201]. No date. http://www.dod.gov/pubs/foi/detainees/csrt_arb/index.html (accessed August 2, 2009).

———. Summarized Detainee Sworn Statement [Abdul Razak, ISN 219]. No date. http://www.dod.gov/pubs/foi/detainees/csrt_arb/index.html (accessed August 2, 2009).

———. Summarized Detainee Sworn Statement [Adel Abdulhehim, ISN 293]. No date. http://www.dod.gov/pubs/foi/detainees/csrt_arb/index.html (accessed August 2, 2009).

———. Summarized Detainee Sworn Statement [Ahmed Mohamed, ISN 328]. No date. http://www.dod.gov/pubs/foi/detainees/csrt_arb/index.html (accessed August 2, 2009).

———. Summarized Detainee Sworn Statement [Bahtiyar Mahnut, ISN 277]. No date. http://www.dod.gov/pubs/foi/detainees/csrt_arb/index.html (accessed August 2, 2009).

———. Summarized Detainee Sworn Statement [Haji Mohammed Ayub, ISN 279]. No date. http://www.dod.gov/pubs/foi/detainees/csrt_arb/index.html (accessed August 2, 2009).

———. Summarized Detainee Sworn Statement [Huzaifa Parhat, ISN 320]. No date. http://www.dod.gov/pubs/foi/detainees/csrt_arb/index.html (accessed August 2, 2009).

———. Summarized Detainee Unsworn Statement [Abdul Ghappar Abdul Rahman, ISN 281]. No date. http://www.dod.gov/pubs/foi/detainees/csrt_arb/index.html (accessed August 2, 2009).

———. Summarized Detainee Unsworn Statement [Abdul Helil Mamut, ISN 278]. No date. http://www.dod.gov/pubs/foi/detainees/csrt_arb/index.html (accessed August 2, 2009).

———. Summarized Detainee Unsworn Statement [Abdulla Abdulqadir, ISN 285]. No date. http://www.dod.gov/pubs/foi/detainees/csrt_arb/index.html (accessed August 2, 2009).

———. Summarized Detainee Unsworn Statement [Abu Bakr Qasim, ISN 283]. No date. http://www.dod.gov/pubs/foi/detainees/csrt_arb/index.html (accessed August 2, 2009).

———. Summarized Detainee Unsworn Statement [Akhdar Qasem, ISN 276]. No date. http://www.dod.gov/pubs/foi/detainees/csrt_arb/index.html (accessed August 2, 2009).

———. Summarized Detainee Unsworn Statement [Arkin Mahmud, ISN 103]. No date. http://www.dod.gov/pubs/foi/detainees/csrt_arb/index.html (accessed August 2, 2009).

———. Summarized Detainee Unsworn Statement [Sabir Osman, ISN 282]. November 5, 2004. http://www.dod.gov/pubs/foi/detainees/csrt_arb/index.html (accessed August 2, 2009).

———. Summarized Detainee Unsworn Statement [Salahidin Abdulahat, ISN 295]. No date. http://www.dod.gov/pubs/foi/detainees/csrt_arb/index.html (accessed August 2, 2009).

———. Summarized Detainee Unsworn Statement [Yusef Abbas, ISN 275]. No date. http://www.dod.gov/pubs/foi/detainees/csrt_arb/index.html (accessed August 2, 2009).

———. Summary of Evidence for Combatant Status Review Tribunal – Khalik, Saidullah. October 29, 2004. http://www.dod.gov/pubs/foi/detainees/csrt_arb/index.html (accessed August 2, 2009).

———. Unclassified Summary of Basis for Tribunal Decision [Hasan Anvar, ISN 250]. No date. http://www.dod.gov/pubs/foi/detainees/csrt_arb/index.html (accessed August 2, 2009).

U.S. Department of Defense, Office for the Administrative Review of the Detention of Enemy Combatants. "Summarized Detainee Unsworn Statement" [Abdullah Abdulqadirakhum]. http://www.dod.gov/pubs/foi/detainees/csrt_arb/Set_20 _1606-1644.pdf (accessed April 11, 2009).

U.S. Department of State. "Patterns of Global Terrorism 2002." April 2003. http://www .state.gov/documents/organization/20177.pdf (accessed August 27, 2009). p. 132.

———. "Patterns of Global Terrorism 2003." April 2004. http://www.state.gov/ documents/organization/31912.pdf (accessed August 27, 2009). p. 144.

U.S. Department of State, Bureau of Public Affairs. "Additions to Terrorist Exclusion List." April 30, 2004. http://www.highbeam.com/doc/1G1-116080093.html (accessed August 24, 2009).

U.S. Department of State, Office of the Coordinator for Counterterrorism. "Fact Sheet: Foreign Terrorist Organizations." July 7, 2009. http://www.state.gov/s/ct/rls/ other/des/123085.htm (accessed August 23, 2009).

———. "Fact Sheet: Terrorist Exclusion List." December 29, 2004. http://www.state.gov/ s/ct/rls/other/des/123086.htm (accessed August 23, 2009).

U.S. Department of State, Office of International Information Programs. "Kelly Stresses U.S. Cooperation, Consultation with East Asia; Assistant Secretary of State Remarks on Terrorism, Other Threats." December 11, 2002. http://www.america .gov/st/washfile-english/2002/December/20021211155813nsiak@pd.state.gov .1011011.html (accessed August 29, 2009).

———. "Text: Craner Says Government Can't Ignore Human Rights in War on Terrorism (Security and Human Rights Support Each Other)." Includes transcript. December 26, 2002. http://usinfo.org/wf-archive/2002/021226/epf402.htm (accessed August 29, 2009).

U.S. Department of the Treasury, Office of Foreign Assets Control. "What You Need to Know About U.S. Sanctions." July 2, 2009. http://www.treas.gov/offices/enforcement/ofac/programs/terror/terror.pdf (accessed August 27, 2009).

U.S. Department of the Treasury, Office of Public Affairs. "Press Statement on the UN Designation of the Eastern Turkistan Islamic Movement." September 12, 2002. News release. http://www.treas.gov/press/releases/po3415.htm (accessed August 15, 2009).

———. "Treasury Targets Leader of Group Tied to Al Qaida." April 20, 2009. News release. http://www.treas.gov/press/releases/tg92.htm (accessed August 20, 2009).

U.S. District Court for the District of Columbia. Declaration of Joseph S. Imburiga. September 19, 2005. http://www.dod.gov/pubs/foi/detainees/csrt_arb/index.html (accessed August 2, 2009).

———. Memorandum Opinion: Granting the Petitioners' Motions for Judgment on Their Pending Habeas Petitions and Denying as Moot the Petitioners' Motions for Immediate Release of Parole into the United States. October 9, 2008. https://ecf.dcd.uscourts.gov/cgi-bin/show_public_doc?2008cv1310-45 (accessed August 9, 2009).

———. *Nag Mohammed v. George W. Bush: Civil Action No. 05-1602 (ESH).* September 19, 2005. http://www.dod.mil/pubs/foi/detainees/csrt_arb/publicly_filed_CSRT_records_698-814.pdf (accessed September 12, 2009).

U.S. House of Representatives, Foreign Affairs Committee. "Exploring the Nature of Uighur Nationalism: Freedom Fighters or Terrorists?" Hearing before the International Organizations, Human Rights, and Oversight Subcommittee. Federal News Service transcript. June 16, 2009.

U.S. White House. "The National Security Strategy of the United States of America." September 2002. http://georgewbush-whitehouse.archives.gov/nsc/nss/2002/index.html (accessed August 22, 2009).

———. "The National Security Strategy of the United States of America." March 2006. http://georgewbush-whitehouse.archives.gov/nsc/nss/2006/ (accessed August 22, 2009).

Vidaillet, Tamora. "U.S. Seeks Nod for FBI Post in Beijing—Says Muslims in Xinjiang Are Not Necessarily Terrorists." Reuters News Agency, published in the *Washington Times*. December 7, 2001. http://www.infoweb.newsbank.com/.

Volkert, Lilith. "Public Enemy No. 1: The World Uighur Congress Champions the Rights of China's Muslim Minority." *The Atlantic Times*. August 2009. http://www.atlantic-times.com/archive_detail.php?recordID=1856 (accessed October 5, 2009).

Wahidi, Hashir. "East Turkistan or Uyghuristan?" Translated by Erkin Sidick. January 7, 1998. http://www.uyghuramerican.org/articles/38/1/East-Turkistan-Or-Uyghuristan/East-Turkistan-Or-Uyghuristan.html (accessed August 4, 2009).

Wang, Hongjiang. "Tibetan Separatists Attack Chinese Embassy in Washington." Xinhua. April 2, 2008. http://www.china-embassy.org/eng/gyzg/t420556.htm (accessed March 28, 2009).

Wang, John Z. "Eastern Turkistan Islamic Movement: A Case Study of a New Terrorist Organization in China." *International Journal of Offender Therapy and Comparative Criminology* 47, no. 5 (2003): 568–584.

Watts, Alex. "Beijing: A Protest-Free Zone?" Sky News. August 20, 2008. http://news.sky
    .com/skynews/Home/World-News/Beijing-Olympics-Protest-Free-Despite-Protest
    -Zones/Article/200808315082849 (accessed September 13, 2009).
Watts, Jonathan. "Chinese Police Officers Stabbed to Death at Checkpoint." *The Guardian.*
    August 12, 2008. http://www.guardian.co.uk/sport/2008/aug/12/olympics2008
    .china?gusrc=rss&feed=networkfront (accessed August 23, 2009).
Wayne, Martin. *China's War on Terrorism: Counter-Insurgency, Politics, and Internal
    Security.* New York: Routledge, 2008.
Weimer, Calla. "The Economy of Xinjiang." In *Xinjiang: China's Muslim Borderland,*
    edited by S. Frederick Starr, 163–189. Armonk, NY: M.E. Sharpe, 2004.
Wingfield-Hayes, Rupert. "Language Blow for China's Muslims." BBC News. June 1, 2002.
    http://news.bbc.co.uk/2/hi/asia-pacific/2020009.stm (accessed September 13,
    2009).
Wong, Edward. "Arrests Increased in Chinese Region." *The New York Times.* January 5,
    2009. http://www.nytimes.com/2009/01/06/world/asia/06china.html (accessed
    April 24, 2009).
———. "Attack in West China Kills 3 Security Officers." *The New York Times.* August 13,
    2008. http://www.nytimes.com/2008/08/13/sports/olympics/13china.html?ref
    =world (accessed August 17, 2008).
———. "Group Says Video Warns of Olympic Attack." *The New York Times.* August 8,
    2008. http://www.nytimes.com/2008/08/08/sports/08iht-08china.15100553.html
    (accessed August 23, 2009).
———. "Warning of Attacks on Olympics Is Said to Be Linked to Muslim Separatist
    Group." *The New York Times.* August 10, 2008. http://www.nytimes.com/2008/
    08/10/sports/olympics/10uighurs.html?ref=asia (accessed April 10, 2009).
Wong, Edward, and Keith Bradshier. "China Orders Highest Alert for Olympics." *The
    New York Times.* August 4, 2008. http://www.nytimes.com/2008/08/04/sports/
    olympics/04china.html (accessed August 22, 2009).
World Uyghur Congress. "Brief History of the Uyghurs." http://www.uyghurcongress.org/
    En/Uyghurs.asp?mid=1195916276&mid2=-1500528155 (accessed August 30,
    2009).
———. "Introducing the World Uyghur Congress." http://www.uyghurcongress.org/En/
    AboutWUC.asp?mid=1095738888 (accessed September 3, 2009).
———. "List of Political Prisoners." http://www.uyghurcongress.org/En/humanrights
    .asp?mid=2125209830&mid2=979265169 (accessed September 6, 2009).
Xiao, Katie. "China Continues to Persecute Religious Groups, State's Birkle Says." July 21,
    2005. U.S. Department of State: United States Diplomatic Mission to Italy. http://
    www.usembassy.it/viewer/article.asp?article=/file2005_07/alia/a5072204.htm
    (accessed March 28, 2009).
Xinhua. "Bus Explosions Leave Two Dead in SW China, Police Say Deliberately Set."
    July 21, 2008. Xinhua News Agency. http://news.xinhuanet.com/english/2008-07/
    21/content_8739304.htm (accessed August 19, 2009).
———. "Chinese Court Rejects Appeal of Convicted Xinjiang Terrorist." Supplied by
    BBC Worldwide Monitoring. July 10, 2007. http://www.lexisnexis.com/.
———. "Fatal Explosion Linked to Gambling Dispute in East China." May 19, 2008.
    Embassy of Switzerland in Beijing. http://www.sinoptic.ch/embassy/presseschau/
    2008/20080519-0523.htm#21 (accessed August 18, 2009).

————. "Police Destroy Terrorist Camp, Killing 18." January 8, 2007. *China Daily*. http://www.chinadaily.com.cn/china/2007-01/08/content_777852.htm (accessed March 13, 2009).

————. "Police: Eastern Turkistan Terrorists Wanted." *China Daily*. October 21, 2008. http://www.chinadaily.com.cn/china/2008-10/21/content_7125363.htm (accessed August 29, 2009).

————. "Report: Tibetan Population Grows Fast, Language Education Stressed." April 1, 2009. http://news.xinhuanet.com/english/2009-04/01/content_11112488.htm (accessed September 13, 2009).

————. "Serial Explosions Kill Two in China's Remote Xinjiang." August 10, 2008. *People's Daily Online*. http://english.people.com.cn/90001/90776/90882/6470889.html (accessed February 1, 2009).

————. "Seven Killed, 36 Injured in China Truck Explosion." March 13, 2008. http://news.smashits.com/NewsPrint.asp?nid=234790 (accessed August 19, 2009).

————. "16 Police Officer Die in Kashgar Terror Strike" [*sic*]. *China Daily*. August 5, 2008. http://www.chinadaily.com.cn/china/2008-08/05/content_6903132.htm (accessed March 8, 2009).

————. "Suspect Confesses to Terrorist Attempt on China Flight." *China Daily*. March 27, 2008. http://www.chinadaily.com.cn/china/2008-03/27/content_6570512.htm (accessed May 4, 2009).

————. "Three Chinese Killed in NW Pakistan." July 9, 2007. http://news.xinhuanet.com/english/2007-07/09/content_6346549.htm (accessed September 13, 2009).

————. "Three Firefighters Die, Nine Injured in Factory Fire." *China Daily*. July 18, 2008. http://www.chinadaily.com.cn/china/2008-07/18/content_6858653.htm (accessed August 18, 2009).

————. "Townspeople in Xinjiang Mourn 16 Slain Police." *People's Daily Online*. August 7, 2008. http://english.peopledaily.com.cn/90001/90776/90882/6468861.html (accessed February 1, 2009).

————. "Xinhua Commentary Calls for Long-Term Fight Against Falun Gong Cult." Permanent Mission of the People's Republic of China to the UN. September 7, 2003. http://www.china-un.org/eng/zt/flgwt/t29534.htm (accessed February 28, 2009).

Xinhua General News Service. "First Batch of 'Eastern Turkistan' Terrorist Groups, Individuals Identified." December 15, 2003. http://www.lexisnexis.com/.

Xinhua News Agency. "China Announces List of ETIM Terrorists." October 21, 2008. http://www.china.org.cn/international/photos/2008-10/21/content_16642708.htm (accessed April 21, 2009).

————. "China's Western Provinces Lead by Some Economic Measures." March 26, 2008. http://www.highbeam.com/doc/1P2-15587656.html (accessed August 2, 2009).

————. "China's Xinjiang Sees 48 Mln Tons of Oil and Gas Output in 2008." February 2, 2009. http://www.highbeam.com/doc/1G1-192957597.html (accessed August 2, 2009).

————. "Chinese Foreign Ministry Confirms Death of East Turkistan 'Terrorist' Leader." December 24, 2003. http://www.lexisnexis.com/.

————. "Chinese Police Deny 'Terrorist Attacks' Behind Recent Explosions." July 26, 2008. http://news.xinhuanet.com/english/2008-07/26/content_8775123.htm (accessed August 23, 2009).

———. "Civilian Dies from Injuries in Xinjiang Bombing Attack." August 11, 2008. http://news.xinhuanet.com/english/2008-08/11/content_9179895.htm (accessed October 24, 2009).

———. "Coal Fires Extinguished After 60 Years in Xinjiang." *Xinhua News Agency.* July 2, 2009. http://news.xinhuanet.com/english/2009-07/02/content_11640437.htm (accessed August 2, 2009).

———. "Official: Dalai Lama 'Stubborn in Talks, Not True to His Word.' " March 26, 2009. http://news.xinhuanet.com/english/2009-03/26/content_11076912.htm (accessed March 28, 2009).

———. "Official Says East Turkestan 'Great Terrorist Threat' to China." Supplied by BBC Worldwide Monitoring. September 6, 2005. http://www.lexisnexis.com/.

———. "Police Arrest Three Over Xinjiang Killings." August 29, 2008. http://news.xinhuanet.com/english/2008-08/29/content_9737543.htm (accessed August 23, 2009).

———. "Two Hospitalized After Car Fire in Downtown Beijing." February 25, 2009. http://news.xinhuanet.com/english/2009-02/25/content_10893344.htm (accessed April 25, 2009).

Xinhuanet. "Anti-Terrorism Law Urged After Urumqi Riot: Expert." Last updated July 22, 2009. http://en.ce.cn/subject/urumqiriot/urumqirioto/200907/22/t20090722_19594550.shtml (accessed August 23, 2009).

"Xinjiang Foils Air Crash Attempt with an Emergency Landing." *People's Daily Online.* March 10, 2008. http://english.peopledaily.com.cn/90001/90776/90882/6370043.html (accessed February 1, 2009).

Yardley, Jim. "New Spasm of Violence in Western China as 11 Die in Wave of Bombings." *The New York Times.* August 11, 2008. http://www.nytimes.com/2008/08/11/world/asia/11xinjiang.html?pagewanted=print (accessed March 8, 2009).

———. "Police in Western China Kill 5 Suspected Militants After Bombing Attack." *The New York Times.* August 9, 2008. http://www.nytimes.com/2008/08/10/sports/olympics/10blasts.html?_r=1&ref=asia (accessed March 8, 2009).

Yin, Sim Chi. "Potential in Qinghai." *The Straits Times.* August 21, 2009. http://www.straitstimes.com/Breaking%2BNews/Singapore/Story/STIStory_419561.html (accessed September 13, 2009).

Yom, Sean L. "Uighurs Flex Their Muscles." *Asia Times*, January 23, 2002. http://www.atimes.com/china/DA23Ad01.html (accessed August 22, 2009).

Yu Song. "BBC Allegedly Has Received a Videotape Showing Masked Men from the East Turkestan Liberation Organization Declaring War on China." Zhongguo Tongxun She News Agency [Hong Kong], supplied by BBC Worldwide Monitoring. October 1, 2005. http://www.lexisnexis.com/.

Yu Zheng. "Woman Behind Xinjiang Riot Caught Self-Contradictory." Xinhua News Agency. July 11, 2009. http://news.xinhuanet.com/english/2009-07/11/content_11689948.htm (accessed August 29, 2009).

Zhang Yumo. "The Anti-Separatism Struggle and Its Historical Lessons Since the Liberation of Xinjiang." Translated by Turdi Ghoja for the Uyghur American Association. In *Pan-Turkism & Pan-Islamism*, edited by Yang Faren, Li Ze, and Dong Sheng. August 1993. http://www.uyghurnews.com/ReadNews.asp?UighurNews=the-anti-separtism-struggle-and-its-historical-lessons-since-the-liberation-of-xinjiang&ItemID=ZH-2172008573115318274840 (accessed September 5, 2009).

Zhu Zhe. "Experts: Anti-Terrorism Law on Cards." *China Daily*. May 31, 2007. http:// www.chinadaily.com.cn/china/2007-05/31/content_883861.htm (accessed August 23, 2009).

———. "Police Foil Terrorist Attempts to Derail Games." April 11, 2008. *China Daily*. http://www.chinadaily.com.cn/olympics/2008-04/11/content_6607933.htm (accessed August 23, 2009).

Zissis, Carin. "Media Censorship in China." Council on Foreign Relations. March 18, 2008. http://www.cfr.org/publication/11515 (accessed March 8, 2009).

Index

About the Authors

J. TODD REED works for BAE Systems in the Washington, DC, area. His education includes two years studying at Xi'an Foreign Language Institute in China and an MA in political science (Chinese politics and international relations) from the University of Missouri–Columbia.

DIANA RASCHKE works for Global Defense Technology & Systems, Intelligence Solutions in the Washington, DC, area. She also teaches in the Johns Hopkins University's Division of Public Safety Leadership. She holds an MS in intelligence analysis from Hopkins.